The Quick and the Dead

Lazy minds cleave to the simple comfort of certainty.

The striving, enquiring Soul thrives on ambiguity,
yearning to sift and weigh the evidence,
judiciously filtering information to winnow out the chaff
in order to distil the underlying and quintessential Truth.

The Truth Will Set You Free

FIRST EDITION

Part Four

The Truth Revealed – What Jesus Really Taught

Piecing together the evidence suppressed and distorted by the early church

GLYN THOMAS

TRUTH PUBLICATIONS

Truth Publications
truthmakesyoufree@icloud.com

Printed by Ingram Spark and affiliates – Lightning Source UK Ltd,
Milton Keynes, United Kingdom (see inside back for this copy).
Second Edition, published August 2022.

Paperback ISBN: 9789887448983
Ebook ISBN: 9789887448990

Typeset, layout and cover design by Greg Thomas
Bullet Design, London, United Kingdom
www.gregthomas.design | www.bulletdesign.com

Contents

Contents

1

Introduction

1.1 So, my friends, now you arrive at the final destination – at least so far as my modest opus of musings is concerned.

1.2 We, as humans, all live in our own skin. Sadly, most of us seem to despair of ever finding out the truth – are we just an accident of biochemical reactions? Or, are we something more?

1.3 I never felt despair but a sense of purpose, that despite the enormity of the questions – the answers lay there for us to fathom out. To my great surprise, over the past decade, my very fundamental questions have generally been answered, and answered in ways I have found profoundly surprising.

1.4 Let me place a marker ahead of writing this last part of my Quintology. I can honestly say, that from my earliest recollections, I have felt utterly convinced that our spirit is immortal – either that our spirit is newly born with us and continues to exist (at least until the end of our universe, which has been estimated at some 36 billion years from now), or our spirit was pre-existing and continues to exist until the end of our universe. Such belief, I confess, was originally utterly devoid of any foundation, but now my belief finds a measure of conviction from what I have learned.

1.5 Those who have persevered in reading the preceding four books will sympathise with my tortured struggle to reconcile the current extent of our multi-disciplinary knowledge with our conventional understanding of history and Christian beliefs. The previous booklets in this series have demonstrated our current understanding of history is different in some major respects from that conventionally taught in our schools, whilst the beliefs of conventional Christianity have been ruthlessly distorted from those originally taught by Jesus.

1.6   This series started with an eye-opener to acquaint readers with a more accurate view of the sweep of history, subsequent parts have challenged both the accuracy and the relevance of the Old Testament of the Bible and challenged the integrity of the gospels and epistles comprising the New Testament.

1.7   Those readers who have struggled through my feeble writings will now doubt whether the Old Testament is talking about a single supernatural Creator, aka God, or about a number of what are conventionally termed 'pagan' gods. In reality, all of the gods referred to in the Old Testament, including El Elyon (translated to English as the Lord Most High or God Almighty) and Yahweh, were more likely to have been an extended family of elite, intelligent, advanced humans who managed to perpetuate their leadership over many generations.

1.8   Part Three looked at how the Gospels seem to have been embroidered to market a popular vision of Jesus to non-Jews and how the Roman authorities took control and developed Christianity for purely political purposes.

1.9   This final part of the series provides the stunning conclusion – hopefully providing the reader with insight into the underlying Truth which many forces have tried successfully to keep hidden. I promise, you will be stunned to learn the real Truth.

1.10   We will proceed methodically, of course! We start by looking at the better-known aspects of the early development of Christianity within the Roman Empire. We will trace the persecutions, the development of dogma through Church Councils and the compromise reached with Emperor Constantine that in a few generations led to Christianity becoming the state religion across the Empire.

1.11   If you believe you are a Christian then you really need to understand the history of the Catholic Church and the origin of its teaching and, at least assess, whether elements of your belief actually originate from Jesus, or from the church. Where beliefs may be shown as formulated only by the church, it is interesting to learn the origin and basis of such beliefs.

1.12   Let's examine the 'Dark Ages of Christianity, the 2nd and 3rd centuries, say AD100 to AD300. The radical new teaching of Jesus, see chapter 15, appears to have spread rapidly and widely – spearheaded by the original disciples. Outside the Roman Empire, the teachings of the original Nazarene church spread east as far as India and westwards around the fringes of the Empire – across North Africa and northwards along the Atlantic coast to Ireland and Britain. Within the Roman Empire a different version of the gospel was spread, led by Paul.

1.13   The church readily admits theological debates raged over these early centuries but categorises anything disagreeing with the later establishment of Catholic dogma as heretical. After reading this book, you may conclude that the terms should be reversed! Evidence from Christian sources is sadly lacking, the Roman church managed to destroy almost all copies of almost all texts known to have circulated during the first three centuries after Jesus. Only a few caches of early texts have been recovered in the past century – which are discussed in the following chapters. The earliest substantive collections of surviving canon date back only to early 4th century.

1.14   Almost no attention is given to the religious scene into which Christianity advanced. We tend to think of Roman citizens worshipping a range of pagan gods – all of which were swept away by the new religion. Predictably, this is not quite true. Long before the rise of Rome, the original family of 'gods' held in esteem by people of both the Sumerian and Egyptian cultures had been assimilated by all successive cultures in the Middle East. Whilst the Sumerian civilisation collapsed soon after 2000BC, the Egyptian theology continued to permeate each new empire, including the Greek and later the Roman. The major deities across the Roman Empire were Isis, collecting additional names including Aphrodite and Venus, her husband Osiris and her son Horus.

1.15   As we saw in Part Three, chapter 23:16-41, those who authored the canonised gospels seem to have assimilated many elements of the beliefs of Isis and her babe Horus – weaving these stories into the birth narrative, some of the miracles and the idea of the bodily resurrection when narrating the life of Jesus.

1.16   Then we shall look at evidence of how the Roman Church further embellished dogma and ruthlessly rooted out anything that contradicted its rulings – labelling such aberrations as heresies and its practitioners as Gnostics. As usual, the victors wrote the history of these events – but increasing evidence has appeared that enables us to retrieve the suppressed truths.

1.17   We look at how the Roman Church persecuted those who believed that they were sincere Christians, and consider what it was that the Church was so frightened of. We shall review the heresies and assess whether they were indeed heretical or just inconvenient for the Church. In this light we shall look at the evidence of how many of the 1st Century texts were destroyed and how those adopted as canon were altered over the centuries to conform with the dogma that was being developed.

1.18   Then we shall examine the evidence of the original beliefs taught by Jesus and see why the politicians and bureaucrats suppressed it. Surprisingly, there appears to be sufficient evidence to support the conclusions reached – but you the reader will be your own arbiter. One benefit from reading this series is that you will be able to detect new meanings in many biblical passages – revealing the original message. I hope you find the journey enthralling and illuminating.

2

Why I came to focus on what the Church deemed heretical

2.1 Few Christians are aware of the traumatic events of the 4th and 5th centuries when Church Councils hotly debated profound articles of faith. Today, these key issues sound almost absurd:- was Jesus a man who became God, God who became a man, a junior god or was Jesus a manifestation of God? Did Jesus have a real body of flesh and bones or was he an apparition? Was Jesus really conceived, grown to term in Mary's womb or just pass through Mary as water passes through a pipe and thereby contain nothing of her substance? Today, summarising what has been examined in earlier Parts of this series, it is generally assumed that Jesus was conceived miraculously, born of a virgin and manifest as part of the Godhead. The New Testament presented by both Catholics and Protestants is dominated by the four canonical Gospels and the Epistles of Paul. Church teaching generally implies the Gospels were written by eponymous apostles who accompanied Jesus during his ministry – so what could be more authentic. Paul is represented as the legalistic and consummate interpreter and author of a coherent Christian dogma. Both assumptions are far from the original truth.

2.2 How can I, a relative nobody, make such outrageous claims? Firstly, just examine the official Catholic pronouncements – that none of the Gospels were written until well after the destruction of the Temple in Jerusalem by the Romans in AD70 – some 37 years after Jesus crucifixion – surely, given the extreme significance of the material, this is an astonishingly long time after the event?

2.3   Hold that thought – why do we not have writings contemporary with Jesus life? Luke (1:1-2) refers to the fact that *'many have written about these events'* and *'these were handed down to us by those who were eyewitnesses and servants of Jesus'* – immediately one realises that Luke was neither an eyewitness nor a contemporary but feels knowledgeable from the large number of texts by those who had been contemporary with Jesus teaching. Furthermore, where are all these writings – those that were available to Luke? The main reason for the absence of any contemporary texts is the extremely effective campaign of the Roman Church to destroy all copies of any text that challenged their own interpretation. Most Christians are aware of 'heretical' beliefs, beliefs challenging early Church dogma which gradually 'faded out'. 'Gradually' is an understatement – examination of history shows a 1500 year campaign of unrelenting censorship and destruction backed by terror and extermination.

2.4   The inescapable conclusion from the previous paragraph is that ALL the numerous texts that Luke refers to were later judged to be heretical at some point in the 2nd to 4th centuries. So, statements in these earliest authentic texts that Luke did not include (for reasons unknown) must have included material that was later found to contradict doctrine developed centuries later – and pose a sufficiently credible threat to the Roman church's dogma to warrant the huge effort to eradicate all copies of such documents, killing many Christians in the process.

2.5   Historians have estimated that during the ***two years*** following the Council of Nicaea in 325 more Christians were martyred on the orders of Church authorities, because they possessed a copy of a proscribed text, than during the ***three centuries*** between the crucifixion and the Council of Nicaea by the Roman secular authorities (see 11.4 below). This is surely very shocking.

2.6   The pursuit, trial and murder of 'heretics' continued in the centuries after Nicaea in 325, it became institutionalised with the formation of the Inquisition in 1250 and greatly expanded to pursue the wanton murder of the various groups, including the Cathars in southern France. The Inquisition then further expanded to cover the huge Spanish and Portuguese empires becoming a ruthless instrument of suppression until finally reined in by changes implemented as recently as 1908. The extensive repression of individual beliefs perpetrated by the Catholic

Church over more than 1500 years is more Orwellian than anything achieved by the Nazis or any Communist Party.

2.7 The sheer extent and duration of the persecution should make one ponder – why would 'heretical' beliefs endure? Why did so many followers of Jesus choose excruciating deaths rather than submit to the dogma of the Catholic Church?

2.8 The Catholic Church did an amazingly thorough job of censoring texts and eradicating all that they deemed heretical – to such an extent that almost no such texts survived. When the Nag Hammadi cache, discovered in 1945, was examined – scholars were astonished to find that the overwhelming majority of the 52 texts were completely unknown – not only had all copies been destroyed but even all references to such works had been obliterated.

2.9 Why did the Catholic Church devote such huge resources to the task of eradicating all references to texts that it deemed heretical. What made it so important? What were they so afraid of? Most Christians understand the great schism between Catholic and Protestantism arose because of concern at the rampant unpunished sinful behaviour of priests and the extreme commercialism of the church. Already extremely wealthy, by the Middle Ages, the church sought every opportunity to sell the forgiveness of sins and the promise of eternal life – for gold, silver and land.

2.10 However, abuses can be remedied by reform and acceptable standards established, the more fundamental issue was brought about by the invention of printing press and the subsequent availability of bibles in the vernacular. The Catholic church had sought to prevent reading of the bible by laity unless carefully supervised by clergy, and strictly forbid translations into other languages from the Latin Vulgate. When ordinary people starting reading the bible in their own language they were surprised to find no supporting evidence for most Catholic dogma. The Catholic pope's authority and the requirements placed on the congregation were found to be man-made. Hence the key Protestant mantra became *sola scriptura* – only scripture – with articles of faith based only on biblical evidence.

2.11 Unfortunately, the Catholic attempt to prevent the population reading the bible resulted in great jubilation and uncritical acceptance of the bible once it became accessible to the masses.

2.12   However, a moments' thought should make Protestants wary of accepting the bible as being an accurate record. The contents of the Bible were gradually accepted as canon during the 3rd and 4th centuries. Whilst we have evidence, including in the bible itself, that numerous texts were written by Jesus disciples and contemporary eyewitnesses – and evidence that many of these were used by churches in the first two centuries after Jesus, the vast majority were systematically destroyed by the church. The collection of books which the Roman church eventually decided were suitable to be accepted as canon, principally the version known as the Vulgate, was ruled accessible only by ordained clergy.

2.13   The books of the Old Testament can be compared with the Jewish Masoretic texts dating from cAD650 to cAD1000 as currently authoritative in Judaism, or with the older Septuagint versions known to contain dubious translations into Greek. However, a number of variations arise between the Masoretic texts and those recovered from the Dead Sea Scrolls – written c300BC to AD60. Moreover, textual research (as reviewed in Parts 2 and 3 of this series) has identified numerous errors of facts and plentiful anachronisms – indicating much later authorship than claimed and extensive subsequent editing prior to canonisation (i.e. when the text was locked) only in the few hundred years before Jesus. According to Jewish sources, a number of books in the Old Testament were only canonised a few centuries *after* Jesus.

2.14   More concerning, certainly for the author who does not see much connection between the Old Testament and his faith, is the fact that our versions of the New Testament books have come down to us only via the Catholic Church. Whilst numerous changes and additions have been identified, how can we be sure that important facts and statements by Jesus have not been edited out in attempts to conform the evidence to the adopted creed. Certainly, it is now widely accepted that the only two references in the bible to the idea of a 'Trinity' are now known to have been added centuries later – evidence indicates that the text of Matthew 28:19 was changed around AD300 whilst the text of 1 John 5 is only found in a trinitarian form after around AD1200 – evidence the church was actively changing texts for around at least a 1000 years – see chapter 20 of Part Three. Apart from changes which were trying to underpin the dogma of there being a Trinity, what else was being changed?

2.15   When we read the books of the New Testament, we assume that there was an early Greek text which was believed to be the original text or an accurate copy of it. Whilst we understand that numerous translations have been published, for example in English, these all represent attempts to accurately reproduce the meaning of the original Greek text. However, this assumption is far from the truth. When looking at the early Greek manuscripts, we find there exist thousands of variants of every book in the New Testament.

2.16   When comparing these variations, we see numerous examples of scribal edits deliberately changing the text to promote dogma or remove phrases supportive of ideas that had been declared heretical. One near universal trend seen progressively appearing in manuscripts from the first millennium, is the accumulation of titles wherever Jesus is mentioned. This may in part have been to show respect but it also played to underscore dogma. Where the oldest manuscripts refer to 'Jesus', latter manuscripts were written as 'Jesus Christ' to underline he was Messiah (by those who only understood Jesus was ***the*** messiah rather than *a* messiah), then 'Jesus Christ, Son of God' to reinforce Jesus was born of God, sometimes rewriting Jesus own frequent claim he was a Son of Man (see chapter 15) and the fullest expression as 'our Lord Jesus Christ, Son of God' to emphasize the Trinitarian claim that Jesus was both Lord, i.e. God himself, as well as the Son of God. The arguments over Christology, whether Jesus was both human and divine simultaneously, or a man temporarily cohabited by God, etc., were so complex and contradictory that some edits made to defeat one argument had the effect of supporting another. Mark 1:1 is one example of the progressive expansion, from "Jesus' in the oldest manuscripts, then expanded to 'Jesus Christ' and later to 'Jesus Christ, Son of God' in successively younger manuscripts, there are numerous other examples.

2.17   I had personally assumed that the epistles written by Paul that I read in my bible must be based upon authentic Greek originals. But it appears that this is not correct – the source used for biblical canon is derived from collections of Paul's letters assembled in the 3rd and 4th centuries. No two collections contain identical versions of each letter, none contain the same selection of letters. There is some debate over whether Timothy and Titus were even written by Paul. Galatians is generally believed to be formed from merging separate letters Paul sent to each church in Galatia into an illustrative letter. Our text of 2 Corinthians is believed to be derived from at least two separate letters – chapters 1 to 9 being one letter and chapters 10 to 13 forming a separate letter. Some argue that textual analysis indicates that the 2nd epistle to the Corinthians actually comprises elements of five separate letters that were merged into a single epistle.

2.18　Those that promote biblical inerrancy, that the everything stated in the bible is the 'Word of God' and therefore must be correct, are very well aware of the issues raised by widespread scribal editing. The Inerrants emphasize that the original divinely inspired text written by the author, the 'original autograph', is the inerrant text not later variants that have been subject to human editing. This leads to some interesting conclusions. For example, whilst we do not have any original autographs of any book in the New Testament text (and certainly no original text of the Old Testament books), all the evidence indicates that none of the authors of any text referred to Jesus as 'the Son of God'. It would be helpful if a recognized authority amongst the Inerrantist academics admitted that the idea the Jesus is the Son of God is purely a man-made assertion – never once divinely inspired to appear as the Word of God.

2.19　The majority of textual variants are either insignificant or obvious scribal errors, often where a word is repeated in close proximity, the copyist's eye being deceived into repeating a line or omitting a line. The fact that the vast majority of variants are of no consequence is obviously the focus of apologists who seek to dismiss the existence of variants as unimportant. However, there remain hundreds of variations which point to the arguments raging over dogma in the early centuries. These are rather more serious because they can have a direct bearing upon issues that all Christians regard as fundamental – such as: is Jesus actually God? Is Jesus the Son of God? Was Jesus resurrected?

2.20　It is widely accepted, and noted in most versions of the bible, that a series of verses were added later to the gospels of John (7:53 to 8:11, the story of the woman caught in adultery) and most of the coverage of the resurrection in John (chapters 20 and 21) and Mark (16:9-20, the ending which discusses Jesus appearance after his resurrection). The story of the woman caught in adultery sounds like an example of Jesus teaching but does not appear in any of the synoptic gospels. This section appears in whole or part in 1495 Greek manuscripts but is absent in 267 Greek manuscripts – which include all the earliest and those considered most important. It's a great story of how Jesus deflected an attack upon himself, shamed the scheming Pharisees and saved a woman from an awful death in the process. Whether true or not has little bearing on our beliefs. However, the extended endings of John and Mark and are fundamental to Christian belief for they add detailed descriptions of Jesus post resurrection appearances. The two earliest known examples of Mark end at verse 8, with Jesus tomb being found empty and a declaration that his resurrection was foretold. Moreover, these two are regarded as highly authoritative: the Codex Vaticanus dated c325 to 350 and the Codex Sinaiticus dated c330 to 360. That the extra text appears to have been added during the second half of the 4th Century is highly significant – as this period was rife with arguments over all the fundamental aspects of dogma. There seem to be two basic reasons why scribes would decide on such a fundamental addition – it may have been to 'conform' Mark with the other canonized gospels or to support the promotion of bodily resurrection. The authenticity of the last two chapters of John is further undermined by their absence from official Catholic bible commentary on John.

2.21   Thus, without the research resources we enjoy today, one can understand why the leaders of the Protestant Reformation believed by focusing on *sola scriptura* they avoided the fake dogma embroidered by the Roman church. However, it is now clear that key elements of faith embraced by Protestants are also inventions of the early church – including the miraculous birth, the resurrection and the trinity. None would see these as 'minor' articles of faith. But, we may take comfort that the transformational stuff lies in the teaching of Jesus not his 'life story'.

2.22   Protestants, with few exceptions, accepted the Catholic view of heresy – that the heretics had adopted unacceptable beliefs and whilst the Catholic forces had been brutal in eradicating such misguided ideas, such ideas had indeed been heretical and represented false teaching. Given the inappropriate behaviour of the priests and their lust for power and wealth – it does seem a little surprising that no one seems to have really challenged the Catholic Church's standpoint on heresies – no one seems to have revisited the beliefs that had been branded as heretical to assess whether such classification had been justified. Early heretical beliefs are nowadays often labelled 'gnostic' a term used derogatively by theologians. The later heresies, such as belief that the Earth was not flat and that the sun did not orbit the Earth, are so obviously absurd that these are seen as justification for Protestantism and breaking with Rome.

On this basis, it is surely surprising that older heresies have not been similarly re-examined.

2.23   Once you start to research the oldest heresies, and understand the heretical texts rediscovered in the past 100 years – the answers become clear. One is led to conclude that far from being heretical, heresies generally seem more likely to represent the Truth than do orthodox beliefs. I have come to realise that Catholic definitions of what is heretical actually provide the clearest avenue of thought to really understanding exactly what Jesus actually taught. One is on fairly safe ground to assert that actually – Heresy is Truth. Truly Orwellian, I know!!

2.24   But, in case you are now choking, just bear with me – the Truth will set you Free!!

2.25   Nowadays most people know nothing of the beliefs of the 'heretics' – just that they were rounded up, summary 'justice' dispensed – usually based on random unsupported allegations, a guilty verdict announced, supplemented by ecclesiastic seizure of any wealth held, followed by death – usually by burning at a stake. Two issues stand out – firstly, it seems there are very few records of anyone recanting their beliefs – even if only to be saved from a horrendous death; secondly, what were these heretical beliefs and why did such beliefs warrant such barbaric cruelty?

3

Early Christian texts declared heretical by Rome

3.1   According to the Catholic Encyclopaedia of 1914 there were some 50 texts that were rejected for inclusion in the New Testament. Many additional titles have been added since this Encyclopaedia was last updated. My own research has identified credible references to no less than 117 gospels and other works used by early Christian congregations. The vast majority of these were declared heretical by Ecclesiastical Council's during the 4th century, starting with Nicaea in AD325 – which also ruled that all copies of banned books should be surrendered and burned by Church authorities. This Council, presided over by Roman Emperor Constantine, decreed that anyone found harbouring a banned book was to be killed – two historians have independently estimated more Christians were killed enforcing this Edict than the cumulative total killed by the Roman authorities over the previous 300 years (this is examined in detail in chapter 11 below). Constantine was not the Christian emperor that conventional portrayal suggests but was more interested in subsuming the growing power of Christianity into his preferred religion, Sol Invictus. He chaired the Council and his deputy ensured Christian dogma was effectively merged with the beliefs of Sol Invictus – covered in detail in Part Three of this series.

3.2   The Roman church did an amazingly thorough job of finding and destroying texts which were declared heretical. In 1904 Adolf Harnack identified 16 gospels, marked [+] in section 3.6

below, in his *Chronologie* that had survived at least in fragmentary form. The Catholic Encyclopaedia of 1914 listed 30 texts, marked [*] below, as having, at that time, no surviving texts even in fragmentary form.

3.3   The sheer scale of the Church destruction of early Christian texts was revealed by the Nag Hammadi cache discovered in 1945 in Egypt. This carefully hidden cache included 51 texts of which only 9 were previously known and two of these we had only the names of – there being no known, even partial, surviving texts. The two titles, already known of from the Catholic Encyclopaedia, which Nag Hammadi yielded complete copies of were the Gospel of Philip and the Gospel of Truth. The contents of the 13 codex discovered at Nag Hammadi included no less than 42 early Christian scriptures that we had never even heard of – titles which appeared in no lists, no correspondence and no surviving document of any kind. The texts recovered from Nag Hammadi are marked [#] in the list in section 3.6 below.

3.4   The importance of the Nag Hammadi cache may be judged from the fact that it is believed to have been buried in 325 when Bishop Athanasius returned to Alexandria, triumphant from Nicaea, and then enthusiastically set about rooting out heretics harbouring banned books. Therefore, the cache comprises manuscripts likely to have been copies written mainly during the 2nd and 3rd centuries – the earliest texts and certainly the oldest almost complete texts about Jesus that we have. The oldest complete texts of any canonised New Testament books are from the early 4th century – the Codex Vaticanus (written between 300 and 325) and the Codex Sinaiticus (written between 330 and 360). Around a dozen fragments of canonical works have been dated to the 3rd century – but most are very short. Given the rampant textual variations found in the Greek manuscripts, invariably by scribes trying to earnestly "improve" the reading, it is likely that the oldest texts from Nag Hammadi present the least corrupted versions of Jesus teaching.

3.5   Other early Christian texts we only know from references made to them in other surviving documents. No texts have survived even in fragmentary form that we can say were part of these documents. Given the experience of Nag Hammadi, it is more likely that there are many, many, other texts, some written in the first century by those who may have heard Jesus teaching first hand, which we may never recover copies of. These include the many eyewitness accounts of Jesus ministry used by Luke and referred to in the opening verses of his gospel – none of these seem to have survived.

3.6 Below are listed the titles of all the non-canonical texts that have been recovered in whole or part, or which have been quoted or criticised as heretical by early theologians. To enable ease of navigation, I have sorted the titles by reference to the alphabetical listing of the attributed authors and tried to group the texts into categories reflecting different types of works: Gospels, Acts of the Apostles, Epistles, Apocryphon (secret writings and treatises) and Revelations (mainly apocalypses):

Gospels

1(#) The Gospel of Andrew
believed to be early 3rd century, quoted by Pope Innocent I and by Augustine, discovery in Nag Hammadi confirmed this was not another title for the Acts of Andrew

2(+#) The Gospel of the Twelve Apostles
until Nag Hammadi, known only from a reference by Origen in his Homilies on Luke, and a fragment in Syriac. Tells of Jesus life from conception to ascension

3 The Gospel of Barnabas
quoted by Gelasius I, Pope 492-496 in Decretum Gelasianum

4 The Gospel of Bartholomew
quoted by Pope Gelasius I in Decretum Gelasianum and others

5(+) The Gospel of Basilides
quoted by Origen

6 The Gospel of Cerinthus
Cerinthus wrote c100, quoted by Irenaeus, describes Earth as formed by divine angels subordinate to the Creator God, the Jewish god as also being an

angel and Jesus as born of two human parents but, because very righteous,
being granted extra Spirit at his baptism. Some references by 4th century
Epiphanius are taken as giving this work the name Gospel of Merinthus

7   The Gospel of the Ebionites

not even a fragment of text survives, only 8 quotations by Epiphanius in
his work Panarion, 'voice at baptism, today you are born as my Son'. The
Ebionites were Nazarene Christians who fled around the Mediterranean in
face of Roman forces bent upon the eradication of Jews from Judah

8(+)   The Gospel According to the Egyptians

believed to be used by Gentile Christians in Egypt, only quotations survive –
six by Clement of Alexandria, overlaps with Mark and Gospel of Thomas

9   The Gospel of the Encratites

a sect quoted by Irenaeus (130-202), Clement of Rome and Hippolytus who
described them "abstaining from meat and wine, they are forbidden to marry"
– despite which, sufficient numbers endured for Emperor Theodosius to issue
an Edict in 382 declaring the death sentence for all followers

10(*#)   The Holy Book of the Great Invisible Spirit (*aka* The Gospel of
the Egyptians)

2 copies found in Nag Hammadi cache, relates that the incarnation of Jesus
was to release souls from the prison of evil

11(+)   The Gospel of Eve

quoted by Epiphanius

12(+)   The Gospel according to the Hebrews

emphasises importance of James as head of the church, similarities
with Gospel of Thomas, only quotations survive – seven by Clement of
Alexandria, Didymus the Blind, Jerome and Origen

13   The Gospel of Hesychius

first bishop ordained by Peter in Rome, mission to Spain, quoted by Pope
Gelasius I in Decretum Gelasianum

14(+)   The Proto-Evangelium of James (*aka* The Infancy Gospel of
James)

known to Origen and Clement of Alexandria, it is believed to have been
written before 150. Appears to be a source of both Islamic and non-biblical

Catholic beliefs, including that Mary herself was born of a virgin; her parents Ann and Joachim not consummating their marriage; Mary being brought up in the Temple; married at 12 to Joseph but perpetually remaining a virgin and of Jesus siblings being children from Joseph's former marriage. Condemned as heretical by Pope Innocent I in 405 yet became the foundation of belief in the Immaculate Conception of Mary

15[(+)]   The Gospel of Judas Iscariot
conversation between Jesus and Judas, text discovered in Codex Tchaco, near El Minya, Egypt in 1970's, thought to date from early 2nd century, referred to by Irenaeus in Against Heresies

16   The Gospel of Jude
copy in Coptic dated to 280, referred to by Epiphanius

17   The Gospel of Lucianus
by Lucianus 240-312, produced revised versions of gospels later condemned as heretical but died a martyr and became a saint

18[(+)]   The Gospel of Marcion
quoted by Tertullian and Epiphanius

19   The Secret Gospel of Mark
according to a letter by Clement of Alexandria, this was a longer version of Mark with additional passages, he quotes one where Jesus raised a rich young man from his tomb and stayed with him for 6 days

20[(*)]   The Gospel of Mary
three fragments remain, two in Greek, one Coptic, but not the complete text. Gives prominence to Mary Magdalene, whom Jesus loved and told secrets not shared with the Apostles – so clearly heretical!

21[(+)]   The Gospel of Matthias
quoted by Pope Innocent I

22   The Gospel of Merinthus
quoted by Epiphanius but may be an alternative name for the Gospel of Cerinthus

23   The Gospel of the Nazareans
some argue that this was the original Gospel of Matthew, the same text

referred to by Eusebius as the original manuscript of Matthew written in Aramaic and held in the library of Caesarea; no text, even partial, survives, only ten quotations by Eusebius, Jerome and Origen

24[+]   The Gospel of Nicodemus (aka Acta Pilati)
plausible details, describes the members of the Sanhedrin laying complaints to Pilate over Jesus healing sick on the Sabbath and Pilate questioning why that was considered wrong

25   The Gospel of Perfection
believed to be Ophite, an obscure 3rd century sect who believed the Son of God did not appear as human but as a wise serpent, same as to Eve who obeyed the serpent believing it was the Son of God

26[+]   The Gospel of Peter
popular in the early church, a large section of 60 verses was discovered in the 19th century in the tomb of a monk in Egypt. Other fragments indicate the full text covered all of Jesus ministry but the surviving section covers Jesus trial, crucifixion and resurrection with some unique details

27[+*#]   The Gospel of Philip
the only text comes as substantial fragments from the Nag Hammadi cache, text difficult to understand in parts, criticises those who take references to a virgin birth and bodily resurrection as historically true

28   The Gospel of the Saviour
substantial fragments discovered in Egypt and purchased by Berlin Museum in 1967, fragments focus on the Last Supper, where Jesus tells them he will go down to Shoel to give news to the souls of the dead, and the crucifixion

29[*]   The Gospel of Scythanius
1st century theologian of Alexandria, quoted by Hippolytus, Cyril of Jerusalem and Epiphanius, the Gospel is noted in the Catholic Encyclopaedia

30[+]   The Gospel Teleioseos

31[#]   The Gospel of Thaddaeus
quoted by Gelasius I, Pope 492-496 in Decretum Gelasianum

32[+*#]   The Gospel of Thomas (i.e. The Gospel of the Twin)
a section in Greek and a complete copy in Coptic found at Nag Hammadi

in 1945, comprising 114 sayings of Jesus, some startling for conventional Christians, a number of sayings have parallels with synoptic Gospels. Highly regarded in 1ˢᵗ century and possibly quoted by Paul

33   The Infancy Gospel of Thomas
a number of copies in Greek and Latin have been found. Contains amusing anecdotes of Jesus from age 5 to 12, was very popular and suggested as the source of Luke's telling of Jesus at 12 visiting the Temple

34   The Gospel of Titan
referred to by Eusebius in his Ecclesiastical History

35⁽*#⁾   The Gospel of Truth
complete copy found at Nag Hammadi in 1945, attributed to Valentinus, c150, treats the Holy Spirit as a power of the Father, serving as the basis of Orthodox Church dogma

36⁽⁺⁾   The Gospel of Valentinus
quoted by Tertullian, some fragments identified although others claim fragments are of an earlier version of the Gospel of Truth

37   The Unknown Gospel, fragments known as 'Papyrus Egerton 2'
purchased by the British Museum in 1935 and believed to have been found in Egypt, comprises parts of four stories, 3 similar to ones appearing in canonised gospels, 1 unique

Acts of the Apostles

38   The Acts of Andrew
believed to date from c260, only surviving source from a Latin translation made by Gregory of Tours 538 – 594. Describes Andrews missionary work across modern Turkey

39   The Acts of the Apostles by Lentitus
quoted by Augustine

40   The Acts of the Apostles by Leucius
quoted by Augustine and Gregory of Tours

41   The Acts of the Apostles by Leontius
quoted by Augustine

42   The Acts of the Apostles by Leuthon
quoted by Eusebius

43   The Acts of the Apostles by Seleuccus
quoted by Eusebius

44   The Acts of John
*large fragment of long text survives in Greek, quoted by Eusebius, Epiphanius
& Priscillian. Relates John's acts in Ephesus and Smyrna including
many healings and resurrections, Jesus described as changing in form and
appearance from time to time*

45   The Acts of Paul
*tells of Paul's time in Rome, meeting with Nero and execution. Quoted by
Origen, Tertullian c190 and Eusebius*

46   The Acts of Peter
*a substantial text describing Peter's missionary works, mainly a contest of
miracles with Simon Magus in Rome, ending with his martyrdom, written
mid 2nd century; seen as a substantial source of the Homilies of Clement,
quoted by Eusebius and Epiphanius*

47(*#)   The Acts of Peter and the Twelve Apostles
found at Nag Hammadi, comprises an allegory followed by its explanation

48   The Acts of Philip
quoted by Pope Gelasius I in Decretum Gelasianum

49   The Acts of Thecla
*some fragments appear to come from a combined text. Converted by Paul's
teaching of chastity, Thecla abandoned her fiancé and family and joined
Paul's journey. Estimated late 2nd century. Quoted by Tertullian, Eusebius &
Pope Gelasius I in Decretum Gelasianum*

50   The Acts of Thomas
*a substantial surviving text documenting Thomas journey to and across
India, quoted by Epiphanius, Athanasius & Pope Gelasius I in Decretum
Gelasianum*

Epistles

51   The Epistle of Jesus to King Abgar V of Edessa
*an exchange of letters in which the king invites Jesus to visit Edessa to heal
the sick and Jesus politely declines due to pressure of work and promises to
send an apostle, Eusebius claims he verified these by reference to the public
records of that city*

52   The Epistle of the Apostles
*written originally in Greek, a mutilated Coptic version found in Cairo in
1895 and a complete Ethiopic version found in 1913. An anti-gnostic tract,
believed to date from c150, promotes bodily resurrection*

53   The Epistle of Barnabas
*written between 100 and 132 when much discussion concerning the
rebuilding of the Temple. Main thrust is that Judaism is a false religion as
the Jews misunderstood Mosaic Law trying to follow it literally, claiming
that it is really a Christian text prefiguring Jesus. May be the source of the
deliberate mistranslation of Psalm 110, 'The Lord says to my Lord' and
of the change in the Sabbath day. Prohibition of abortion. The complete
text appears in the Codex Sinaiticus, Eusebius argued for it to be included in
canon. Attribution to Paul's companion, Barnabas, unreliable as he would
have long been dead*

54   The First Letter of Clement
*consensus dating now to c96, written by Clement I to the church in Corinth –
key source of doctrine of primacy of apostolic succession as basis of authority
and of continued practice of Jewish animal sacrifices. Addresses church
administration and hierarchy with extensive quotes from Hebrews and Paul's
epistles*

55   The Second Letter of Clement
*originally accepted as scripture but later found heretical, essentially a sermon
directed at converts from pagan gods, warning against idols and extensive
quotes from Isaiah, Gospel of Thomas and other unknown sources, generally
viewed as not from Clement I, but from Corinth or Alexandria c 150*

56   The Homilies of Clement
*believed to have been a set of 20 booklets describing Clements journey
with Peter from Caesarea to Rome, includes Clements life history, his close
relationship with the Emperor and his letter to James. References to duality.*

Written from a Jewish Christian perspective, some scholars believe references to Simon Magus may be code for Paul

57   The Third Letter to the Corinthians
reads as Paul responding to questions from the Corinth church on heretical teaching of Simon Magus, Paul reaffirms the proto-orthodox views of Jesus being human, born of Mary & Holy Spirit and that believers will be bodily resurrected. Regarded as canon in the Orthodox church but rejected by the Catholic – presumably because it mentions heresies even if only to refute them.

58   The Didache (*aka* Teaching of the Twelve Apostles)
scholars date to between 100 and 120, rediscovered 1873, may have been commissioned by Jerusalem Council in 49, has sections with prayers, ethics, church rituals and church organisation, canonised by Ethiopian Church. Copy found is intriguing, it contains an early pre-Orthodox version of the Lord's Prayer but no verses which might be seen as heretical, however the baptism formula in three names indicates a 3rd or 4th century editing – so what we have seems to be a cleaned up version

59   Epistles between Paul and Seneca
comprising 8 epistles from Seneca, a Roman philosopher contemporary of Paul, and 6 replies from Paul, regarded as genuine until the Renaissance but then challenged and now dismissed as dating from the 4th century, in the words of Philip Schaff "They are very poor in thought and style, full of errors of chronology and history, and undoubtedly a forgery". Whilst Paul dominates the NT, he is not referred to by any Roman or Jewish historian and it suggested that this correspondence with a leading intellectual was forged as a remedy

60   Paul's epistle to the Laodiceans
Paul refers to such a letter in Colossians 4:16 "And when this letter has been read to you, see that it is also read before the church at Laodicea, and that you yourselves read the letter which will be forwarded from there". One text purported to be such a letter was condemned as heretical in the Muratorian Fragment, itself dated to c150. However, two ancient copies of a text with the same title have been found, one at the Sorbonne and another in Padua. The surviving text appears consistent with Pauline theology and devoid of any heretical statements, leading some to claim a revised letter was forged to replace the original heretical forgery!

61   The Epistle of Peter to James
*states that accompanying set of sermons should only be given to the
circumcised, i.e. not Gentiles, and of six years standing in the church, warns
against the preaching of the enemy – possibly referring to Paul; complete
text has survived as a preface to the 'Homilies of Clement', also quoted by
Tertullian 160-220*

62(*#)   The Epistle of Peter to Philip
*found in Nag Hammadi and in Codex Tchaco in 1970's, Peter expresses
his wish that Philip re-join the evangelising work, positions Peter having a
leadership role amongst the apostles and tells of post crucifixion teaching and
the nature of Jesus*

63   The Epistle of Ptolemaeus to Flora
*known only from what seems to be a complete quote in Epiphanius work
'Panarion', an interesting work addressing the conflicts between Jesus
teaching and the rules laid down in the Torah, argues that whatever God
had originally laid down as the laws for men, other men had confused and
distorted through multiple redactions, the text then tries to identify what truth
lies in the Torah, dated between 130-150, appears to have the first of a series
but no trace of any others has been found*

64   The Epistle of Themison
referred to by Eusebius in his Ecclesiastical History

65   The Epistle of Titus (aka Pseudo-Titus)
*found in the Codex Burchardi discovered in 1896, written in poor Latin
presumed to be a translation from Greek. Attributed to Paul's companion,
teaches against sex even in marriage as a temptation from the devil which
jeopardises your relationship with God, a slave cannot serve two masters –
therefore a Christian cannot marry but should remain a virgin. Judged to be
authored in 5th century*

Apocryphon (secret writings & treatise)

66(*#)   Allogenes (*meaning* Stranger)
*a mystical text from Nag Hammadi with parts missing. Allogenes speaks
of the invisible, spiritual Triple-Powered-One, existing as an Invisible One
incomprehensible to all. Containing them all within himself, they all exist
because of him. He is perfect and blessed. He is always One and he exists in
them all. Perhaps this inspired Athanasius on his way to Nicaea!*

67(*#)   The Hypostasis of the Archons (*The Reality of the Rulers*)
found at Nag Hammadi, is a blend of Genesis 1 to 6 and Greek mythology

68(*#)   Asclepius Ch21-29
a discussion between Trismegistus and Asclepius, nine chapters concerning creation talks of God and the Father creating man after the creation of the gods, men are mortal but may become immortal if they attain learning and knowledge. God has created a daimon to judge the souls of man, allowing the good to ascend to heaven and casting down the evil ones

69(*#)   Eugnostos the Blessed (*meaning* Right Thinking)
two complete copies from Nag Hammadi, this text focuses on creation, the spirits and immortality

70   The Book of the Helkesaites
referred to by Eusebius in his Ecclesiastical History

71(*#)   Hypsiphrone (*meaning* She of Exalted Thought)
only small fragments from Nag Hammadi referring to revelations which 'replaced' her virginity

72(*#)   The Apocryphon of James (*aka The Secret Book of James*)
complete text from Nag Hammadi describing secret teachings of Jesus to James and Peter during a return 550 days after the Resurrection, dwelling at length on the role of the spirit, the soul and the flesh

73(*#)   The Dialogue of the Saviour
badly damaged text from Nag Hammadi, presents a dialogue between Jesus, Judas the Twin, Mary and Matthew, some see as two texts with one inserted into the other, dated to c150

74(*#)   The Sophia of Jesus Christ *(Sophia meaning wisdom)*
first discovered in 1896 as part of a collection on sale in Egypt, known as the Codex of Berlin, another text from Nag Hammadi, comprises 13 questions put to Jesus by his apostles and the responses given by Jesus

75(*#)   The Apocryphon of John (*aka The Secret Book of John*)
known to Irenaeus and therefore written before 180, 4 extant copies. Appearing after his ascension, Jesus relates the story of creation to John. Jesus describes the Invisible Spirit as much more than a god, as there is nothing above him. One of the Spirit's creations, Sophia, made a new entity,

Yaltabaoth, without the consent of the Spirit – which became the god of the Old Testament. Yaltabaoth made mankind and then claimed he was God, led man astray and hence Jesus came to save the souls of mankind trapped in mortal bodies.

76(*#) The Interpretation of Knowledge
damaged text found at Nag Hammadi, parallels with Gospel of Truth, dark view of the world and need to resist its temptations

77 The Books of Lentitus

78(*#) Marsanes
the only partial and very damaged text is from Nag Hammadi, tells of multiple levels of the heavens and of multiple successive incarnations of Jesus, believed to be 3rd century

79(+) The writing Genna Marias *(meaning the Descent of Mary)*
our only source is Epiphanius writing in Panarion with four quotes concerning Zacharias, father of John the Baptist being killed in the Temple after seeing a vision

80 The Traditions of Matthias
quoted by Clement

81(*#) Melchizedek
a subject of much speculation, in Genesis described as the King of Jerusalem and as the High Priest to El Elyon, roles normally combined at that time, later speculation that Melchizedek may have been a previous incarnation of Jesus, plausible as Melchizedek is described as 'not born of woman', a phrase implying he might have been a Son of Man – can you dig it!

82(*#) The Thought of Norea
a short text from Nag Hammadi, about Seth reincarnated as Jesus, dated to 2nd century

83(*#) The Prayer of the Apostle Paul
a damaged text found at Nag Hammadi, missing its opening lines, references to the Redeemer, a term used by Paul might support its authenticity, otherwise might date as late as 300

37

84   The Preaching of Paul
       *quoted by Clement of Alexandria, Gregory of Nazianaus and John of
       Damascus*

85   The Doctrine of Peter
       quoted by Origen

86   The Judgment of Peter
       quoted by Eusebius

87   The Preaching of Peter
       quoted a number of times by Origen, Clement and Eusebius

88(*#) The Treatise on the Resurrection (*aka* the Epistle to Rheginus)
       *a short 8 page text from Nag Hammadi, an author writing to his son,
       Rheginus, explaining Jesus was human and divine, a Son of Man and a
       Son of God, refers to the Transfiguration, holds that bodily life is a short
       intermission during our spiritual lives. Indicates a high respect for Paul*

89(*#) The Three Steles of Seth
       *three hymns of adoration to Seth, who was believed to have reincarnated as
       Jesus, quoted by Josephus*

90(*#) The Second Treatise of the Great Seth
       *a strange book, found amongst the Nag Hammadi cache, the title referring to
       the third son of Adam and Eve, the text purports to be Jesus telling readers
       of how he descended and occupied a human body departing just before the
       crucifixion, dismissive of Jewish patriarchs and Yahweh, believed to be 3rd
       century*

91(*#) The Sentences of Sextus
       quoted by Origen c250, promotes self-castration to avoid sin

92(*#) The Paraphrase of Shem
       *a Nag Hammadi text, describes the Spirit as unbegotten, the Flood, the
       destruction of Sodom and recension of Shem (Jesus) to save our spirits from
       darkness*

93(*#) The Teachings of Silvanus
       *a Nag Hammadi text dated to c150, God is seen as the one true Creator
       and Jesus as the 'incarnate Wisdom of God' – close to the idea of Sophia/*

Serpent and not far from the 'Logos'. Jesus is described as a single hypostasis – a hidden spiritual reality and a term adopted at Nicaea in relation to the definition of the Trinity

94(*#)   **The Exegesis on the Soul**
found at Nag Hammadi, teaches that the Soul is feminine, has fallen from perfection into evil but the <u>Father</u> will restore to perfection – NB a pointer to the Father not being God to whom Spirit returns but more closely related to Jesus

95(*#)   **The Prayer of Thanksgiving**
Nag Hammadi text, c250, concludes "with such hope we turn to a pure meal that includes no living thing" – implying vegetarianism

96(*#)   **The Book of Thomas the Contender**
found at Nag Hammadi, the text is a dialogue between Jesus and his twin brother Judas. Jesus describes those focused on only what is visible are endangering themselves to an internal fire which will corrupt their souls and lose their souls to darkness. The author names himself as Matthias stating he had listened to the conversation between the brothers, leading some to suggest this might be the lost Gospel of Matthias

97(*#)   **The Thunder, Perfect Mind**
discovered at Nag Hammadi, comprises a mysterious long poem written as from a feminine divinity, has triggered many books

98(*#)   **The Tripartite Tractate**
text from Nag Hammadi, describes God as a unique transcendent entity from which have descended a Son and the Church. Describes relationship between life forces granted freewill and the Son saving the righteous who achieve unity with their souls. Some see Origen's thinking, Eusebius saw a proto-trinity of natural forces

99(*#)   **The Testimony of Truth**
badly damaged and fragmentary recovery from Nag Hammadi, seems to ridicule the Genesis account of God in the Garden of Eden. Those who listen with ears to the laws of the Torah are blind to the light as the Son of Man who, empowered at the Jordan, talks to the mind (soul), Jesus had descended to Hades to save souls and heal wounds. Describes martyrdom as achieving nothing, God does not want human sacrifice, those who wait for carnal resurrection misunderstand scripture

100[*#] Valentinian Exposition on Anointing, Baptism & the Eucharist
Valentinus c100-180, developed a structure of rituals which we only understand from Irenaeus criticism of them from which it is difficult to piece together. A primal Father created 15 pairs of powers, one of whom Sophia created the material world populated with life – the highest form of which, mankind embodies both spiritual and material natures. Christ is the son of Sophia, who descends into the body of Jesus at his baptism to preach salvation, freeing man from the material world through knowledge not faith

101[*#] Zostrianos
badly damaged text from Nag Hammadi concerning a vision castigating women as evil bondage – "Flee from the madness and the bondage of femaleness and choose for yourselves the salvation of maleness. You have not come to suffer; rather, you have come to escape your bondage. Save yourselves so that your soul may be saved"

102[*#] The Concept of Our Great Power
found at Nag Hammadi, this describes God as the Great Power invisible and using fire to cleanse, one born to man came to know the Great Power, he opened the gates of Heaven with his words, was seized by the rulers and sent to Hades, but they could not hold him and the Logos abolished the law and gave the power of life

103[*#] The Discourse on the Eighth and Ninth
attributed to a Greek named Hermes Trismegistus, only survives as Coptic translation found at Nag Hammadi

Revelations and apocalypses

104[*#] The Apocalypse of Adam
found at Nag Hammadi dating from c100-150, a confusing tract featuring Adam's 3rd son, Seth

105 The Revelation of Cerinthus
quoted by Irenaeus and Eusebius, describes the Christ descending into Jesus at his baptism & departing from him at the crucifixion

106 The Shepherd of Hermas
scholars believe to be written c150 by Hermas, a brother of Pope Pius I, although some link to Hermas addressed by Paul in Romans 16:14 and reference to Clement likely to be Pope Clement I who was pope from 88 to 99

– therefore this could be very early. Early Christians believed sins committed after baptism could not be forgiven, Hermas taught there was a single second chance at repentance after baptism. Refers to our divine spirits and need to nourish our souls. Teaches to avoid thoughts of sexual immorality but "if you always keep thinking about your own wife, you will never sin". Considered canon by Irenaeus, included in the Codex Sinaiticus

107(*#) The First Apocalypse of James
narrates two conversations between Jesus and his brother James, one prior to the crucifixion and one after his ascension

108(*#) The Second Apocalypse of James
copy found in Nag Hammadi cache, describes James trial and martyrdom

109(*) The Apocalypse of Paul
believed written c390 in an Egyptian monastery. Fragments found in numerous languages:- Greek, Syriac, Coptic, Ethiopic and Amharic. Tells of a sealed box found during reign of Theodosius (347-395) containing the original text of a revelation to Paul. Text mainly concerning judgment, heaven and hell. Tells of angels preparing souls for judgment and of spirits rejoicing when they had dwelt with righteous souls, angels make reports about souls to God. Also tasks souls with remembering the body they had left in order to return at resurrection. One version relates Paul successfully negotiating a weekly day of rest every Sunday for the wicked burning in hell

110(#) The Coptic Apocalypse of Paul
found at Nag Hammadi, dated circa 150 to 180, unrelated to the Apocalypse of Paul. Tells of Paul's encounter with a child en-route to Jerusalem who speaks to him about souls being imprisoned in mortal bodies and to focus on things which cannot be seen, then the child becomes a spirit taking Paul up to the third heaven (qv 2Cor 12:2) and to higher levels. Quoted by Irenaeus

111 The Revelation of Paul
quoted by Epiphanius and by Pope Gelasius I in Decretum Gelasianum

112 The Hymn of the Pearl (aka The Hymn of the Soul and The Hymn of Judas the Twin)
believed written in Edessa, maybe late 1st century, found in a book of psalms. Allegorical tale of Jesus and his twin, as royal princes sent down to Egypt to retrieve a pearl (believed to represent human souls), closing with a triumphal return to the father's kingdom

113(*#)   The Apocalypse of Peter
three quite different texts have been found bearing this title. The first
fragmentary Greek text was found in a monastic tomb in Akhmim, Egypt,
in 1887. The second much longer Ethiopic text with little commonality was
uncovered in 1910. The third, clearly gnostic, Coptic text was amongst the
Nag Hammadi cache. Refers to the souls and the spirits of people. Peter
dreams of Jesus talking to him, in which Jesus warns of those who will
name themselves 'bishops' and 'deacons' as if they had received their authority
from God

114   The Revelation of Peter
quoted by Clement and Eusebius

115   The Revelation of Stephen
quoted by Pope Gelasius I in Decretum Gelasianum

116(*#)   Trimorphic Protennoia (*aka* The First Thought in Three Forms)
scholars date to c200, describes a female Creator who is present in all beings,
and has made three descents to Earth – as the Thought, the Voice (the Father)
and the Word (the Perfect Son). The Word was sent to illuminate those who
dwell in darkness and took on the shape of their likeness. The great Demon
emerging from Chaos is Yaltabaoth, who had snatched power from Sophia.
Some ideas similar to The Apocryphon of John

117(*#)   On the Origin of the World (*text without a title, this describes its*
         content)
a Nag Hammadi text, a blend of ancient creation myths loosely linked
to Genesis 1. Judged to be written c300, at least 100 years after The
Apocryphon of John, it provides an alternative explanation for the creation of
Yaltabaoth from darkness beyond the edge of the celestial realm. Yaltabaoth
believed he was the only God and was angry and jealous, but the Immortals
brought light (Sophia) to his son Sabaoth. After the creation of mankind,
Sophia appeared as the Serpent in the Garden of Eden bestowing wisdom
upon Man

3.7   The most interesting texts, which I vouch you will find much easier to
         follow after completing this book, are:

32   The Gospel of Thomas
53   The Epistle of Barnabas
58   The Didache (*aka* Teaching of the Twelve Apostles)

3.8   The texts which tell of the Acts of one or more of the Apostles and those attributed to Paul's companions (such as the Epistle of Titus) seem to all share a disturbing emphasis on sex, even between married couples, as being inherently sinful and to be avoided if one is seeking a closer relationship with God. The texts mostly date from the 2nd century and tell of the missionary activities of individual apostles, recording their heroic deeds combating the adherents and priests of pagan deities, debates, beatings and a variety of natural disasters. A common theme of the teaching is the stress placed on acetic lifestyles, urging denial of pleasures described as promoted by pagan beliefs – sexual love of married couples, raising of children and family commitments. Forbearance from sex was emphasised as the path to a closer acquaintance with God. Such views were also central to Marcion and his followers. One can understand both the Roman political and religious leaders took a dim view of such ideas – to maintain and defend an empire one needed a good supply of young men. Hence it is easy to understand why most were considered heretical and only a sole survivor of this genre was admitted to canon. Consider the contrast with the Shepherd of Hermas – which states that sex with one's spouse can never be sinful.

3.9   Digging deeper, one finds that the cause of the orthodox church obsession with sex being linked to sin arises from a misunderstanding of the original teaching of Jesus and arose from attempts to suppress the original teaching that humans must unify their Spirit and their Soul to enter the Kingdom of Heaven – see chapter 15 below.

3.10   The overwhelming imperative of destroying texts which challenged Roman doctrine led to wholesale destruction. Some texts appear to have very early origins, arguably written by or dictated by members of the original apostles, others show indications of later authorship as they reflect doctrinal arguments that arose only in the 2nd or even 3rd century. Given the ruthlessness shown in destroying texts, even an authentic letter from Jesus would certainly not have survived if it contradicted Roman doctrine – as most of the documents we do have, even where fragmentary, include statements attributed to Jesus which contradict orthodox doctrine. Likewise, of the many documents attributed to his closest Apostles, surely some may have been genuine and it shows rank hypocrisy and total disregard for the truth that the Roman church authorities acted to destroy all copies of such texts.

3.11   Further evidence of the likelihood that the original orthodoxy was turned on its head by the Roman church may be found in citations by the earliest 'Church Fathers'. One may find quotations from texts later ruled 'heretical' long before any from NT canon: Dionysius the Areopagite in 96; Clement of Rome in 99; Epiphanius between 130 to 150 e.g. in *Panarion*; Polycarp c156; Papius in 163; Tertullian from c160 – yet the earliest reference to any of the four canonised gospels dates only from 171.

4

Christians martyred on the orders of the Roman State

The Rise of the Roman Church

4.1   Initially, those who heard Jesus preaching in the Temple or at other public gatherings saw him as a rabbi (teacher) but, as word spread of his wisdom and healing, he was acclaimed as a Messiah, specifically a King Messiah, appointed by God to free his people from the yoke of the Roman Empire.

4.2   In addition to the biblical gospels, we have in recent times rediscovered some additional evidence of what Jesus said about his role and purpose that had been ruthlessly suppressed and destroyed by the Roman authorities. Whilst, for 1700 years, such ideas have been successfully tainted as heretical by the Catholic Church – we now realize that we also have a biblical reference where some argue that Paul attributes equivalent reverence to one of these texts as he does to the Torah.

4.3   Until the discovery of the Nag Hammadi texts, unearthed in an Egyptian village in 1945, there were virtually no surviving Christian texts from the first two centuries – such was the thoroughness of the book burning destruction wrought during the first few centuries after the Council of Nicaea in AD325. However, from authoritative works by respected early church theologians, we know at least the titles of many texts that were in circulation during these first few centuries.

4.4   Today we have no certainty as to the complete theology that Jesus taught.

The vast majority of early texts having been destroyed and the few
surviving texts incorporated into the New Testament being restricted
to only four canonized gospels and various letters, mostly believed to
have been written by Paul. There are many references to what became
described as heretical ideas – but generally we know neither the full
explanation of most of these ideas nor the details of any theological basis
for such beliefs.

4.5   We know that there were disputes on theology from an early date – there
       are references to concern at Paul's teaching recorded in Acts 15 and 21,
       Galatians 2:16, Philippians 3:9 and James 4:13-16. As the rebellions in
       AD66-70 and AD133-136 led to widespread killing of the Jews in Judah
       and Samaria, leadership of the Jewish culture reverted to the large Jewish
       communities in Babylon and Alexandria, whilst the headquarters of Jesus
       original Nazarene church had migrated out of the Roman Empire to
       Pella, in AD65. Hence it was easy for 'Pauline Christianity' to become
       dominant within the Roman Empire. Others, including the descendants
       of Jesus family (known as the Desponsyi) campaigned for the church
       to be headquartered in Jerusalem – it is reported that at least two and
       maybe up to eight Desponsyi appealed to Pope Sylvester on this point in
       AD318.

Christianity in the first two centuries

4.6   We have already examined how in the second half of the first century,
       the fledgling church seemed to splinter into two movements. The original
       Nazarene Church, spreading largely around the edge and outside of the
       Roman Empire, established a flavour of Christianity which was clearly
       derived from Judaism and retained many aspects of Jewish ritual. This
       branch spread east, establishing churches across what is now Syria, Iraq,
       and across the Indian sub-continent (by Thomas); south into Egypt
       (Coptic) and Ethiopia; and westwards across North Africa and then
       northwards along the west coast of the Iberian peninsula (where James
       was revered), and establishing strongly in Ireland.

4.7   The other main outgrowth was into the heartlands of the Roman
       Empire, spearheaded by Paul. Pauline Christianity largely dismissed
       Jewish practices, Paul gradually concluded that God had decided that the
       laws he had laid down for the Jews, set out in the Torah, were impossible
       for men to comply with and, as any breach constituted sin, the Jews

could never attain salvation through the Law. So, despite being a chosen people, they needed Jesus for their salvation. In contrast, Paul taught that the Gentiles were now also embraced by God and offered salvation though belief in Jesus but need not follow the Jewish laws – their salvation would be from faith not legal compliance.

4.8   These two strands increasingly emphasised different aspects of Jesus teaching. Discoveries of hidden texts and academic analysis of these surviving documents, not seen for over 1500 years, has revealed both the nature of the heresies and why they were so reviled by the Roman church. Paul himself was familiar with the teaching that was later written out of the dogma of the Roman church, as can be found in several parts of his Epistles and indeed what some claim is a direct quote from what is now regarded as the foremost of the heretical texts, which he quotes in a way signifying he believes it highly authoritative.

4.9   It seems that in the centuries after Jesus taught on Earth, numerous versions of his key messages developed and various disputes arose over theological definitions. One hotly debated issue was over the nature of Jesus himself – was he God in human form, or a man who became divine, or a dual personality – man and God in one.

4.10   The arguments concerning the nature of Jesus fall into several categories. These ideas are generally understood almost exclusively from surviving polemics arguing against such beliefs as most of the texts which promulgated such ideas were destroyed. The attempts by the Roman church to counter these views, the theological critiques of them and evidence of edits to eradicate supportive phrases from the canonised texts of the New Testament can be better understood by remembering these broad categories:

• Adoptionist beliefs – that Jesus was born as a normal son of Mary and Joseph without any divine involvement. Jesus righteousness as a man led to his divine adoption (the grant of sonship) at his baptism by John in the Jordan. This was almost certainly the majority view during the first century, giving rise to numerous 'anti-adoptionist' theses;

• Separationist beliefs – that two entities co-existed within Jesus, the normal man and the divine being. The divinity was associated with Jesus period of ministry, as with adoptionists, separationists believed the divine entered the man at his baptism and also departed from Jesus on the cross – causing Jesus to exclaim "Father, why have you abandoned me". These writings were challenged by the 'anti-separationist' school;

- Docetic belief – that Jesus was not what he appeared, he only appeared to be of flesh and blood but was actually a spiritual being cloaked in a human form – hence Jesus could not have really experienced human suffering. These ideas gave us 'anti-docetic' tracts emphasising Jesus was flesh, blood and bones;

- Patri-passianist belief – that Jesus was in fact God, who converted himself into human form and suffered as a normal human whilst in that state – spawning 'anti-patripassianist' texts.

4.11   The definition of the nature of Jesus given by John, in 1:1 of his gospel, has been deliberately mistranslated to conform with Roman dogma. See section 16 of Part One for a full explanation. Those who originally heard John 1:1 understood him to relate that the Logos was the force created by God as an intermediary to convey God's instructions to mankind. John 1:1 might be more accurately written as *"In the beginning when humanity emerged, the Word was also created, and the Word was with God, and the Word was divine, a god in its own right."*

4.12   Origen of Alexandria, c184 to 253, a highly regarded early church leader wrote extensively, including a 32 book series providing a detailed commentary on the Gospel of John. Only 9 books of this series remain, fortunately including book 2, where in section 2.17-18, Origen used John 1:1 to demonstrate that Jesus was subordinate to God.

Political strategy of the Roman empire

4.13   The Romans were consummate administrators, they sought to establish peaceful societies to enable trade to flourish thereby generating strong tax revenues. Therefore, local administration was focused on suppressing dissent and extracting maximum tax revenues. Social unrest disrupted commerce and jeopardized commerce and tax revenues – therefore countering it was a priority for civil administration.

4.14   Across the entire Roman Empire, all populations shared a common heritage of worshipping local traditional gods, as most believed gods were territorial, which led to ready acceptance of the god of the ruling emperor as a natural consequence of being a subject. Traditionally, the ruler always had a special relationship with the territorial god, subjects understood that the ruler must surely have been favoured by the powers that be in order to win the throne. From recognising the emperor of Rome must be godlike to accepting the emperor as the son of a god was a small step. The emperor's majesty and power was visible everywhere – from the ubiquitous and fearsome legions, to the official tax collector, to the very coins in everyday use. Acknowledging that the emperor was in fact divine was a small step, understood and viewed as uncontroversial. Except by one small race – the Jews.

4.15   The Jews were known across the empire for their prickly attitude to all gods except their own and general refusal to share meals with others – because such food was both non-kosher and had usually been offered to &/or blessed by the local god. Roman soldiers and administrators had additional grievances, ever since Judea had been incorporated in the Empire, the province had been a source of trouble. Roman garrisons in Judea had suffered from regular assassinations and ambushes from the Zealots. Outside Judea, across the rest of the empire, the Jews had long established enclaves and tended to keep to themselves, they caused little trouble and were recognised as effective merchants.

4.16   Into this background a new movement emerged, emanating from Judea and spreading rapidly across the Empire, passionate disciples preached of a new type of divine being – offering adherents eternal life after death. Some of the beliefs of this new religion were alarming to the authorities – in particular the stress on rejecting all other gods, including rejecting worship of the Roman Emperor which was seen as obviously seditious! Christians also claimed their god was their king and ruler, which sounded treasonous as well.

4.17   Because Christians had no idol representing Jesus, they were often accused of being atheists, a worse status than a foreigner worshipping the god of his far away homeland – which was widely recognised as OK. Christian rituals spoke of eating flesh and drinking blood suggesting cannibalism whilst married couples addressing each other and others as brother and sister seemed licentious. (Hollywood and a few emperors whose antics shocked their contemporaries have given us a distorted view of Roman morality.) Another quite widespread teaching of many strands of Christianity was abstinence – abstinence from marriage and abstinence from sex, which many understood from Paul's teaching. This alarmed the authorities – if this got out of control, the empire would be doomed.

4.18   One impact of Christian missionary work, as recorded even by Paul, was on the local economy. Where significant numbers converted to Christianity, there was a commensurate reduction in demand for the accoutrements of pagan rituals – impacting a variety of local trades, lower donations, fewer sacrifices, reduced tourism, fewer attendees at festivals, etc – the loss of income and resulting unemployment generated anger towards the Christians. There are many instances recorded of civil disturbances arising from such missionary work – causing the local authorities to view Christian activity as destabilising. One is reminded of the likely fate of Akhenaten – after he triggered an uprising following his announcement that worship was to focus on a single god and thus most of the priestly caste of Egypt was being made redundant.

4.19   The dominant Greek culture, largely adopted by the Romans, accepted that most people worshipped multiple gods. Whilst a few gods were worshipped across the empire, such as Osiris and Isis (sometimes under local names), other gods were believed to be territorial, connected to certain cities or provinces from time immemorial, others were linked to particular festivals or even personal family favourites. The people were god fearing, at mealtimes the food was dedicated to one's god of choice, greetings acknowledged one's gods, celebrations took place at the temples, etc. This created a social glue and significant economic activity and employment. Into this came Christian missionaries declaring all the gods were fake and should be abandoned completely – creating a social shockwave. Converted Christians avoided dressing up in jewels and finery at church, many strands of Christianity preached avoidance of meat and of wine – diverting expenditure into helping feed and clothe the poor and disabled. Where conversion rates to Christianity were significant the economic impact was substantial.

4.20   One of the issues on which Pauline Christianity diverged from the original Nazarene version was in relation to women and sexual activity. The Nazarenes had almost 'added' Jesus teaching to Judaism, which strongly advocated marriage and procreation as a religious duty. Paul, who had tried and failed to win the hand of a daughter of a High Priest, bore a grudge which comes through in his early writing – observing that the other apostles were able to travel around accompanied by good Christian wives – indicating he wasn't.

4.21   There are references to Paul getting himself circumcised as an adult when seeking the approval of the High Priest to marry his daughter, as noted above. Maybe there were complications, maybe this explains the 'thorn' he complained about during his missionary travels. Certainly, Paul's views on circumcision underwent a complete 180 degree turn, from being compulsory to being an act which cut off a person from God permanently. Paul's teaching can be seen as quite negative towards women, starting a trend which resulted in many missionaries and early texts equating women with evil temptations designed to entice men into sin and sex. Many taught that even sex between married couples was a degrading lustful act.

4.22   Paul writes at length against sexual immorality, promoting the purity of remaining single and chaste like himself but warning those men burning with desire – to get a wife first (almost any wife). There are many references in 1 Corinthians promoting remaining single, extending his exhortations to married couples refraining from sex in order to be closer to righteousness.

4.23   Paul was also crystal clear in his views about women in the church: *"Women should remain silent in the churches. They are not allowed to speak, but must be in submission, as the law says. If they want to inquire about something, they should ask their own husbands at home; for it is disgraceful for a woman to speak in the church."* 1 Corinthians 14:34-35. And again in 1 Timothy 2:12 *"A woman should learn in quietness and full submission. I do not permit a woman to teach or to assume authority over a man; she must be quiet."* In 1 Timothy 3:1-7, Paul lays down the qualifications for anyone being considered for any role in the church, including being faithful to their wife – clearly assuming that any candidate must, of course, be male.

4.24   This indicates Rome was a totally male dominated society and the Catholic church remains so today. In his 1994 apostolic letter, Pope John Paul II declared that "the church has no authority whatsoever to confer priestly ordination on women and that this judgment is to be definitively held by all the church's faithful".

4.25   Despite Paul's views on women, it did not seem to hinder his success in converting women to Christianity. This led to many instances of women abandoning marriage offers to remain single. Thecla, betrothed to a rich young man, abandoned her plans and elected to follow Paul on his mission, bequeathing to us the Acts of Thecla (see 3.6 #49) – telling her story of elective chastity. Titus, a disciple who accompanied Paul on other missions, in a text known as Pseudo-Titus, (see 3.6 #65) warns against sex within marriage and urging abstinence. Another text, the Sentences of Sextus (see 3.6 #91), went further – promoting self-castration to avoid sin.

4.26   Considering the impact of Pauline Christianity on Roman society, the economic dislocation, the apparent treason towards the Emperor, the attacks on marriage and teaching against sexual activity of any kind – some must have seen Christianity undermining the very survival of both society and state. One might have expected Roman authorities to have taken a much harsher line against the new religion – the economic impact would have reduced tax collections and converting women to abstain from sex threatened men whilst the prospect of fewer young Romans threatened the future of the Roman state and the maintenance of her legions.

4.27   The truth, as ever, is more prosaic. Roman concern at the destabilisation of the social structure by this new Christian religion, was seen as another product of the troublesome Jews, leading to a number of edicts which affected Jews and by extension Christians both Jewish and Gentile. There are many historical references to Christian martyrs but it has been estimated that the actual number killed was actually far less than the Roman church ordered once it became the state religion.

4.28   The Edicts issued by Roman Emperors remained in force only whilst they were in office – and for many periods the turnover in emperors was very high, the 3rd century witnessed 29. Only two Roman Edicts stand out as specifically targeting Christians and seeking destruction of the faith on an empire wide basis – edicts of Decius and Diocletian, which occurred late enough for the faith to be firmly established. Languishing in a Roman prison was unhealthy and it could be a small step from arrest to becoming fodder for the lions. Edicts took time to be distributed to all corners of the empire and their enforcement depended upon the diligence, priorities and resources of each provincial administration.

4.29 Persecution of Christians was really an inevitable extension of action against Jews, stemming from Jewish rejection of local gods, refusal to recognise the Emperor as divine, terrorism by the Zealots and their social separateness. This led to many actions against Jewish communities. There were regular expulsions from Rome, but such actions were not exclusively against Jews – the historian Josephus tells us that in AD19, Tiberius expelled both Jews and worshippers of Isis from Rome and ordered 4000 Jews to serve in the Roman army. Under Emperor Domitian, between AD90 and 95, many Jews refused to pay the annual poll tax leading to reprisals against both Jews and Christians – many of whom were Jewish and widely still regarded as the same by many local authorities. Jews and Christians stood out by refraining from local social customs, most social events related to the worship of local and Roman gods, food being dedicated to the respective god – such separateness drew ostracism.

4.30 To the Romans, the province of Judea was a hotbed of terrorism and religious fanatics. Given the indications that up to half of Jesus 12 disciples may have had some connection with the Zealots, see chapter 11 of Part Three, it is surprising that the Romans did not take earlier action against the Christians. The most severe actions against the Jews were the military campaigns during AD66-70 and AD132-136, which today would be classified as genocide. Initially, the Roman authorities viewed Christians as just another squabbling Jewish sect. It may have been Claudius expulsion of the Jews from Rome in AD49, which helped define Christians as a distinct group in Roman eyes. Evidence indicates that up to this time Christian groups in Rome originated in Jewish circles and were led by Jews and attracted Gentiles. During the last five years of Claudius, without Jews in the predominantly house churches, they became exclusively Gentile and separately identifiable, with Jewish Christians trickling back into Rome only after AD54. This change of perception converted Christianity from a sect within a legally recognised religion, into an unrecognised and illegal religion.

4.31 Hollywood has bolstered the general impression that the Roman authorities were responsible for killing huge numbers of Christians. However, the conclusion reached by historians that have studied the issue is that Roman persecution was actually very limited. Edicts attacking Christians were rare and short-lived, the records identify few being issued and those were in force for a total of less than 10 years during the three centuries before AD313, when the joint emperors, Constantine and Licinius, issued the Edict of Milan granting full legal rights to Christians.

4.32   Whilst there were various local actions by Roman authorities which were directed against Christians, estimates of the total number of Christians martyred by Roman authorities are in the 5500 to 6000 range. W. Frend in *The Rise of Christianity* and N. Harari in *Sapiens, a Brief History of Humankind* both arrive at similar figures.

4.33   If the above estimates are realistic, the numbers martyred were really surprisingly small. From Jesus crucifixion in 33 to the Edict of Milan of 313 is 280 years – even using the higher estimate of 6000 deaths, indicates an annual average of only 22. During this period, the empire consisted of 33 provinces plus 11 regions of mainland Italy – therefore, on average, each Roman Governor killed one Christian every two years. It suggests that, whilst there were a handful of horrific targeted massacres of Christians, generally during the centuries prior to the Roman church merging with the Roman state – Christians were able to profess their beliefs largely unmolested.

4.34   The Edicts that specifically targeted Christians were:

   (i)   By Nero in 64 – which applied only to Rome and resulted from Nero looking for a community to blame for the Great Fire.

   (ii)   Under Marcus Aurelius (161-180), a Stoic, who thought martyrdom accepted by Christians was theatrical nonsense. Opinions differ as to whether Aurelius himself promoted persecution of Christians or sought to dampen civil disturbances. Whilst no imperial Edict appears to have been promulgated, there is evidence of regional governors seeking guidance from Rome which indicates support for action against Christians. It is recorded that Aurelius agreed with a rule proposed by the governor of Lyons in 177 that the property of Christians who refused to recant would be given to their accusers. But, the only evidence we have of this event is from Eusebius, who quotes a long letter in his *Ecclesiastical History* writing some 120 years later, in 300. The letter Eusebius quotes describes numerous tortures in such excessive gory detail that some query the accuracy. However, no other author of the period makes any reference to the events in Lyon. On the contrary, we have Irenaeus, Bishop of Lyon, who wrote his massive work *Against Heresies* only three years later, 180, in the same city. Irenaeus not only omits any reference to the alleged slaughter but writes that "The Romans have given the world peace, and we Christians travel along the roads and across the seas wherever we will". Another highly regarded church father, Tertullian, a contemporary of Marcus Aurelius, testifies that Aurelius was a "protector" of Christians.

(iii)   By Emperor Decius during 250-251. Decius became emperor at a time when Rome was reeling from a series of natural calamities and was the first to attack Christians right across the empire. In 250, Decius issued an Edict demanding an annual offering to the Roman gods and the wisdom of the Emperor, audited by the issue of a certificate (libellus) when citizens performed. Christians who refused to worship were stripped of their property and cruelly tortured to death. Fortunately, Decius died the following year and the edict lapsed.

(iv)   By Diocletian during 303-305. Diocletian was a strong military leader who became emperor in 285. He sought to establish order across the empire following a century of political turmoil. Diocletian ended the shared authority of Senate and Emperor established by Augustus in 27BC, he saw no place for religions that denied the Roman state gods. In 303, one Edict ordered the cessation of Christian meetings, the destruction of church meeting places and the imprisonment of all bishops, elders and deacons who were to be tortured until they denied Jesus and the burning of all Christian texts. A second edict ordered all Christians to sacrifice to Roman gods, upon pain of death if they refused. The pace of persecutions slackened after Diocletian abdicated in 305 and his successor, Galerius, realised eradication of Christianity was impossible and was damaging the empire. In 311, Galerius issued an Edict permitting Christian meetings again.

4.35   The darkest period, the Diocletian persecutions, had indeed come just before the dawn – two years later, the Edict of Milan granted full legal rights to Christianity as a religion.

5

The formation of dogma by the Roman Church

5.1   The conventional view of the development of Christianity is that
      the early church showed great unity of belief and relied on apostolic
      authority to root out heretical ideas that emerged This view has been
      handed down to us mainly through Eusebius, whose *Ecclesiastical History*
      originally in Greek has also survived in various early translations.
      Originally, *Ecclesiastical History* comprised ten books, published as a series
      between 313 and 324. It established a belief that the Roman Church
      had inherited the right beliefs (Orthodox view) tracing its origin back to
      apostolic teaching. All deviations from the creed adopted by the Roman
      church being labelled as heretical.

5.2   One nugget comes down to us from Eusebius, who spent years in
      Caesarea studying at the famous Theological Library. This library was
      founded by Pamphilus, an avid collector of early Christian texts, who was
      martyred in 309, probably when Eusebius was living there. Many early
      church 'fathers', including Jerome, also studied there and by 630 the
      library was reputed to hold over 30,000 documents, making it the second
      largest collection after Alexandria. Eusebius wrote many pamphlets
      quoting from the original manuscript of the Gospel of Matthew, which
      he stated was held at the Caesarea Library, specifying that it did not
      contain the 'orthodox' trinitarian text of 28.19 but a commission to
      go out and teach in Jesus sole name. In *Ecclesiastical History*, Eusebius
      stated that he had studied the *Gospel according to the Hebrews*, written by
      the apostle Matthew in Aramaic. Today, Christians study the *Gospel of
      Matthew*, originally written in 'Semitic Greek' and drawing heavily on the

Gospel of Mark (incorporating some 600 verses of the 661 verses of Mark), and other material generally attributed to two other sources nowadays referred to as the 'M' source and the 'Q' source.

5.3   The majority of scholars place the writing of the *Gospel of Matthew* <u>after</u> the destruction of the Temple in 70, hence the inclusion of a tortuous and patently fake genealogy of Jesus (the Temple records having been burned); and <u>after</u> the *Gospel of Mark* upon which it draws heavily – hence a date of between 75 and 85 is widely accepted. Some point to a later date and a minority to an earlier date prior to the destruction of the Temple. It is generally agreed that the author was not the apostle Matthew but another who most likely had never met Jesus. However, whilst this very second-hand *Gospel of Matthew* was adopted by the Roman Church and tweaked to conform with the 'orthodox' creed, the authentic apostolic *Gospel to the Hebrews*, which Eusebius states was written by the apostle Matthew, was found to be 'heretical' by the Roman authorities and all but eradicated from history. NB The *Gospel to the Hebrews* should not be confused with the *Epistle to the Hebrews* which is included in the New Testament and is generally attributed to Paul, although some question whether Paul was the author.

5.4   The *Gospel to the Hebrews* is one of the few early texts later ruled heretical that was widely quoted by preeminent church fathers. It is quoted by Papias (died c130); and by both **Hegesippus** (writing c170 in his five books of *Commentaries on the Acts of the Church*) and Eusebius (writing c320) who refer to this gospel but do not quote from it. Fragments of the *Gospel to the Hebrews* are preserved in the writings of Clement of Alexandria (150-215), Origen (184-253), Cyril (Bishop of Jerusalem, 313-386) and Jerome (347-420). The full extent of this gospel is no longer known. Some complete copies survived until at least the 9th century, as Nicephorus (Patriarch of Constantinople between 806 and 818), noted in his listing of 'canonical' and 'apocryphal' texts that the *Gospel of the Hebrews* contained 2200 lines.

5.5   A number of early writers noted the use of the *Gospel to the Hebrews* by the Nazarene and Ebionite churches – which may have contributed to the Roman church declaring it heretical.

Which was the aberration – the Orthodox or the Heretical

5.6   The victors always write the history, but recent research is increasingly concluding that what today is deemed the orthodox dogma was originally viewed as an aberrant minority view and what the Roman church declared as heretical was in fact the original mainstream dogma.

5.7   As Bart Ehrman states in *The Orthodox Corruption of Scripture*, what later became known as the Orthodox view of Christianity was simply one of many competing interpretations of Christianity during the first two centuries. The power and authority of Rome became the arbiter of dogma, texts were accepted for future canonization or rejected, based upon how close they hewed to the dogma determined by successive Church Councils.

5.8   The earliest Council making determination of the current set of New Testament books was that in Rome in 382, presided over by Pope Damascus – who then commissioned the Latin Vulgate based upon this selection the following year. This was not definitive, there were earlier collections of texts widely referred to and preserved – including the Codex Vaticanus (c310) and the Codex Sinaiticus (c345). These early collections included a number of books later ruled heretical – including the *Book of Wisdom*, the *Apocalypse of Peter*, the *Epistle of Barnabus, 1 Clement, 2 Clement* and the *Shepherd of Hermas*. On the other hand, these early bibles often excluded books that later were canonized – such as *2 Peter, 2 John, 3 John, Jude* and *Revelations*. Other successors to the original Nazarene church each adopted differing collections of books for their bibles – with significant variations arising between Roman Catholic, Eastern Orthodox, Coptic, Syriac, Ethiopian, etc.

5.9   Once a Council of the Roman church determined what was accepted as canon, all copies of any books that had been rejected were systematically hunted down and destroyed. However, many orthodox views are neither self-evident interpretations of events nor an original apostolic view – this is a very important point, as orthodox interpretations frequently claim to be founded upon apostolic texts. For example, even in the gospel texts as presented to us today, no apostle described Jesus using any of the following terms which were adopted in the Nicaean creed: *begotten of the Father before the creation of all worlds, God of God, light of light, very God of very God, begotten not made, being of one substance with the Father....who for us and for our salvation came down from heaven and was incarnate from the virgin Mary.* The Catholic Catechism attributes none of these phrases to an apostolic source but merely to Catholic officials and councils.

5.10   These competing views can all be traced back as being in circulation during the second century and became the battleground for continuing controversy over the next two centuries. The dearth of early texts which survived scrutiny by the Roman church (our current NT) compares with around 200 texts we now know were used by early Christian churches. This variety of texts originally in use reflects the popularity of various beliefs that all became condemned as heretical.

5.11   The evidence from the earliest texts points strongly to the initial belief being that Jesus was born fully human from the union of two human parents, being adopted by God at his baptism – when he was endowed with divine powers. The main issue that early theologians struggled with was the idea that, if Jesus was clearly junior to God, how could Jesus be seen as having the power to grant eternal salvation – surely only God himself had the power to do this? One can imagine how paramount this concern would have been in that contemporary setting – when the consensus was that one world existed, the stars in the sky were arranged to provide lighting for mankind – who was the central purpose of creation. From this point of view, there was a huge gulf between God, the array of gods recognized by most people and the man Jesus – how could such a man claim to have the ultimate power of God?

5.12   Today, our knowledge of the universe makes us feel very insignificant. If a Creator God has helpers, even one per _galaxy_ would mean Jesus is part of a team of 10 billion 'sons' of God. Even so, as a direct report, Jesus could wield enormous authority. Reading the NT texts, even in the form we have today (after millennia of possible editing), the overwhelming thrust of Jesus' recorded pronouncements is that he was instructed by his Father, doing his Father's work and had been granted authority over humans by his Father. There is evidence, as we shall examine below in section 15, whether Jesus believed or described his Father as God.

5.13   The Roman Church was formed and supported by devout Christians who came together to celebrate their belief in Jesus and live in accordance with his teaching, undertaking great charitable works and dispensing care and relief to the impoverished and the sick. The social care provided by Christians across the Roman Empire was a key factor in the political calculation to reverse policy and support the Christian religion – far from a threat to the Empire, Christian works were seen as supportive of social peace and prosperity.

5.14   Emperor Constantine was a master tactician but he did not live according to Christian standards at all – he murdered his wife and a son, he revelled in mass executions of defeated soldiers and enjoyed torturing his enemies. He marvelled at Christians faith in their God and their steadfast belief in immortality if martyred but their refusal to worship him made him feel weak. He was confused by the myriad arguments raging over dogma and concluded the solution was to absorb and thereby control the church rather than continue to sporadically try to fight it. The strength of faith exhibited by its adherents he found very attractive. So, Constantine invited 1,800 bishops to the Council of Nicaea. However, the overwhelming majority were wary enough to decline the invitation and only 300 attended. If the power of the state was fused with the faith of these Christians he would be in a very strong position. Therefore Constantine wanted a strong centralised church, wielding power and accountable to him.

5.15   During the second and third centuries, theological debate flourished but once Christianity was adapted by Constantine and a few decades later adopted as the state religion – there was an abrupt change. With recognition as a legal religion and later when becoming the state religion, the administrators had to quickly adjust from periodic persecution to enjoying the lavish perks of being high state officials. One might observe that the flow of wealth and status helped the Roman Church sell its soul at the Council of Nicaea – agreeing to the Emperor's demands for a merger with his own religion, Sol Invictus, as the price of the Pauline theology achieving legal dominance.

5.16   Indeed, by the time of Constantine, the tomb of St Peter was in a complex dedicated to the worship of Sol Invictus (aka Shamash to Semitic peoples and Mithras for Persians), so when Constantine begun the construction of a basilica over the tomb St Peter in 322, for Romans it truly represented a merger of the two religions.

5.17   The Roman church became an arm of the state, organized along military lines to enforce loyalty to a standardized set of beliefs. Deviant views were no longer tolerated, questioning the dogma set out by the Roman church was questioning the Chairman of the Church councils which decided upon them – the Roman Emperor or his appointee.

New dogma determined at Council of Nicaea, AD325

5.18   The deliberate distortion of Jesus teaching and the suppression of all records of some of the original teaching begun as a result of the resolutions determined at Nicaea.

5.19   The logic behind the changes forced through at the conclusion of the Council was to establish a powerful religious organization applying a standard agreed dogma. Jesus had been unique and divine, salvation came only through the church and the church could withhold grace and thereby consign one to everlasting hell. This promised huge influence over the lives of the population and a very effective political control mechanism.

5.20   Some key issues needed to sorted out: no one could think Jesus had been born an ordinary man who later became God – if Jesus could do it perhaps others might think they could. Therefore, Jesus had to be described as fathered by a god, just like all other gods had been, and any references to him as being born of normal human parents suppressed. If Jesus was not only fathered by God but was, in fact, God himself then obviously any reference to Jesus having a twin brother had to go, indeed all references to Jesus having any siblings at all had to be excised. To underline the church's monopoly power over access to salvation, all records of Jesus teaching of reincarnation which gave the spirit multiple chances to redeem itself (by uniting with its soul before bodily death) had to be eradicated.

5.21   The dogma of the church became the beliefs of the state religion, to hold other beliefs about Christianity was heretical. To hold heretical texts was treason – and thus begun the great bonfires of banned works and the heretic hunting. Christianity, at least the Roman kind, was not obligatory for another 55 years – one could still worship other gods, including Sol Invictus but if you claimed to be a Christian you had to stick to the official doctrines.

5.22   It was very clear that only a minority really supported the key conclusions tabled at Nicaea – only 10% of the bishops attending agreed with the idea that Jesus had equality with God. There were three main schools of thought amongst the 300 odd bishops who attended the Council of Nicaea, convened in the Emperor's palace and funded entirely by the state:

- Athanasius, a Trinitarian from Alexandria, who believed Jesus was absolutely equal to the Father, has always existed beside the Father and is of the very same substance as the Father. Jesus is absolute God and must be worshipped as God. Around 10% supported this view, including Bishop Hosius – who chaired the meetings when Constantine was not present.

- A much larger minority, led by Arius, believed Jesus was not God but must be divine – as in John 1:1, Jesus is the Logos. Jesus was made by God and therefore God must have existed before Jesus. Jesus is different from God and must not be worshipped as the one true God.

- However, the vast majority, over 200 bishops, led by Eusebius, whose views were very similar to Arius – strongly agreeing that Jesus was not God, had not always existed, had been made by God but was of similar substance to God – but was not equal to God, was subordinate to God and must not be worshipped as God.

5.23   It is clearly recorded that 90% of the bishops agreed with the gospel of John, seeing Jesus as created by God to communicate the Word of God to humanity, a role endowing divine status. Many months of stormy debate ensued before Emperor Constantine forced acceptance of Athanasius views on the Council by threatening them to sign the Trinitarian creed or be exiled and treated as heretics – i.e. be 'terminated with extreme prejudice' !! The creed was amended to incorporate key phrases such as *"begotten not made"* and *"of one substance with the Father"*.

5.24   In line with classical beliefs, Emperor Constantine saw himself as descended from a god – and despite the notion that he was converted to Christianity prior to Nicaea, historical evidence shows he maintained his worship of Sol Invictus long afterwards. It is noteworthy that Sol Invictus was a sect that was already headed by a trinity. Constantine hated the Jews, a common trait amongst Romans who remembered numerous terrorist attacks and years of rebellions across Judea, by a stubborn people that socially isolated themselves (by refusing to eat with other citizens) and who refused to acknowledge other gods, including those Emperors who had decided that they were divine. Therefore, the idea that adopting the powerful new Christian religion that had gripped large parts of the empire also meant acknowledging the Jewish god as supreme was an anathema. Accordingly, Constantine, attracted to the proposals of the Alexandrian school of bishops led by Athanasius, demanded that Christianity adopt a Trinitarian structure. Constantine was familiar with a trinity and saw himself as a far more worthy 'son' of god – after all, as Emperor, he headed the dominant earthly power and he was blessed with numerous military victories – in these terms, he saw Jesus as a failure – and himself as a more worthy member of the godhead, suitably qualified to become part of the Trinity following his own death.

5.25   In the early centuries, debate raged over various aspects of belief, as biblical texts were laboriously copied by hand, it was common for helpful margin notes to get incorporated into the text. Promoters of dubious dogma saw opportunities to tweak accepted texts to support their arguments – Matthew 28:19, a grammatically clumsy insertion to support the idea of a trinity, being one of the most notorious. The prevalence of widespread textual changes being added into transcripts can be judged by the fact that no less than 70 variations of the Lord's Prayer have been identified in surviving early manuscripts. In Part Three of this series we saw that both Luke and Matthew contain opening sections on the birth and early childhood of Jesus which profoundly conflict with each other in many respects whilst containing many assertions that bear no credibility.

5.26   Building upon statements found in the canonized texts, the Roman authorities developed a clear strategy to establish hegemony over adherents lives – and not just their Earthly lives. The Roman church concluded enormous power should be vested in its leader. The Pope was declared to be God's representative on Earth and vested with the power to act as sole arbiter of one's afterlife experience. It was concluded that the Pope had access to God's grace, indeed he was uniquely vested with the grace of Jesus – a reservoir of grace which was held to be infinite. Thus the Pope could dispense unlimited forgiveness as he felt appropriate...

Subsequent Church Councils agonized over dogma

5.27   The adoption of the trinitarian dogma forced through by Constantine in 325 was far from universally established. A much larger and more representative Council held at Rimini-Seleucia in 359, reversed the Nicaea decision and the 500 bishops present adopted the Arian creed that Jesus was not God, was subordinate to God and must not be worshipped as God.

5.28   However, this religious rejection of trinitarianism did not sit well with the Roman political authorities and in 381, Emperor Theodosius I, who saw himself as potentially divine (Theodosius meaning 'giving to God'), convened the First Council of Constantinople. This Council restored the Nicaean concept of the trinity, declaring that God the Father, God the Son and the Holy Spirit were all strictly one being in three hypostases, misleadingly translated as 'persons'. The Christological question then arose as to how Jesus Christ could be both divine and human. This was formally resolved after much debate by the Ecumenical Councils of 431, 451 and 680 (Ephesus, Chalcedon & Constantinople III).

5.29   Power was vested in the clergy, distributed downwards by the Pope, through the bishops, whilst the sacraments disbursed grace. However, the Bible was reserved solely for the clergy – its contents judged too difficult for lay people to understand and carried the risk of people 'misunderstanding' the texts.

Dogma invented by the Roman Church

5.30   Catholic dogma was thoughtfully designed to accrete power to the Church. The Roman church was established with a clear hierarchical structure designed to enable command and control – over both the temporal and the spiritual affairs of every living person and even extending to influence the fate of the poor souls of the dead who were stuck in purgatory. Temporal power over the living aimed high – a document appeared entitled the 'Donation of Constantine' purporting to be a gift by Emperor Constantine. This vested the Papacy with power to appoint and approve the kings and princes of all lands within the former Roman Empire. First used in negotiations by Pope Hadrianus I in 778, use of the Donation was extended so that it became a Papal matter whether one king could attack another; whilst any kingdom which allowed heretical views to prosper was at risk of invasion at the command of the Pope. It was only in the midst of the Reformation in the 16th century that the Donation was admitted to be a forgery.

5.31   We shall look at twelve aspects of the control developed by the Roman church:

A   The term 'messiah' was re-defined as meaning 'son of God'
B   Original Sin, a product of Pauline theology
C   Papal authority, as God's representative on Earth

D	Sacraments, services through which grace is dispensed
E	Indulgences
F	Relics
G	Purgatory, two Limbos & Hades
H	Excommunication
I	Bodily resurrection
J	Mariology
K	Church services exclusively in Latin until 1965
L	Control of clergy through celibacy

5.32 Another aspect, restricting access to the Bible, is covered in the next chapter – something that would certainly be most puzzling to Jesus.

5.33 To gain a more detailed understanding of Catholic doctrine, I recommend reading the Catholic Catechism. It provides a useful explanation for the elements of the Creeds and all other aspects of Catholic dogma. At the end of this chapter, I provide a brief summary and draw attention to a few statements which are particularly noteworthy.

A   The term 'messiah' was re-defined as meaning 'son of God'

5.34 In the definition of the trinity and in liturgy, Jesus is positioned as both the 'son of God' and as co-substantial with God – i.e. Jesus is God. This definition was reinforced by deliberately mistranslating the Jewish term 'Messiah' with the implied meaning 'son of God', as in liberal usage of the phrase: 'Jesus Christ, the Messiah, the Son of God' throughout Catholic liturgy. This phrase jumps out as a classic oxymoron. As detailed in Part Three chapter 7, it is extremely doubtful that Jesus, whilst potentially eligible, was actually ever anointed a Messiah – a process involving use of a special mix of oil and herbs set out in Deuteronomy. Moreover the title Messiah is clearly defined as a male descendant of either Aaron (the first high priest) or of King David – which given the evidence discussed in Part Three, Jesus might indeed have been eligible – but only if he had a human father. But the term Messiah definitely never meant 'son of God'.

5.35 The wider issue of the nature of Jesus, Christology, is discussed elsewhere – in section 16 of Part One.

B   Original Sin, a product of Pauline theology

5.36   Original Sin may be taken to mean: (i) the sin that Adam and Eve
        committed; (ii) a consequence of this first sin, the hereditary stain of our
        natural inclination to commit sins (concupiscence) with which we are
        born on account of our origin and descent from Adam & Eve.

5.37   The term Original Sin is unknown in Judaism and mainstream Church
        teachings on this doctrine seem to contradict the core principles of the
        Torah. According to traditional Christian belief, when Adam and Eve
        ate from the forbidden Tree of Knowledge all their descendants became
        infected with sin and all were committed to die. Being a slave to sin,
        man is lost in a state of sin and held captive since the 'fall'. Because of
        man's uncontrollable lust to sin, man cannot be saved from everlasting
        damnation – except through faith in Jesus.

5.38   Statement 402 of the Catholic Catechism sources its assertion on the
        universality of sin from Paul: *By one man's disobedience, many (i.e. all) men were
        made sinners: sin came into the world through one man and death through sin, and so
        death spread to all men because all men sinned.* (Romans 5:12) Paul's technique
        of balanced argument led him to theorise that because the first man had
        sinned, all men became sinners and therefore all men died; whilst the
        arrival of Jesus meant all would be saved and thereby all would live. Thus
        the foundation of Pauline theology was based upon confusing mortal
        bodily death, which is universal for lifeforms, with the second death –
        which, indeed, Jesus did teach is linked to sin.

5.39   The rationale for the Church to take this extreme position appears to
        have been simply political. The early Roman church saw that reliance on
        the Torah and Jesus own teaching indicated that man can, through his
        devotion and obedience to God, save himself from eternal damnation.
        This was a threat to the power of the church. Moreover, if righteousness
        can be achieved through submission to the commands of Jesus, what
        benefit could Jesus' death provide for mankind?

5.40   Christians who also accept and believe the Old Testament face a
        quandary. Near the end of his life, Moses declared to the Israelites that
        it is man alone who can and must merit his own salvation. Moreover,
        Moses dismisses the idea that obedience to God is "too difficult or far
        off." Moses declared to Israel that righteousness has been placed within
        man's reach. Deuteronomy 30:10-16 states: *"if you obey the Lord your God
        and keep his commands and decrees that are written in this Book of the Law and*

turn to the Lord your God with all your heart and with all your soul. Now what I am commanding you today is not too difficult for you or beyond your reach. It is not up in heaven, so that you have to ask, "Who will ascend into heaven to get it and proclaim it to us so we may obey it?" Nor is it beyond the sea, so that you have to ask, "Who will cross the sea to get it and proclaim it to us so we may obey it?" **No, the word is very near you; it is in your mouth and in your heart so you may obey it.** *See, I set before you today life and prosperity, death and destruction. For I command you today to love the Lord your God, to walk in obedience to him, and to keep his commands, decrees and laws; then you will live and increase, and the Lord your God will bless you in the land you are entering to possess."*

5.41 If Judaism draws great comfort from this encouragement, how can Christianity conclude man's condition makes it impossible to save himself – when Moses declares it is "not far off", "not too hard", and "you may do it"?

5.42 Thus the Torah presented Paul with quite a problem in explaining his newly devised faith. Paul writes in Romans and Galatians that man is utterly depraved and incapable of saving himself through his own obedience to God. How could Paul, a pupil of the leading expert of the Torah at that time and acknowledged himself as an expert, make such an assertion? Paul managed to conceal this vexing theological problem with unparalleled literary manipulation – setting an early standard for scriptural revisionism for future New Testament authors.

5.43 Romans 10:8 is a classic example, here Paul proclaims that he is quoting Deuteronomy 30:14 – yet he stops short of the vital conclusion and expunges the remaining phrase of this crucial verse. In Romans, Paul writes:- *But what does it say? "The word is near you; it is in your mouth and your heart."* But the final phrase of 30:14 *"that you may do it"* seem deliberately omitted by Paul as contradicted his theology, whilst creating the illusion that his theological message conformed to the principles of the Torah – easily convincing the Gentiles who had a poor knowledge of the texts.

5.44 The Old Testament identifies many who are judged righteous by God – including Noah, Job and Abraham. Even Cain is told he can save himself, soon after the sin of Adam and Eve is narrated, God declares that man can master his passionate lust for sin. In Genesis 4:6-7, God explains to Cain: *Then the Lord said to Cain, "Why are you angry? Why is your face downcast? If you do what is right, will you not be accepted? But if you do not do* *what is right, sin is crouching at your door; it desires to have you, **but you must rule over it.***"

5.45 Likewise the concept of Original Sin is completely absent from the Gospels. Indeed, it appears that Luke unwittingly undermined Paul's teaching on Original Sin by stating that the parents of John the Baptist were righteous in the sight of God:- *"Both of them (Zechariah and Elizabeth) were upright in the sight of God, observing all the Lord's commandments and regulations blamelessly".* (Luke 1:6)

5.46 It is generally believed that the Luke who wrote the eponymous gospel was the same Luke who authored Acts. Luke writes that Elizabeth and Zechariah were to be regarded as "blameless", that this couple observed "all the Lord's commandments" – which radically contradicts Paul's central teaching that no one is capable of keeping the myriad rules of the Torah. According to Pauline theology, Luke's claim that Zachariah and Elizabeth were sinless, is untenable.

5.47 Sequentially, the consensus view is that Acts was written first, before AD57, whilst Paul's epistle to the Romans was written in AD57 and the gospel of Luke sometime after AD70. As on other big issues (such as circumcision), Paul's theology on Original Sin may have evolved over time – a development that Luke may not have been aware of when writing his gospel.

5.48 Not only does the Torah make no reference to Original Sin but it specifically limits inherited sin to the fourth generation. The original Jewish god, El Elyon, makes no reference to either original or inherited sin. His successor, Yahweh, does – twice in warnings to those who worship other gods (other rocks, or idols) and another more generally – but each time specifically stating that the iniquities of the fathers will be visited upon their sons unto the fourth generation, women seem to be exempted. In both versions of the Ten Commandments, inherited sin is specified as caused by Yahweh's jealousy aroused when a father worships an idol – Exodus 20:5 and Deuteronomy 5:8-9. In Numbers 14:18 the inheritance of sin is declared to be from both parents, for any type of sin, and to all children – but is still limited to the 4th generation: *The Lord is slow to anger, abounding in love and forgiving sin and rebellion. Yet he does not leave the guilty unpunished; he punishes the children for the sin of the parents to the third and fourth generation.* But in all these references, sin is only inherited until the 4th generation.

5.49   So, there is no foundation for the concept of original sin being inherited by all generations in the Torah – something Paul would have been fully aware of. What does Jesus say? As one might expect, Jesus seems to refute the Torah – in John 9:3 states: *"Neither this man nor his parents sinned," said Jesus, "but this happened so that the works of God might be displayed in him"*. Jesus appears to refute inherited sin completely.

5.50   Many Christians believe sin is something existing in the world, something which can tempt them to do wrong – as if sin is an external force they must try to resist. But Jesus is quoted quite clearly stating that sin only comes from man's deliberate actions: *Peter asked "Since you have explained everything to us, tell us this also: what is the sin of this world?" The Saviour replied "there is no sin in the world, but it is you that make sin when you do the things that are like the nature of adultery. Beware no one leads you astray, for the Son of Man is within you – follow after him. Those who seek him will find him."* (Gospel of Mary)

5.51   Paul's idea that everyone is a slave to sin, unable to escape, and his solution – merely belief in Jesus (no works) may have been born of his own experience. The idea of Original Sin inherited by all and inescapable without grace dispensed by the Church was enthusiastically taken up by Augustine – at a time when the Jews and their scripture was very unfashionable.

5.52   Claims that man can restrain his lust for sin, e.g. by Pelagius, was declared to be heresy. The fact that Genesis places the promise of self-salvation immediately following the sin in the Garden of Eden must be a challenge for orthodox theologians. It directly contradicts Paul in Romans repeatedly insisting that man can do nothing to release himself from sin's powerful grip.

5.53   Judaism contends that God did not give mankind desires that we could not control or commandments that we could not keep. Why would God command people to observe laws he knew they could not keep? And then punish us for not being obedient to commandments that he knew we could not keep. Would any loving parent raise his child that way?

5.54   The Roman Church realised it had created quite a problem – it was so busy developing dogma to exert and maintain control over the population that it overlooked the fact that most of its doctrine either lacked any scriptural basis or flatly contradicted both scripture and Jesus teaching. The solution was obvious – prohibit the laity from reading the bible – a policy which was vigorously maintained right up until 1943, yes 1943.

5.55   The origin of the debate challenging Paul's concept of Original Sin has been linked to Theodorus (350 – 428), who was writing biblical commentaries when only 18 and ordained as Bishop of Mopsuestia in 392. Theodorus wrote that the sin of Adam was not the origin of death. Celestius, a friend of Pelagius and in Rome during the period 398 to 410 when they both fled from the sacking by the Visigoths, took Theodorus idea further: "Adam was to die in every hypothesis, whether he sinned or did not sin. His sin injured himself only and not the human race." Pelagius (354 – 418), argued that if mankind was created by God, mankind must be inherently good, why would God create man as inherently sinful? Pelagius saw man as a moral creature, fully capable of doing good things and needing only to be given divine teaching to be able to voluntarily obey Jesus – firmly rejecting the idea that every person is born sinful.

5.56   Paul's assertion of Original Sin as the cause of every man needing salvation was taken up by Augustine of Hippo. Augustine was Bishop of Hippo (in modern Algeria) from 396 to 430. In his work 'De nuptiis et concupiscentia' (II xxvi 43), Augustine wrote *"the deliberate sin of the first man is the cause of Original Sin"*. Augustine focused on the 'hereditary stain' of Adam's sin rather than the circumstances of the event or its aftermath – because he too had developed Pauline theology beyond anything in the Torah or the Gospels. Like Paul, Augustine had an unsavoury past and may have seen inherited sin as a good excuse for his past behaviour.

5.57   Augustine argued that Pelagius and Celestius had overlooked the operation of divine grace. Augustine asserted that Adam's sin meant that mankind lost the ability not to sin and that therefore any good deeds done by Christians required grace from God to be done. Pelagius believed that God had granted free will to all mankind, not just Christians and that no one inherited a predisposition to sin. Celestius went further and denied that grace was required for Christians to do good deeds – because if any Christian sinned it would imply that God's grace had failed.

5.58   Naturally the church authorities bristled at such open debate and at the Council of Carthage in 411, Celestius was condemned for holding six views regarded as heretical. We have no record of whether Celestius agreed with the formulations asserted by his accusers, but the minutes list his heresies thus:

       (i)   Adam would have died whether he had sinned or not; citing Romans 5:12

       (ii)   Adam's sin did not harm the entire human race;

       (iii)   Children are born into the same state as Adam was born into, i.e. sinless;

       (iv)   The entire human race neither dies through Adam's sin nor is saved through Jesus resurrection;

       (v)   The Torah gives entrance to heaven as well as the Gospel;

       (vi)   Before Jesus, some men lived without sin.

5.59   I must say, if Celestius did make these claims, I personally feel close alignment with Celestius.

5.60   The central tenet of what became known as Pelagianism lived on. Ideas evolved, with parental transmission of death (as with hereditary diseases) being admitted but not parental transmission of sin. They argued that when Paul wrote of the transmission of sin he was referring to death not that sin was inherited. This position was condemned as heretical at the First Council of Orange in 441.

5.61   The Second Council of Orange, in 529, took the orthodox view further, declaring that: "One man has transmitted to the whole human race not only the death of the body, which is the punishment of sin, but even sin itself, which is the death of the soul." As death of the body results from the deprivation of life, so the death of the soul results from the loss of sanctifying grace – which according to all theologians is the principle of supernatural life. Therefore if original sin is the death of the soul – it is the loss of sanctifying grace. Mankind is therefore captive to sin and unable to save himself.

5.62 Thereafter, Pelagianism persisted but whilst admitting Adam had caused mankind to sin – this was not due to the stain of sin being inherited but adults committing sin in imitation of Adam. This position was finally ruled heretical at the Council of Trent, 1545 – 1563.

5.63 This left the Catholic church with an enduring problem – one effect of Adam's sin is the absence of sanctifying grace from the new-born child. If a child is still born, or dies before baptism, does it die without grace? This is explored further under section G "Purgatory, two Limbos & Hades" below.

5.64 The Roman Church still maintains that mankind only suffers mortal bodily death as a consequence of Adam eating a piece of fruit – as per Statement 1018 of the Catechism: *"As a consequence of original sin, man must suffer bodily death, from which man would have been immune had he not sinned"*.

5.65 According to the Roman Church, if you don't believe in Original Sin you can't really believe in Jesus: indeed, Statement 389 rather arrogantly asserts that: *The Church, which has the mind of Christ, knows very well that we cannot tamper with the revelation of original sin without undermining the mystery of Christ.*

5.66 A number of leading philosophers have continued to question the concept of original sin. Eric Fromm (1900-1980), in *You will be like Gods*, wrote that the first act of disobedience was the beginning of human freedom, the first act of liberation. Fromm noted that the ability to distinguish good from evil is regarded as a virtue and that, acting independently, man became self-aware and begun the process of establishing moral values. This interpretation strikes a chord with my thinking – that partaking of the knowledge offered by the serpent Enki, the source of wisdom, was the crucial step for mankind to transition from being just another animal species towards becoming a civilised sentient species. It is noteworthy to consider Fromm's background – he studied the Talmud under two highly regarded rabbis: J Horowitz and Salman Baruch Rabinkow. Fromm also studied the Hasidic codification of Jewish law, the Tanya, at the University of Frankfurt. Fromm's grandfather was a rabbi as were two great grandfathers – therefore Fromm's view of the events in the Garden of Eden cannot be dismissed as ignorance of Judaism. Paul Ricoeur (1913 to 2005), was a highly regarded French philosopher – in the 1935 Baccalauréat, Paul scored the second highest mark nationally. Whilst at the Sorbonne, in 'The Symbolism of Evil', Paul wrote "It will never be said enough how badly it has done souls, during centuries of Christianity, the literal interpretation of the story of Adam". Immanuel Kant, the great German philosopher, considered 'inconvenient' the idea that evil comes to us by inheritance from our ancestors.

5.67   Senior ordained Catholics also raised serious objections. Vito Mancuso, an Italian theologian born 1962 and a prolific author, has argued for theology to be freed from the captivity of history. The narration of original sin should not be understood as historical truth, but as a mythical representation, since the myth is truest of the story. The snake is just a symbol: the symbol of ambiguity, between good and evil, between intelligence and cunning. However, papal defense of the indefensible continues unabated – a great example being the announcement of the ultimate punishment, the excommunication of Tissa Balasuriya, on 5 January 1997 in the Vatican's newspaper, L'Osservatore Romano. Tissa, 1924 to 2013, was a Sri Lankan priest and theologian. In 1975 he founded the Ecumenical Association of Third World Theologians. In 1990, Tissa published 'Mary and Human Liberation', in which he stated that "*original sin was invented by the clergy in order to exercise power over the souls of the faithful*". Despite the self-evident truth of this statement, Tissa was challenged by the Congregation for the Doctrine of the Faith – a sort of successor to the Inquisition. He responded by submitting a 55 page explanation to support his views. No doubt incensed, the Congregation for the Doctrine of the Faith demanded he sign a specially crafted 'Profession of Faith and submission to the teaching of the Roman pontiff'. Tissa responded by signing the then current standard Profession of Faith as composed by Pope Paul VI. Exasperated, Rome excommunicated him and on 24 January 1997, Joseph Ratingzer, the head of the Congregation, who went on to become Pope Benedict XVI in 2005, pointed to his heretical statement quoted above as sufficient justification.

5.68   To conclude, neither the Old Testament nor the gospels make any reference to original sin – it is a concept invented by Paul.

5.69   Eye opener – as we shall see, the 'wages of sin' is death but it is **not** the death of the body.

C   Papal authority, as God's representative on Earth

5.70   The Pope, is held to be God's representative on Earth, empowered to dispense both divine grace to speed a person to heaven, and excommunication to commit someone to everlasting damnation in hell. The Pope's function is to intercede between God and Man.

5.71   The Catholic justification for the authority vested in the pope is principally derived from Matthew 16:13-20. In these versus, Jesus declares to Simon, called Peter, that he is the rock upon which he will build his church. The original pun is lost on most people as Simon's nickname 'Peter' can be translated as 'Rocky'. Moreover, Jesus goes on to tell Simon he will give the keys of the kingdom of heaven to him and explains that decisions Simon makes on Earth will bind decisions in heaven.

5.72   Matthew 16:13-20. *When Jesus came to the region of Caesarea Philippi, he asked his disciples, "Who do people say the Son of Man is? They replied, "Some say John the Baptist; others say Elijah; and still others, Jeremiah or one of the prophets." "But what about you?" he asked. "Who do you say I am?" Simon Peter answered, "You are the Messiah, the Son of the living God." Jesus replied, "Blessed are you, Simon son of Jonah, for this was not revealed to you by flesh and blood, but by my Father in heaven. And I tell you that you are Peter, and on this rock I will build my church, and the gates of Hades will not overcome it. I will give you the keys of the kingdom of heaven; whatever you bind on earth will be bound in heaven, and whatever you loose on earth will be loosed in heaven." Then he ordered his disciples not to tell anyone that he was the Messiah.*

5.73   On the face of it, this appears to fully justify the elevation of Simon to being Jesus representative on Earth, granted powers that could justify the dispensing of grace and of sentencing sinners to excommunication. The Catholic church then contends that these powers were vested in the office of the leader of the church and could be passed on to Peter's successors.

5.74   However, the verses quoted from Matthew contain markers that indicate tampering during scribal copying. In verse 13, Jesus describes himself in his standard phrase as 'the Son of Man' – which has a clear meaning, lost to most Christians, that explains the answers Jesus elicited. The disciples responses offer various identities that persons that they believe Jesus is a reincarnation of. Jesus persists asking them who they themselves think he is – and Simon's response "You are the Messiah, the Son of

77

the living God" clearly shows late tampering with the text by a gentile scribal community maybe in the 3rd or 4th century. No one in Jesus entourage would say Jesus is **the** messiah, they would have said **a** messiah – please see Part Three chapter 7 for more detail. Further, the idea that a messiah could be divine is an oxymoron to Jews and, finally, in the 1st Century, no one believed Jesus was a son of God. The final instruction, not to tell anyone that he was 'the' messiah is also odd, as in public Jesus behaved very much as a king messiah – and the crowds on Palm Sunday clearly identified Jesus as such. So, there is ample evidence that the very foundation of papal authority is very suspect.

5.75   One has to consider why Jesus would have given any single human the sweeping powers specified in the above verses. The Great Commission to spread the gospel was given to all the apostles – why would only one alone be given such vast powers? It just does not make sense, and as we shall see, the church has plenty of form in creating authority to bolster the powers of the Pope.

5.76   Because Peter was martyred in Rome, it was assumed Rome should be the head of the Church – but this was debated even in Constantine's time. Catholic records indicate that a deputation of eight Nazarene Desposyni – i.e. leaders directly descended from Jesus family, met both Pope Sylvester and Emperor Constantine in 318 requesting that the Jerusalem Church be regarded as the Mother Church and that Desposyni should be appointed bishops to the sees' of Jerusalem, Alexandria, Antioch and Ephesus.

5.77   When Constantine transferred the capital of the Empire from Rome to his new capital of Constantinople in 330, Rome's civil power was weakened but its spiritual authority was strengthened as the title Pontifex Maximus (Supreme Priest) previously held by the emperor was devolved to the bishop of Rome. Initially, the pope had been merely a Prime Minister, now Constantine granted him the religious Presidency.

5.78   The construction of papal authority was a continuing process. Forging the alliance with the Roman state led the Roman church and its bishop to develop pre-eminence through the formulation of theological terms. Whilst a number of churches were acknowledged as founded by apostles, Pope Damascus I, bishop of Rome from 366 to 384, begun to refer to the Roman church as **the** apostolic see.

5.79   During the 5th Century various principals of Roman law were used to define the prerogatives of the bishop of Rome. Leo I, pope from 440 to 461, witnessed the collapse of the Western Roman Empire and the start of the theological split with Constantinople. Leo worked to suppress heresy and formulate theological support for orthodox dogma, whilst strengthening papal authority under the guise of unifying the church. Leo I was instrumental in extending the power of the Roman See. He used the Council of Chalcedon in 451 to extend the jurisdiction of the Roman See over Spain, Gaul and North Africa. He also gained huge influence by his personal interventions: dissuading the forces of Attila the Hun from attacking Rome in 452 (assisted, according to papal tradition, by the Apostles Peter and Paul plus an angelic host) and again in 455 he persuaded the Vandals not to sack Rome.

5.80   Pope Gelasius, pope from 492 to 496, argued for the primacy of the Roman See over all others, presenting his doctrine as based upon succession from the apostle Peter. Gelasius described himself not simply as Peter's successor but also as his representative, declaring himself to be the Vicar of Christ. As Peter's 'unworthy heir', under Roman laws of inheritance, Gelasius wielded the full powers granted to Peter as these powers were 'monarchical' because Peter had been granted 'principatus' – pre-eminence and rule over the entire church.

5.81   Gelasius formulated a doctrine which established the relationship between spiritual and secular authority. According to the Gelasian doctrine, as it became known, set out in a letter entitled *Famuli vestrae pietatis* issued in 494, secular authority is subordinate to spiritual authority since priestly authority is responsible for the eternal condition of those with secular authority but in the secular domain, the priestly authority is inferior to the secular authority. This doctrine led to the legal doctrine of sovereign immunity, as it gave political protection to the papacy and the monarchies – who promised not to violate each other's respective jurisdictions.

5.82   One audacious bid for power and influence was highly effective for over seven centuries but ultimately found to be based upon a forgery. The Donation of Constantine (Emperor 306 to 337) purported the transfer of authority over the lands of the Roman Empire and the Sees' of Antioch, Jerusalem, Alexandria and Constantinople to the Pope as a gift in recognition of God healing Constantine's leprosy. The 'Donation' gave the Pope enormous political authority:- magnifying claims to be vested with the authority of God in relation to secular matters, the Donation was used as authority to choose who was crowned king in respect of all territories once within the realms of the former Roman Empire. By extension, it became a Papal matter whether one king could attack another; a kingdom which allowed heretical views to prosper was at risk of invasion at the command of the Pope. No clear evidence has been found of who wrote the Donation but from terms used in the document and references made to its text, even the Catholic sources agree, fix its authorship to the period between 752 and 795.

5.83   Following the collapse of the western Roman Empire under successive waves of invading Germanic tribes, the Roman Church gradually gained a patchwork of landholdings across northern Italy – holdings built from gifts, legacies and warfare, which became known as the Papal States. Some popes had to devote significant attention to protecting and developing their terrestrial estates and the purported legal rights set out in the Donation begun to be deployed in papal negotiations. Pope Hadrianus I (772-795), has been identified as using phrases from the Donation in his correspondence. Certainly the Donation proved helpful to papal efforts to extend papal governance over the area of modern Italy and as a countermeasure to the crowning of Charlemagne as Holy Roman Emperor in 800.

5.84   Controlling a continental religious empire from a central authority was underpinned by an extensive body of laws mostly developed from Roman legal theory. The exercise of this power was greatly helped by a massive codification undertaken by a Benedictine monk named Gratin c1140. His *Decretum Gratiani* was based upon a collection of almost 3,800 texts covering all aspect of church laws and regulations. Contradictions and differences in rules accumulated from different sources were generally resolved by applying the principles of Roman Law. Two important principles were enshrined in the *Decretum Gratiani* – that a church Council may only be convened by a Pope and that "the Roman See is under the judgment of nobody". It certainly stood the test of time, forming the basis of canon law, known as the *Corpus Juris Canonici* until 1917 when replaced by a new *Code of Canon Law*.

5.85   The 14th and 15th Centuries were a period of almost continuous crisis for the church. Elected under a disputed papal conclave in 1294, Pope

Boniface VIII triggered crises by engaging papal troops against other church forces and becoming deeply involved in political disputes with Philip of France, the Hapsburgs and even Scotland. The French king ruled that clergy in France should pay tax and should be excluded from matters of temporal law – Boniface responded by excommunicating King Philip and his leading nobles. Philip retaliated by sending troops to capture Boniface in his palace and beat him for three days culminating in his death. French influence led to the papacy relocating to Avignon in 1309 – where it remained almost continuously for over a century.

5.86   There was an attempt to move back to Rome in 1377 but the long absence had led to the College of Cardinals filling the administrative vacuum created by the long absence of a pope, whilst the papacy based in Avignon had become under the political and religious domination of France. The new pope, Urban VI, tried to re-establish the monarchical style of papal rule but within a year he was ruled mentally incapacitated and the next pope, Clement VII, decided to return to Avignon. This resulted in the Roman cardinals deciding to elect their own pope – triggering the Great Schism which lasted until 1417 when attempted reconciliation led to there being three popes for a short period.

5.87   This turmoil at the head of the church coincided with the Hundred Years War (1337 to 1453), the Black Death (1348-9) and a series of powerful attacks on dogma – by Michael of Cesena, William of Ockham, Marsilus of Padua, Wycliffe, the Lollards and Jan Hus. The first two were senior leaders of the Franciscan Order who compared Jesus poverty with papal wealth; Marsilus dismissed papal authority to dispense spiritual sanctions – grace and excommunication; Wycliffe attacked the luxury and pomp of the clergy whilst translating the Vulgate into English; Jan Hus refuted transubstantiation. All were laying the groundwork for the forthcoming Protestant Reformation.

5.88   The experience of the Great Schism, illustrating the risks of power being vested in a single man, led to efforts by cardinals to establish primacy of Church Councils over popes. The Council of Ferrara-Florence, 1438-1445, sought but failed to link this with reunion with the Eastern Orthodox Church. The Eastern Emperor and the Orthodox archbishop both attended and big concessions were made – the Roman bishop was to be acknowledged as senior, whilst married clergy would be accepted in eastern provinces. The codification of papal primacy set out in the draft unification document, *Laetentur Coeli*, was adopted 430 years later by Vatican I in 1870. The text asserted the primacy of Peter and the succession of popes in that primacy was an article of faith. This primacy granted the full power of nourishing, ruling and governing the church, including the pope's judicial supremacy, stating there is no higher authority, not even an ecumenical council from which appeal can be made to a papal judgment. The stumbling block was arcane – the Eastern church maintained that the Holy Spirit came forth only from the Father but the Roman church insisted the Holy Spirit could come forth from both Father and Son. The Council was abandoned and the pope retained primacy over the cardinals.

5.89   In the midst of this turmoil, an Italian priest, Lorenzo Valla, proved conclusively in 1440 that the Donation of Constantine was a forgery (as it used terms dating only from the 8th century) but remarkably the Vatican managed to suppress the evidence of this until 1517.

5.90   Papal authority has been buttressed by the doctrine of papal infallibility. Scripturally derived from Luke 10:16, where Jesus says to his apostles "*He who hears you, hears me*", Pope Hormisdas (514 -523), used this in decreeing that the Roman see had always preserved the true faith against heresies. The general belief was that succession from Peter granted popes a privileged teaching authority. Papal infallibility was even promoted during periods when papal authority was openly questioned – by the Franciscans in their debate over poverty and during the Great Schism of competing popes. Efforts by papal supporters during the Reformation led to the 'ultramontane school' (those who looked south over the Alps to Rome) who linked the supreme teaching authority of the church to the infallibility of the pope acting as its head. This they argued guaranteed the inerrancy even of the pope's doctrinal pronouncements.. This was adopted by Vatican I in 1870 which pronounced that even the ex-cathedra statements by the pope, those made from the papal 'chair', "are irreformable of themselves".

5.91   The Catholic Catechism lays out the source for the claim of papal power but, even after finessing for almost 2000 years, the claim is based on the dubious extension of power granted to one being available to many and also being indefinitely transferable, supported by phrases taken out of context. Statements 1444 and 1445 set out the basis for the papal power of judgment and of excommunication:

1444   *In imparting to his apostles his own power to forgive sins, the Lord also*
give them the authority to reconcile sinners with the Church. This ecclesial
dimension of their task is expressed most notably in Christ's solemn words
to Simon Peter: "I will give you the keys of the kingdom of heaven, and
whatever you bind on earth shall be bound in heaven, and whatever you loose
on earth shall be loosed in heaven."

1445   *The words bind and loose mean: whomever you exclude from your*
communion, will be excluded from communion with God; whomever
you receive anew into your communion, God will welcome back into his.
Reconciliation with the Church is inseparable from reconciliation with God.

5.92   The sources for these claims of authority are given as Matthew 16:19;
18:18 and 28:16-20. However, only the first is relevant. Even accepting
that the quote from Matthew 16:19 is an accurate quotation of Jesus,
various aspects are left unsupported:

- Matthew 18:18 repeats the phrase about what is bound on earth shall
be bound in heaven – but in the context of any Christian counselling
his brother or sister to avoid or desist from sinning and clearly points
to sins or good works occurring on Earth being considered when the
perpetrators are judged in heaven.

- Matthew 28:16-20 contains the doctored text claiming Jesus asked
his followers to baptise in the name of a set of Offices rather than his
own name, but whilst stating that he, Jesus, had been given authority
over humanity it is silent concerning granting and powers to anyone
else.

- Nowhere does Matthew claim that the power granted to Simon
extends to any other person, apostle or otherwise;

- Nowhere is it stated that the power granted to Simon may be
bestowed or transferred to anyone else;

- Nowhere is it claimed that Simon or anyone else may exclude people
from the church, let alone the power of sentencing another to eternal
damnation – i.e. excommunication.

5.93   Statement 1444 goes on to claim that *"The office of binding and loosing which*
was given to Peter was also assigned to the college of the apostles united to its head"

quoting only an internal church authority, namely: LG 22 # 2.

D   Sacraments, services through which grace is dispensed

5.94   As the Vicar of Christ, God's representative on earth, the Pope is held
to be endowed with full powers and authority to act in God's name.
Technically, with the grace created by Jesus sacrifice determined to
be unlimited and with Jesus defined as one facet of a triune God, the
Pope is therefore not only the Vicar of Christ but also acts as God's
representative. It is taught that all God's grace flows to mankind through
the Pope. Only the Pope has the power to ordain bishops, and they in
turn to appoint clergy – these became the people sanctioned to turn on
and off the taps of grace. Whilst the church claimed its administrators
had access to unlimited volumes of grace to wipe out sin, it carefully
balanced how much was dispersed. The congregants must be supplicant
(deserving) and compliant, they must pay, often literally, and if causing
trouble, in the opinion of the administrators – grace could not only
be withheld but awkward types could be punished with everlasting
damnation – consigned to hell for all eternity through excommunication.

5.95   The taps of grace are the seven sacraments: baptism, confirmation,
penance, Eucharist, marriage, ordination and the last rites. These
sacraments were sometimes described as the seven arteries of Jesus
body through which grace flowed. Historically, this suited the intended
audiences, in the main uneducated and illiterate, who just had to attend
church, stand under the taps and receive grace. The key sacrament is the
Mass, a daily sacrifice of Jesus body on the alter to appease God's anger
for the sins committed that day. During Mass, the Eucharist is celebrated
to commemorate the Last Supper where Jesus told his disciples to
commemorate him when taking bread (his body broken for them) and
drinking wine (his blood spilt for them).

5.96   The concept of sacraments developed from the 5th Century, with
the number of sacraments varying over time between 5 and 12. The
definition of the seven sacraments was given by the 2nd Council of Lyon
in 1274, reviewed and endorsed by the Council of Florence in 1439.
Then, under assault from Protestants who challenged the biblical basis of
the idea that the service of a sacrament transmitted grace, the Council of
Trent (1545-1563) dogmatically ruled as its 1st Canon (ruling) that *"anyone
who says that there are not the seven sacraments, or that they were not all instituted by*

Jesus or that even one of these is not truly and properly a sacrament – then let him be an anathema", i.e. excommunicated. Furthermore, the 4th Canon ruled that anyone who claims that the sacraments are not necessary for salvation, or that men can gain salvation through faith alone, then let him be excommunicated also. No room there for any theological debate!!

5.97   The following clauses of the Catholic Catechism explain the doctrine of how the sacraments deliver grace to celebrants. All were formulated by the Council of Trent in 1547.

- Statement 1127 Celebrated worthily in faith, the sacraments confer the grace that they signify. They are effective because Jesus himself is at work, it is he who undertakes the baptism, and acts in the celebration of the other sacraments. God the Father always hears the prayer of his Son's Church which, in the epiclesis of each sacrament, expresses her faith in the power of the Spirit.

- Statement 1128 The Church affirms the sacraments act ex opere operato (literally: "*by the very fact of the action's being performed*") by the power of God. As a sacrament is celebrated, the power of Jesus and the Holy Spirit acts in and through it, independently of the personal holiness of the minister.

- Statement 1129 The Church affirms that for believers the sacraments of the New Covenant are necessary for salvation. '*Sacramental grace*' is the grace of the Holy Spirit, given by Jesus, which heals and transforms those who receive by conforming them to the Son of God.

5.98   Elsewhere, Catholic law defines a sacrament as "*an outward sign instituted by Jesus to give grace*". Generally, Protestants challenge this on the basis that there is no biblical support for most of the sacraments nor the notion that any sacrament of itself actually bestows grace. Most Protestants recognise only baptism and communion as rituals ordained by Jesus – the former as an outward sign of belief and the latter as a commemoration of Jesus life on earth.

5.99   The Catholic concept of salvation is not derived from biblical sources but from the teaching of Augustine (354-430). Augustine taught that we exist to love God, something we cannot do without praying for help – which comes in the form of grace which God pours into us. Thus the

Catholic view became that God poured grace into believers through the celebration of the sacraments – making us more loving and thereby 'justifying' us – making us righteous in God's sight – and ultimately meriting salvation.

5.100   The idea that the rites of the sacraments, in and of themselves, bestowed grace quite apart from any personal submission to the will of God may be traced to the writings of Hugo of St. Victor (1096-1141). Hugo entered the Abbey of Saint Victor in Paris around 1118, where he rose to head the institution and spent the rest of his life there. An enthusiastic proponent of Augustine's theories, Hugo viewed the sacraments as outward and visible signs of an inward and spiritual grace.

5.101   However, papal power to forgive Original Sin through baptism and one's own sins through the dispensation of grace is contradicted by at least two statements in the Catholic Catechism:

Statement 430: *Jesus means in Hebrew: "God saves". At the annunciation, the angel Gabriel gave him the name Jesus as his proper name, which expresses both his identity and his mission.* **Since God alone can forgive sins**, *it is God who, in Jesus his eternal Son made man, who "will save his people from their sins".* This seems to contradict unfettered and unlimited papal power to forgive sins through the taps of grace? Statement 431 repeats the same definition: *Because sin is always an offence against God,* **only he can forgive it**.

5.102   The seven sacraments codified by the 2nd Council of Lyon in 1274, comprise:

- Baptism
- Confirmation
- Reconciliation (Penance or Confession)
- The Eucharist (Holy Communion, *or simply,* Mass)
- Sacred/Holy Orders – Ordination
- Holy Matrimony
- Extreme Unction, *renamed* Anointing of the Sick *by Vatican II*

Baptism

5.103   According to Catholic teaching, the sprinkling of water over a candidate's head bestows grace of pardon for that person's original sin inherited from their parents. Baptism is a ritual for new born babies, usually only 10 to 15 days old, to literally wash out the stain they carry of inherited original sin. But this definition has no biblical basis – which is where 'tradition' and 'papal authority' are used to support dogma. For Protestants, baptism is a symbolic burial in water and resurrection therefrom for a penitent believer, it is a public affirmation of the individuals belief in Jesus and commitment to try to live accordingly (Luke 13:3-5). In turning from sin and repenting, the baptized seeks the remission of his sins (Acts 2:38 and 22:16). Baptism does not signify inward grace already received but an outward act of obedience which leads to forgiveness and a clear conscience before God (1 Peter 3:21).

5.104 There is a valid debate over the name in which persons are baptised into – the biblical record clearly shows Jesus instructing his followers to convert people in His name. However, the Roman church edited two books in the New Testament to insert references to the 4th Century invention of a Triune God and its baptism services gradually followed this man-made formula. Please see Part Three chapter 20 for detailed analysis of these two edits – the Comma Johanneum and Matthew 28:19.

5.105 As I understand, orthodox Catholic doctrine explains baptism as God's grace entering the soul of the baptised, being the sacrament of salvation and opening the door to all the other sacraments. This is another example of where the invention of the Trinity has disguised the truth.

Confirmation

5.106 As a standalone rite, divorced from baptism, this sacrament has no biblical foundation. The idea evolved from that of Original Sin, if a new born inherited Original Sin and died before baptism the infant was unsaved and was doomed to everlasting hell. Therefore, baptism should be carried out at the earliest possible occasion – when the infant had no conscious part in the ritual. Originally, early Christians were only baptised when making a conscious decision to declare in public their belief in Jesus and to be baptised in his name. As the decision to be baptised was an individual one by an adult, there was no concept of confirmation. Without Original Sin there was no need to worry about unbaptised infants.

5.107 Until the 5th Century, the practise was for a bishop to welcome newcomers into the church with a single rite combining Baptism,

Confirmation and the Eucharist. After Baptism, the new members donned a white robe and the bishop laid hands on each anointing them with oil in Confirmation, after which the gathering then celebrated the Eucharist together for the first time. However, with growing numbers joining the church, it was not possible for the bishop to always be present and the sacrament of Confirmation came to be administered separately at a later date. The Eastern church decided that bishops should bless the oil to be used but delegate the three sacraments of initiation to the priests. The Orthodox church still follows this practise. In the Western church, bishops delegated Baptism to the clergy and delayed Confirmation until a later date when they were in the locality. The date when children were judged ready to participate in Communion varied between 10 and 14, whilst Confirmation became practiced at age 7. Nowadays, Confirmation is associated with the 'age of discretion' and carried out after a course of study at an age of 10 or 11.

5.108   The theological basis for the sacrament of Confirmation is attributed to Petrus Lombardus (c1096 to 1160), better known as Peter Lombard, a theologian who studied for most of his life in Paris and who was appointed Bishop of Paris the year before his death. Known to be an associate of Hugo of St. Victor, Lombard's most famous work is the *Four Books of Sentences* which became a standard textbook in medieval universities. In *Book IV Sacraments*, Lombard laid out his definition of Confirmation.

5.109   In 1910, Pope Pius X lowered the age children could participate in Mass to 7. Today, the normal practice is that Confirmation occurs after children start to receive the Eucharist, often when a teenager.

Reconciliation (Penance or Confession)

5.110   The history of the sacrament of Reconciliation illustrates the amazing ability of the Roman church to progressively develop doctrine over time.

5.111   In the early church, the concept of reconciliation and the forgiveness of sins was baptism – as in John 20:23. Initially, Christians could confess their sins to one another at their gatherings (James 5:16).

5.112   Early theologians believed repentance and forgiveness of sins was only available once, at baptism, after which it was very difficult to gain further forgiveness. Sometime around 150, the idea arose of there being a one-time chance of a reconciliation (between the sinner and God) after baptism – for serious sins, identified as apostasy, murder and adultery. This was popularised by a text known as *The Shepherd of Hermas*, which some claim was written by a brother of Pope Pius I, bishop of Rome from c140 to 154. To gain this second forgiveness, the penitent must do penance – in the early years, this was very much a public affair. The penitents' sin was seen as a sin not only against God but against the neighbour and against the community – hence the need for penance to be public. Since this reconciliation could be granted only once after baptism, for many centuries most powerful men postponed baptism until late in life and targeted their final chance at reconciliation for their deathbed.

5.113   The move to private confession and private penance arose around 250 under Cyprian, bishop of Carthage. A large number of Christians in Carthage had renounced their beliefs under severe persecution following an Edict issued by Emperor Decius 249-251 (see 4.34(iii) above). Afterwards, many wanted to reconcile with the church and gain readmittance but public penance would lead to immediate arrest – so penance became possible in private.

5.114   The Decian persecution also led to another development in dogma – the lifetime transfer of merit between the living. The original idea was good works that you do here on Earth can lay up treasure (religious merit) for you in heaven. This was based upon Colossians 1:24-25, where Paul appears to claim that his good works and suffering are adding to the infinite merits earned by Jesus to enable all the sins of mankind to be forgiven. Thus it became established that each of the Saints had generated religious merit, adding to the already infinite treasury of merit created by Jesus. The Bishop of Rome was already vested with the authority to grant forgiveness, so naturally papal authority could make withdrawals from the treasury of merit to relieve the deserving of the burdens of their sins. From this grew the notion that all good works earned merit and thence the idea that this merit could offset the penalties created by sinful acts. This led to the idea that merit earned by one person might be credited to reduce the penalties attaching to another.

5.115   For those persecuted under the Edict of Decius in 250, the merit earned by the sufferings of those that had refused to deny their faith, referred to as 'confessors', created credits which could be compensate for the sins of the fallen, the 'lapsi', who under persecution had denied their faith. The church begun to allow intercession by confessors to reduce the term of penance for those seeking readmittance to the church.

5.116   The Council of Ancyra (modern Ankara), 314, reserved exclusively for bishops, the power to allocate merit from the treasury to reduce the term of the penance.

5.117   When Christianity became the official state religion of the Roman Empire in 380, sin was transformed. Bishops became judges and sin was seen as breaking the law rather than fracturing one's relationship with God. Cases held before episcopal courts became legalistic, with a schedule of payments devised to satisfy divine judgment. Augustine and Pope Leo I interpreted John 20:23 as if the apostle rather than God granted forgiveness, thereby transferring power of forgiveness to the church hierarchy. Henceforth, an ordained priest could grant forgiveness to sinners. During the 4th to 6th Centuries, those classed as penitents were banned from Mass until their local bishop had reconciled them.

5.118   The origin of indulgences has been traced back to the Council of Epaone, 517, held in Burgundy, where the idea of *relaxiato* was adopted by which a severe penance could be substituted for a lighter sentence. The original practise of a penance being of lifelong duration was replaced with a term of two years. Various other elements were proscribed for the penitent during the two years: fasting every third day, entry to church via the penitents door and exclusion from parts of the Eucharist.

5.119   In the 7th century, beginning in Ireland and England, the practice of *redemptio* arose under which the original terms of penance could be commuted to a lesser obligation including prayers, good works and alms and also the payment of fixed sums of money depending upon the offense – known as tariff penances.

5.120   The Council of Chalon-sur-Saône (644 to 655) concluded that it helped the salvation of the faithful when their bishop proscribed penance as many times as the sinner fell into sin. This led to the idea that penance is the imposition of a punishment for sin (the 'binding' referred to in Matthew 16:19 and John 20:23). These punishments may be relieved by 'indulgences' – the partial remission of the penalties by virtue of the prayer or penitence of others in the church. As the church claimed authority to apply merits earned by one person against the penalties payable by another – a sort of spiritual central clearing system came into force. Paul is quoted as the authority for imposing a penance on a sinner and later relaxing it – however, the quote does not quite work as it is not Paul who later relaxed the penance (1 Corinthians 5:3-5).

5.121 Starting with Pope Benedict III (855 – 858), a number of popes (including Nicholas I, John VI and Stephen V) started to grant reductions of penance for those completing a specific pilgrimage.

5.122 Indulgence is defined in Canon Law (#992) as the remission of the temporal punishment due for sins, the guilt of which has been forgiven by the church. A believer who is properly disposed and who fulfils certain specific conditions, may gain an indulgence from the Church utilising its power to dispense grace. Catholic theology progressed to define the apostle (and his legal successors) as having the power to forgive, displacing God. Furthermore, a monetary fine could be substituted for any punishment scheduled in the 'penitentials' which defined the level of punishment for every sin. This progressed to allow penitents to pay others to do penance for them.

5.123 From the 9th Century, the regularity of deathbed absolution, divorced from the performance of any penance, further separated repentance from forgiveness. Originally, absolution by the church applied to the punishment rather than to the sin – as the punishment was controlled by the bishops. By the 9th Century, the effect of absolution begun to be understood as applying to the absolution of the sins as well. Theologians such as Peter Lombard taught that repentance and confession (even to a layman) assured the sinner of God's forgiveness – so long as one was truly repentant. But Lombard maintained that absolution applied not to the punishment but to the sins.

5.124 The matter came to a head with the Fourth Lateran Council, 1215, which ruled that confession had to be made to an ordained priest, normally in private, and had to be within one year of the sin being committed. A distinction was made between mortal sins and venial sins – mortal sins were deemed to sever the relationship with God and lead to eternal damnation unless confessed; whilst venial (forgiveable) sins were those that weakened but did not sever the relationship with God. Mortal sins were mandatory to confess, whilst venial sins were judged optional.

This distinction, backed by extensive scheduling of tariffs, related to the severity of the sin committed, and enabled penitents to budget for their confessions. It also opened the path to the growth of a considerable body of canon law The new ruling was reflected in the formula used by the priest. The Fourth Lateran Council changed the formula spoken by the priest after hearing confession from "*May God have mercy on you and forgive you your sins*" to "*I absolve you from your sins*". Thomas Aquinas 1225-1274, an Italian Dominican friar, with little knowledge of the early centuries of the Church, mistakenly asserted that clerical remission of sins was an ancient formula, and this has led to its widespread use ever since.

5.125   The term *indulgentia* can be traced to the 9th century but, at this time, indulgences were very difficult to obtain – granted only by a pope upon application from a bishop.

5.126   Around 1230, a Dominican monk, Hugh of St Cher, devised the concept of the 'treasury of merit' – which remains the basis for the theological explanation for indulgences. Indulgences had arisen from the idea that when a very righteous person died they departed with more merit than required to enter heaven. Conveniently, this excess righteous merit was somehow credited to the papal 'treasury of merit' and was then available to the pope to dispense by granting indulgences (the remission of punishment in purgatory for sins committed) as he wished. Indulgences can be partial – granted for specific sins or specific periods of time (i.e. a reduction in the number of days spent in purgatory) or for all sins (termed 'plenary') which enables the beneficiary to bypass purgatory entirely. Jesus had left a super abundance of such merit and other saintly persons contributed more.

5.127   Meanwhile in parallel developments, a succession of popes identified the potential for using the unlimited treasury of merit to further geopolitical aims – specifically the recruitment and resourcing of crusades against Moslems and heretics. In 1063, Pope Alexander II initiated the practice of granting partial indulgences in respect of penances for those who fought in Spain against the Moors. In 1095, at the Council of Clermont, Pope Urban II announced in his Bull of the Crusades, that all those who participated in a crusade against Muslims or heretics (including the Cathars and the Hussites) would have their full penance remitted – a plenary indulgence. In 1187, Pope Gregory VIII went even further, offering a full plenary indulgence to anyone unable or unwilling to go on a crusade – they could be granted remission of all their sins in exchange for a cash contribution! After the Crusades to the Holy Land, the same facility was used extensively during the Spanish campaigns against the Moors in Iberia – with Bulls published in 1478, 1479, 1481, 1482, 1485, 1494, 1503 and 1505.

5.128 A theological debate arose in the 11th Century over whether acts of reconciliation granted close to death without any chance to perform penance could result in a complete remission. But, with full plenary indulgences granted by direct papal authority to crusaders whether they even reached the Holy Land before dying, the idea arose that plenary indulgences should be available to anyone at the moment of death.

5.129 By 1350, it is recorded that the faithful had begun to apply certain indulgences (such as Jubilee and Crusader indulgences) they had been granted in favour of the souls of the dead as well.

5.130 In 1457, Pope Callixus III (1455 to 1458) granted King Henry IV of Castille indulgences for a crusade against the Moors which provided a plenary indulgence for the living and for a fixed monetary amount for an indulgence for the dead.

5.131 In 1476, Pope Sixtus IV (1471 to 1484) issued a Bull relating to the financing of the construction of the Cathedral of Saintes in France. Valid for 10 years, this provided financial subscribers for plenary indulgences for both the living and the dead.

5.132 Indulgences, originally linked to piety and charity, became debased into primarily fund raising devices – and became a key issue for clergy and laity appalled by the behaviour of the senior hierarchy of the church in the 14th and 15th Centuries. Indulgences were a major factor behind the Protestant Reformation but their blatant abuse continued for centuries before major reform was announced at the Council of Trent, albeit after no less than 18 years of debate, in 1563. The abuse of indulgences is explained in more detail in section E below, paragraphs 5.145 to 5.159.

5.133 The Council of Trent also rowed back a bit from the 1215 Fourth Lateran Council formula of absolution of *"I absolve you from your sins"* to reintroduce God into the process, with the priests declaration changing to *"I absolve you from your sins in the name of the Father, and of the Son, and of the Holy Spirit"*.

5.134   The Council of Trent ruled that from the age of discretion (7 years old) each person be obliged to perform Confession in a state of contrition at least once a year. Confession of all mortal sins is obligatory, and of venial sins is recommended but not required. Knowingly failing to confess any mortal sin invalidates the Confession and incurs another sin – sacrilege.

The Eucharist (Holy Communion, or simply, Mass)

5.135   The term Eucharist derives from the Greek *eucharisteo* meaning 'to give thanks' as in Matthew 26:27. The sacrament is a celebration of the Lord's supper performed as if Jesus sacrifice is repeated on a daily basis to atone for mankind's sins that day.

5.136   The Fourth Lateran Council in 1215 determined that when the priest uttered Jesus words during the Eucharist, the bread and wine were literally transformed into Jesus flesh and blood – this became the doctrine of transubstantiation. During the service, grace flowed to the congregation through their merely looking at the wine and the bread. It was further ruled that all consecrated bread and wine had to be stored in secure facilities in case parishioners tried unofficial application of its magical properties.

5.137   Maybe it was thought a bit of magic would keep the audience spellbound, however the practice proved popular and was affirmed at the Council of Trent (1545 to 1563). Trent confirmed that wine was reserved exclusively for the officiating priests (in case clumsy parishioners split Jesus blood) and bread was replaced by thin wafers placed in the mouth by the priest (in case crumbs of flesh were dropped on the ground). Even these wafers were only to be given to the laity once a year – when, although the lay member only eats the wafer, he supposedly receives both elements (flesh and blood) within the bread. This Catholic theological magic is known as "communion under one kind".

5.138   Under Catholic theology, Jesus is allegedly sacrificed again during each Mass for the sins committed since the previous Mass, hence the full title being the 'sacrifice of the mass'. This seems to contradict Jesus own description of the Lord's supper as a memorial – to remember him by. The concept of 'communion under one kind' also flatly contradicts Jesus instruction that *all* are to drink (Matthew 26:27). Finally, it must be noted that the Catholic dogma of multiple messianic sacrifices directly contradicts an explicit testimony in Hebrews 9:28 that Jesus was offered but *once*.

Sacred/Holy Orders – Ordination

5.139   The Catholic sacrament of ordination is tailored for three levels of officials – bishops, priests and deacons. Loyola Press, a Catholic publication, suggests that the rites of the sacrament are derived from how the 11 remaining apostles chose a twelfth to replace Judas (Acts 1:23-26). However, Acts relates that the choice was based on prayer followed by drawing lots – divinely inspired betting?

5.140   The doctrine is that those dedicated to serve Jesus and the Church, receive a permanent spiritual mark, called a 'character', signifying their ordination. The oil used to appoint those ordinated transfers an essence of a special spiritual nature which can never be forfeit. According to the doctrine, no personal sin can ever make the ordained unfit for office. This concept originates from the appointment of government officials of the Roman Empire. This explains the church response to the clerical abuse of minors – a position maintained almost throughout the 20th century until it became totally unsustainable.

Holy Matrimony

5.141   The Catholic church claims marital jurisdiction over all that have been baptised into the Catholic church. The Council of Trent ruled that marriage between two Catholics was a sacrament but marriage between non-Catholics was merely contractual. Catholic doctrine asserts there are no grounds for divorce – which seems to contradict both the Torah and Jesus own teaching – Matthew 5:32 and 19:9 permit divorce for adultery.

5.142   However, in the spirit of the Pharisees, the Catholic hierarchy managed to find creative solutions – if divorce was ruled out, then why not claim the marriage never took place? Find a reason why the marriage was 'ineffective' – maybe some Mosaic type of blood relationship might exist between the parties, maybe claim it was never consummated, etc. With influence in the right places and sufficient financial assistance, an annulment seems to be possible on almost any basis.

Extreme Unction, renamed Anointing of the Sick by Vatican II

5.143   The Catholic sacrament of Extreme Unction doubtless has given succour to those close to death concerned about their future prospects and worried about their past deeds, as well as some measure of closure to their loved ones.

5.144　The 'Last Rites' involves the use of consecrated oils by an ordained priest – the oil is applied to the eyes, ears, nostrils, lips, hands and feet (echoes of ancient Babylonian rites) and, according to the Council of Trent, is alleged to absolve the sins of the dying celebrant. The theological justification refers to Mark 6:13 (which refers to healing the sick by anointing with oil) and James 5:14-15 (which also refers to praying for the sick and anointing them with oil to make them well). James also advises this will forgive sins and urges believers gathered together to confess to each other.

E　　The abuse of Indulgences

5.145　Faced by the constant threat of new penances to be performed every week plus the dire prospect of purgatory afterwards, demand for indulgences soared. The theological challenge to framing a doctrine was defining why an indulgence could be granted or gained. Supply was, by definition, unlimited – who could suggest that Jesus only had a specific numerical excess of righteousness? As the ranks of the saints were steadily swelled by the Church process of sanctification – the supply of indulgences became inexhaustible. This comforting knowledge may have helped drive the demand for greater availability of indulgences. In medieval times, piety was expressed through numerous devotions, ceremonies and pilgrimages – demand sought indulgences for visiting relics, shrines and even just listening to sermons.

5.146　The ability of indulgences to generate funds made it attractive for all sorts of projects – both religious and civil. Revenue from indulgences not only financed the construction and repair of churches but also hospitals, schools, roads and bridges.

5.147　Inevitably, this led to abuses. When an indulgence was announced for contributions to a specific project, *quaestores* were nominated to collect the alms. To maximize collections, some *quaestores* went beyond doctrinal limits – even promising that money could not only reduce time spent by their loved ones in purgatory but even release loved ones from the supposedly eternal existence in hell. Concerns arose from popes granting Catholic kings and princes the right to retain a large proportion of funds collected in respect of crusader indulgences to finance their efforts.

5.148   As early as 1215, church authorities recognised that the use of indulgences was getting out of hand. That year the Fourth Lateran Council ruled that indulgences granted in respect of new churches must be limited to one year and for other occasions limited to 40 days. However, these limits were still ignored and some indulgences lasting for hundreds of years were granted.

5.149   The subject of indulgences raised various debates. St Thomas Aquinas (1225 to 1274) pondered whether the church could grant indulgence to someone who was dead. Aquinas determined that the Church had jurisdiction in the afterlife and therefore indulgences for the dead were valid. He argued that the dead in purgatory could benefit because, like the living, they were on the way to salvation, but the blessed did not need indulgences and the damned could not use indulgences. The extension of indulgences to enable the living to reduce the term of purgatory not only for themselves but for their loved ones and even for those already dead opened up a huge trading opportunity which the church enthusiastically monetised. The abuses arising from the exploitation of Indulgences were probably the greatest contributing factor to the Protestant Reformation.

5.150   The fact that the sale of indulgences had become generally viewed as an abuse is reflected in the treatment of indulgences in The Canterbury Tales, written by Geoffrey Chaucer between 1387 and 1400.

5.151   But the greatest scandal was the infamous sale of indulgences to finance the new St Peter's Basilica. This massive project was directly born out of the decay Rome suffered during the 70 year period of the Western Schism (1309 to 1377) when the Papacy was based in Avignon. Once popes returned to Rome, they desired a headquarters which declared the power and sovereignty of church.

5.152   Pope Nicolas V declared that the old Basilica, dating back to Emperor Constantine and in a very poor state of repair, should be replaced by a new building. In 1450, he announced plenary indulgences for those who made a jubilee year pilgrimage to Rome which refilled the Vatican's coffers but Nicolas argued against the *sale* of indulgences for cash. When he died in 1455 only a small part of St Peter's had been demolished.

5.153   For the next 50 years, popes focused more on personal and family aggrandizement than grand schemes to revive the Vatican and it was not until Pope Julius II that rebuilding plans were revived. During this period the reputation of the papacy was trashed by a series of greedy and immoral popes, of which the following stand out:

- Paul II 1464 to 1467, who promised a finance a crusade but when elected pope then spent the money on art and antiquities. According to Eamon Duffy (*Saints and Sinners: A History of the Popes*), Paul II was a man of lavish tastes who loved games and ceremonies and who was intensely proud of his good looks. He exploited the discovery of alum in lands owned by the papacy and issued a bull requiring Christians to only buy alum from the Vatican.

- Sixtus IV 1471 to 1484, spent compulsively, lavishing a third of the Vatican's annual income on his coronation tiara and then showered money on art, massive feasting and his family members – appointing six of his nephews as cardinals.

- Innocent VIII 1484 to 1492, dappled profitably in Turkish politics whilst furthering the revenue raising use of indulgences. Innocent VIII had two illegitimate sons prior to becoming pope, one of whom he married into the Medici family and then appointed his grandson a cardinal at the age of 13, who later became Pope Leo X.

- Alexander VI 1492 to 1503, a scion of the Borgia family, established new levels of depravity. Alexander VI had nine illegitimate children from seven mistresses who lived openly with him when pope. As a cardinal for 35 years and holding the office of Vice Chancellor, viewed as second only to the pope, Borgia had accumulated a vast wealth in church palaces, castles, bishoprics, estates, etc., assets which upon becoming pope he would have to give up – so he used church assets to shamelessly buy the cardinals votes. In his first year, Alexander VI appointed 13 cardinals – mostly family members and including the brother of one of his mistresses. At one point, in 1497, following the murder of one of his sons, Alexander VI drafted a bull of reform outlawing many practices he himself had used – the sale of church offices, limiting the number of bishoprics held to one, cardinals being appointed on merit, sale of church property, and even outlawing the use of boys as 'body servants' by cardinals. However, Alexander soon recovered from mourning his son and reform was forgotten.

5.154 These popes established the dire reputation of papacy into which the future key reformers were born and grew up – Erasmus c1466, Luther in 1483, Zwingli in 1484 and Calvin in 1509.

5.155 In 1506, Julius II laid the foundation stone for the new St Peter's Basilica and initiated a drive to raise funds for construction through the sale of indulgences. Julius II took direct charge of the building project, visiting kings and princes in person to seek major donations in return for absolving their sins. Levies were put on all types of local church activities and those in the Papal States were directed to leave bequests for St Peter's, failure to comply leading to wills being declared void and a deceased person's entire estate being seized by Julius' officials. Julius II quickly realized that huge sums were required to realize his plan for the new St Peter's, issuing a bull entitled "*Liquet omnibus*" in 1510. The blatant cynical quest for money that was unleashed directly triggered Luther's '95 Theses' seven years later. The bull set out in bold terms that absolution for any sin could be purchased, with prices set to extract whatever individuals could pay. Those wishing to repent only had to "deposit in the chest the price determined by the commissioner or his delegate". The monetary tariff set for the commissioners reflected the prevalence of the clerical class amongst the wealthy – and their widespread appetite for repeated sinning. The Archbishop of Mainz set a standard price of 25 gold guilden for kings, princes and 'great' prelates; 10 guilden for abbots, cathedral dignitaries and nobles; 6 guilden for lesser prelates and traders with an income exceeding 500 guilden; 3 guilden for burgers and merchants with an income exceeding 200 guilden; and so on, with only the very poor offered terms based on prayers and fasting.

5.156 Whilst Julius II ruthlessly exploited the sale of indulgences, he was pursuing the construction of the greatest church ever attempted – the faithful were at least being rewarded with what promised to be the most splendid religious headquarters. But St Peter's was barely beginning to take shape when in 1513 Julius II died – to be succeeded by Leo X, grandson of the infamous Innocent VIII. Leo X was committed to continuing the construction of St Peter's and decided the sale of indulgences had to be supercharged – new commissions and experienced salesmen were recruited. The most infamous was Johann Tetzel, a Dominican, who according to Charles Mee, in *White Robe, Black Robe*, states that Tetzel was retained for a fee of 80 ducati per month plus unlimited expenses and a commission from what he raised which comfortably exceeded his salary. A common technique used by Tetzel and others was to claim that indulgences could be bought for deceased relations held in purgatory – this went beyond the bull that Leo X had issued. It was Tetzel's zeal that most directly triggered Luther's Theses – although Luther assumed that the pope was unaware of how his bull was being misused.

5.157　In his Theses, Luther raised an obvious point, if the pope's main role was to save peoples souls from sin and if, as claimed in the doctrine of indulgences, the pope had access to unlimited merit donated to the church treasury upon the death of Jesus – why does the pope not use that unlimited merit to simply save all souls?

5.158　With many popes simply diverting funds into less admirable activities and into family pockets, the construction went very slowly, further delayed by significant design changes mid-build. Completion was only achieved in 1626 – 121 years after the foundation stone was laid.

5.159　Finally, after some 45 years of condemnation of its practices by Luther and Zwingli and 25 years of Calvin, the Catholic Church finally got the message and at the end of 1563, the Council of Trent denounced the sale of indulgences: *"All evil traffic in indulgences, which has been a most prolific source of abuses among the Christian people, be absolutely abolished"*.

F　Relics

5.160　Jesus message of love and forgiveness got lost somewhere along the way and he became viewed more as a terrifying judge meting out unending punishment which only the very rich might afford to ameliorate. How could common people seek mercy? Surely Jesus would listen to his mother and other wholly righteous persons who had been assessed as being saints? Thus grew the Catholic veneration of Mary and the original apostles. The concept of relics was based upon the idea that contact with a very righteous person would result in some of their surplus grace flowing to the supplicant. This resulted in pilgrimages to those churches claiming to hold relics, creating an early form of tourism – which became highly profitable for the establishments at the destinations.

5.161 With typical administrative relish, Relics were defined by the church as being of three classes: part of a saint's body (usually encased in stone and placed on the alter); an item of clothing from a saint; and, another item associated with a saint. The demand for grace and the desire for relics to display for pilgrims fuelled a huge industry. It became apparent that more saints were also required. The first formal canonization of a saint occurred in 993, of St Ulrich of Augsberg. The process became systemized and undertaken exclusively by the Vatican. Significant numbers were hailed to be saints, from as far back as Mary's mother and father, supporting the discovery of vast numbers of relics. The aggregate number of saints now exceeds 10,000. Officially, followers are supposed to pray to saints to intercede with Jesus on their behalf for themselves or their departed loved ones. In reality, with saints represented by images placed in niches or on alters, the practice seems uncomfortably similar to idol worship.

G   Purgatory, two Limbos & Hades

5.162 The earliest use of the term 'purgatorium' has been traced to around 1160, in usage which implied purgatory was a place. The Catholic doctrine of there being an intermediate state between death and heaven (or hell), where the dead are purified may be found in many ancient traditions where prayers for the dead were believed to help the deceased on their journey. The church found scriptural support for the idea in 2 Maccabees 12:42-45, a work believed to have been written in Alexandria c125BC influenced by then recent belief in Judaism of there being heavenly rewards for the righteous and the potential for the lesser sins to be forgiven. Church theologians see 2 Maccabees as evidence showing the dead can be assisted between death and their final abode, that prayers and sacrifices for the dead must be efficacious.

5.163 Once the practice of Confession was established it became deliberately officious, repeated failure to confess led to eternal damnation (through excommunication), long proscribed lists of questions were provided for priests to cross examine supplicants. Any sins for which due penance was not performed would be carried forward and dealt with after death in purgatory. The result was that the general population feared their sins would imperil their salvation, making them increasingly submissive to church authority. The result was that everyone accepted that the weight of their sins meant they were unlikely to die deserving of salvation –

but the church had a solution. Upon death, Christians arrived first in purgatory – where they were assessed and inevitably found wanting, resulting in rather unpleasant process of purging until they were cleansed sufficiently to pass on to heaven. Without a shred of evidence, even of the existence of purgatory, the process was described as akin to torture, remaining sins were to be excised by fire – in a process that could endure for thousands of years.

5.164   Greek beliefs include something which may have spawned the idea of purgatory. In Greek culture, following death all souls went to Hades, both the wicked and the righteous, directly equivalent to Jewish belief and the Hebrew term 'sheol' was translated as 'hades'. Greek understanding adopted the Egyptian belief that, after death, one's soul arrived at the River Styx where the ferry-man, Charon, would take the souls across the river to judgment. Hence the early practise in Egypt of placing a gold coin under the tongue of the dead to pay the ferry-man. This practise was copied in Hebrew and Greek burials by placing a coin on each eyelid and then carried over into Christian burials – remaining quite common in some Catholic countries even today. Plato, speaking of the judgment of the dead, said all could hope for deliverance but they must first proceed through a subterranean place of judgment where they will receive the punishment they deserve.

5.165   The background Greek cultural influence on the destination of the soul after death seems also to have played a part in the development of Catholic dogma. In Greek culture, Hades was the general name for the underworld where all souls went and after judgment they were then despatched to one of four destinations:

- The irredeemably wicked were sent to Tartarus, an abyss of absolute darkness far beneath the earth, where the wicked were punished for all eternity. There is a reference to Tartarus in 2 Peter 2:4;

- Those who had committed lesser evils went to the Fields of Punishment;

- Those who were considered ordinary but had not achieved anything special were sent to the Asphodel Fields, which had a special section, the Lugentes Campi, for those that had wasted their lives on unrequited love (!); and,

- Those who had made a mark and had achieved something with their lives – military, political, thespian, etc, and also those judged pure and righteous, were sent to Elysium. The Roman era belief in Elysium is well illustrated by Russell Crowe playing the Roman general Maximus Meridius in the 2000 film *Gladiator.*

5.166 Thus it seemed natural to develop specialised sections within the afterlife. Whereas the Greek concept of Hades as the destination for all reflected the Jewish concept of Sheol, the Catholic doctrine reserved Hades as the name for the everlasting hell of Tartarus. Latin translations from c1200 began to translate *Hades* (the combined name for all afterlife areas) as *Purgatorium*, meaning the specific place that everyone went first for judgment. Similarly, the King James version dating from 1611, generally translates *sheol* (where in Judaism all souls go forever) as *hell* reserved only for the wicked.

5.167 The origin of the idea of 'burning' in hell is attributed to biblical references to Gehenna. Gehenna, the valley of Hinnom, was a rubbish dump outside the walls of Jerusalem which usually contained fires where the rubbish and disposed carcases were burned. Bodies of those deemed to have died in sin without any hope of salvation were also burned there. According to 2 Chronicles 28:3, King Ahaz of Judah sacrificed his sons in the valley of Hinnom, which as he was succeeded by his legitimate son Hezekiah born by the daughter of the High Priest, those sacrificed are understood as meaning his children by unrecorded concubines. Although often translated differently, as hell or hades, Gehenna appears in the Greek NT texts many times referring to a horrible place one would not wish to end up in. References to Gehenna include: Matthew 5:22, 5:29, 5:30, 10:28, 18:9, 23:15 and 23:33 as well as Mark 9:43, 9:45 and 9:47, Luke 12:5 and James 3:6. However, it is stated in many Jewish sources that the maximum amount of time a sinner can spend in Gehenna is one year – a much shorter time than generally understood as the likely duration spent in purgatory! The image of a purifying fire was described by Origen (c184 – c253) quoting from 1 Corinthians 3:10-15 – by which the dross of lighter transgressions will be burnt away and the soul thus purified will be saved. Origen also described a refining fire melting away the lead of evil deeds, leaving behind only pure gold. Plato also described the ritual sacrifice to Mercury on the 30th day after death as an offering for both the living and the dead, to free both from suffering they were liable to endure after death resulting from wicked acts they had committed. Sounds like we have justification for purgatory and indulgences!

5.168   Given the accepted description of conditions in Purgatory and the sins borne by everyone courtesy of Original Sin, various objections were raised about whether the truly righteous, such as patriarchs and saints, and the truly innocent such as unbaptised infants should still suffer painful purification processes in Purgatory.

5.169   Catholic interpretation of scripture established (i) the idea that as a result of the Fall (eating the fruit in Eden) heaven was closed to mankind, and (ii) the rule that no one will subsequently enter heaven until Jesus comes again in glory to establish his kingdom. However, there also seem to be scriptural references, including quotes by Jesus, that indicate some at least are not held in purgatory until that future time. Therefore there must be another place which accommodates those described in scripture as righteous and those infants guilty only of inherited original sin. Accordingly, new spaces were devised – the Limbus Patrum and the Limbus Infantium.

5.170   Support for the existence of a Limbus Patrum may be found in Jewish apocryphal writings and in statements by Jesus from which one may conclude some souls are held in a condition of happiness awaiting their final admittance to heaven once Jesus new kingdom is established. Matthew 8:11 is quoted as evidence of a fun place for good types from amongst the Gentiles to enjoy spending time 'feasting with Abraham, Isaac and Jacob'. However, Jesus also refers to this being 'in the kingdom' so maybe it is after he has established his kingdom after his second coming? In other cases it seems clear that not all those dying have to pass into the torment of purgatory. In Luke 16:22, Jesus speaks of an angel carrying a dead beggar directly to Abraham's side. On the cross, Jesus tells the penitent criminal next to him: today you will be with me in paradise. Doctrine concludes that those who had lived under the Torah (the Old Dispensation) and who, either at death or after purgatory cleansing, had attained righteousness and were eligible for heaven still had to await Jesus second coming – in prison but in a state of happiness.

5.171   As is often the case, the truth is hidden in plain sight. Jesus explained many times during his visit 2000 years ago that he was the Son of Man – therefore his life on Earth 2000 years ago was his second coming *for he was not born of woman.* Jesus harvested the souls of those who died before him during the period between the crucifixion and the resurrection (as told by James and Peter, e.g. 1 Peter 3:18-20) and thereafter it became an option, for all those subsequently dying, simply to follow the light. (Yes, a lot to take in but all will become clear by the time you finish this book!)

5.172   The doctrinal barrier for the still-born and for those dying before baptism is the absolute necessity of having been born again as a prerequisite for entry to heaven – as attributed to Jesus in John 3:5. Further, Catholic doctrine states that scripture and tradition tells us that baptismal regeneration is only available in this life and not after death. However, as always, some checking may be instructive. Some Catholic websites quote scriptural passages in support of this claim, including Luke 12:40, Luke 16:19, John 9:4 – none of which remotely support the specific claim. Surprisingly Matthew 19:14, suffer the little children for they shall inherit heaven, is not used to support Limbo Infantium but doctrinal explanations conclude *"that, as the result of centuries of speculation on the subject, we ought to believe that these souls enjoy a state of perfect natural happiness"*. (Er? So, if one thinks about something long enough, one is entitled to conclude that everything will turn out fine – surely there must be a Latin term for this astonishing process? Yes there is – it is called *'tradition'*!!)

5.173   Likewise, 'tradition' is quoted in support of Limbus Infantium and that relies upon theologians such as St Gregory of Nyssa, who died c 385. St Gregory, the author of a theory known as Apokatastasis in which he labours at great length to argue that eternal damnation might not be absolutely eternal as sustained purging of sins should eventually purify every sinner. For his boldness in questioning the eternal duration of hell, St Gregory was even attacked by some as being heretical. Another Gregory, St Gregory of Nazianzus 325 to 389, wrote that *"those just mentioned (infants dying without baptism) will neither be admitted by the just judge to the glory of heaven nor condemned to suffer punishment, since, though unsealed (by baptism), they are not wicked. For from the fact that one does not merit punishment it does not follow that one is worthy of being honoured, any more than it follows that one who is not worthy of a certain honour deserves on that account to be punished"* from Oration 40. However, it is Augustine (354 to 430) that is most widely quoted as the source of the concept of Limbus Infantium as the destination for unbaptised children who then shelter in relative peace, despite inheriting original sin, whilst they await salvation by Jesus at the end times.

5.174 'Tradition' is held as one of the three pillars of true doctrine but it seems unfortunate that the 'New Advent' website quotes the Catholic Encyclopaedia as giving its first example of tradition as being that Jesus was born on December 25th. Seemingly unaware that Jesus birthday can be readily calculated from Luke as being in September but its celebration was moved to December by Emperor Constantine as part of the negotiations at the Council of Nicaea – December 25th being the annual feast day of his god – Sol Invictus, and of the far more popular (in the 4th century) birth of Horus (the immaculately conceived son of the perpetual virgin, the Mery Isis).

5.175 At this point a little digression, don't you just love digressions!! It is puzzling that the combined brains trust of the Catholic church has been unable to discern Jesus birth date from its own canonised versions of the gospels – maybe to conceal the embarrassment of the deal with Emperor Constantine, which remained safe – so long as only ordained insiders were allowed to read the bible.

5.176 If one believes the biblical texts, as the church does, it is quite straightforward to find in Luke that Jesus birth was during the month of September. The first chapter of Luke reveals when John the Baptist was born: John's mother, Elizabeth, was Mary's cousin and the wife of Zacharias, who was high priest for the "course of Abijah". Luke 1:5 *There was in the days of Herod, the king of Judea, a certain priest named Zacharias, of the division of Abijah.* This reference provides the calendar clue – Priests were divided into 24 courses for their service in the Temple, and they served for one week, beginning on the Sabbath (1 Chronicles 24:7-19). The course of Abijah was the 8th course which places it around mid-July. It was at this time that Zacharias returned home to find his wife had conceived.

5.177 Mary visited Elizabeth soon after Mary had conceived, at a time when Elizabeth was six months pregnant: In Luke 1:31, Mary is told: *You will conceive and give birth to a son, and you are to call him Jesus.* Very soon after Mary goes to visit Elizabeth: with Luke 1:36 stating: *Even Elizabeth your relative is going to have a child in her old age, and she who was said to be unable to conceive is in her sixth month.*

5.178 Therefore Luke points to John the Baptist being born in mid-April and

Jesus six month later in mid-September. The Catholic church obviously has plenty of learned scholars who must have worked this out long ago – but truth was sacrificed on the altar of the secular-religious act of union with the Roman Empire. Oh, and what occurs around mid-September – Sukkot, the Feast of the Tabernacles. Some draw attention to John 1:14 to claim Jesus was born during the Feast of the Tabernacles, as it states that *"And the Word was made flesh and dwelt (using the word: tabernacled) among us"*. Of course the Feast of the Tabernacles, celebrating the grape harvest, originated as the Sumerian worship of Dionysus – which was already popular in Abraham's time, some 2000 years earlier.

5.179   End of digression, let us return to Purgatory. The idea of purging sin through enduring fire gained papal backing from Pope Gregory I (590-604). Gregory I wrote of a *purgatorius ignis*, a cleansing fire to purge venial sins (wood, hay and stubble) but not mortal sins (iron, bronze and lead) prior to Judgment. This Catholic development of the idea of purgatory as a waystation for purification, purging sinners of the stain of their sin through a regime of fire and torture sponsored a wave of imagination amongst writers and artists.

5.180   The Second Council of Lyons (1274) ruled that worthy souls are purified in purgatory after death and that such souls benefit from prayers and pious acts that are dedicated to them by the living. The concept of purgatory was confirmed by the Council of Florence in 1439 as part of an agreement for the unification of the Eastern church with the Western, which included Eastern acceptance of the doctrine of purgatory. It was declared that the truly penitent having died before completion of their penance and therefore undergoing cleaning through purgatorial punishments benefitted from observances, prayers and alms given by the living. The attempted unification failed – with the Russian church declaring autonomy and just a few years later, in 1453, Constantinople fell to Moslem forces.

5.181   Such was the general fear of purgatory that the church hit upon a great idea. The living could act to alleviate the suffering of the deceased in purgatory. The grace which was released by holding a Mass could apparently be channelled to benefit one's deceased loved ones held in purgatory, reducing the period of their suffering. This idea caught on, with rich benefactors setting up and endowing 'chantries', where Mass was said hundreds or thousands of times over to speed their passage after death.

5.182 The extra scriptural elaborations and public imagination led to the Council of Trent (1545-1563) issuing a decree 'Concerning Purgatory' as part of its final rulings. Whilst reaffirming previously defined doctrine, the ruling instructed bishops to keep strictly to the teaching of the pope and church councils – excluding "more difficult and subtle questions from popular discourse with uneducated people". Public discussion of matters with the appearance of falsehood, curiosity and superstition should not be permitted.

5.183 In 2005, the then Cardinal Joseph Ratzinger indicated the concept of Limbo should be abandoned because it was "*only a theological hypothesis*" and "*never a defined truth of faith*". In 2007, as Pope Benedict, he published "The Hope of Salvation for Infants Who Die Without Being Baptised" which triggered headlines such as "*The Pope closes Limbo*". But, the 41 page document makes no conclusion either way – merely that the Limbo of Infants is "*consistent with the Church's teaching, though it is not an official expression of that teaching.*" It states that the theory of Limbo "*remains a possible theological opinion*". The document endorses the hypothesis of a Limbo of Infants as one of the existing theories about the fate of children who die without being baptised, a question on which it states that there is "no explicit answer" from Scripture or 'tradition'. The traditional theological alternative to Limbo was not Heaven, but rather some degree of suffering in Hell.

5.184 Islam has a more refreshing view, the concept of Limbo exists as Barzakh, the period from death until resurrection. During this period sinners are punished and those adequately purified may then rest in peace. However, without any concept of original sin, all children are exempt from this stage, as they are regarded as innocent and are automatically classed as Muslims (whatever their religious upbringing). After death, children (defined as not having reached the 'age of accountability', meaning not showing the first signs of puberty) go directly to Paradise, where they are cared for by Abraham.

5.185 One must ponder the unquantifiable anguish of Christian mothers caused by this Catholic doctrine for the past 2000 years. Already suffering from the impact of a still birth or the death of a young baby, which was extremely common in most Catholic countries even 100 years ago, the overwhelming majority of mothers would fear the immediate consignment of their innocent babes to purgatory.

H   Excommunication

5.186   Excommunication was, and still is, a powerful weapon used by the Catholic Church to control its adherents. Growing out of the old Jewish concept of banishing outlaws from the settlement, putting them 'beyond the pale', excommunication can be declared in respect of any baptised individual. The act deprives the person from receiving grace through the sacraments, although they can attend Mass and do penance, they will receive no grace and upon dying will be denied a Catholic burial in sanctified ground. Therefore, upon death the excommunicated go directly to hell where they can expect eternal damnation. Moreover, under medieval church belief, family members could not alleviate the suffering of the excommunicated by dedicating Masses, undertaking pilgrimages and buying indulgences – which could only benefit those in purgatory. Heretics would be excommunicated, then burnt at the stake and their ashes scattered – depriving them of the Last Rites, a proper burial from which they might hope for resurrection. Excommunication condemned them to immediate and direct despatch to everlasting damnation in the fires of hell – a terrifying and terminal end for any stout believer who had the temerity to question any aspect of doctrine and then refuse to recant.

5.187   Under Canon Law, Excommunication is the usual punishment for heresy (post baptism denial of any article of Catholic dogma), schism (rejecting any authority vested in the pope), apostasy (post baptism denial of the faith), abortion, breaking confidentiality of the Confession and impersonation of a cleric.

5.188   Now, one may appreciate the full horror of Excommunication for Catholics – the power vested in the Pope allows the miscreant to be fast tracked through judgment by an earthly consignment direct to Hell with no chance of judgment by God in Purgatory.

I   Bodily resurrection

5.189   The resurrection of Jesus is regarded by mainstream Christians as the essential basis of their faith – the unique and divine aspect which foretells their own salvation through belief. Given its centrality to Christian faith, it is surprising that the biblical record is rather sparse and quite contradictory. One might assume all the gospels provide a detailed and consistent account. The gospels we have do not quite provide this.

5.190　John does provide a detailed account of Jesus resurrection and provides the basis for the conventional understanding. Matthew and Mark explain that Mary Magdalene and either one or two other women visit the tomb and found Jesus body gone – then, what they presumed were, angels informed them that Jesus has risen and to tell the apostles he will visit them in Galilee. Matthew tells of Jesus appearing near the tomb and repeating the message for his disciples to go to Galilee. Originally the gospel of Mark ended with two terrified women leaving the empty tomb – a very unsatisfying ending and no doubt a good reason for a scribe adding the final verses some 4 centuries later – a fact even footnoted in the NIV. The added verses seem to contradict the old ending by saying Jesus did indeed appear to Mary Magdalene near the tomb.

5.191　Mark then switches to tell of two men walking 'in the country' who encountered Jesus, followed by Jesus appearing before his disciples when they were eating, giving them the Great Commission and then ascending to heaven without visiting Galilee. Luke is similar to Matthew, the women are told of Jesus resurrection by angels but Jesus does not appear to them. The Marys' tell the apostles of their discovery and Peter and John go to check. Luke also tells of two men walking in the country, naming one as Cleopas, who were joined by another man who, after they stopped at an inn for the night, revealed himself as Jesus.

5.192　In Luke, Jesus then appears before the 11 apostles who recognise him, whereupon Jesus goes to Bethany (on eastern side of Jerusalem) instead of Galilee (c125km north) and ascends to heaven. In Matthew, the disciples meet Jesus on a mountain in Galilee whereupon Jesus gives them the Great Commission and then nothing – no departure, no ascension or anything – an odd ending for a document of such importance. The end of Luke is also controversial: the earliest manuscripts of Luke 24:51-52 omit the phrases "he left them and was taken up to heaven" and "they worshipped him". For example, in the Codex Sinaiticus, Luke concludes: "he blessed them. Then they returned to Jerusalem with great joy." Thus, the original gospel of Luke seems to have made no reference to an ascension. This is contradicted in the opening of Acts where the author claims he has already written about Jesus activities over a period of 40 days between his resurrection and ascension and provides a summary in verses 1-11. This rather suggests that either the author of Acts was not the author of the surviving gospel of Luke or that the original ending of Luke was much longer and lost at some point.

5.193 As with the nativity story, most Christians learn of the resurrection from lessons in school or sermons in church – all being based on a pastiche assembled from contradictory texts. A deceptive foundational belief is laid in our minds at a tender age and later anyone actually reading a gospel concludes that they know more detail and what they already understood is not contradicted by what they just read.

5.194 In conclusion, John, who was the only gospel writer who had first-hand experience of Jesus, seems to provide the most detailed account. By contrast, the synoptics look weak – in two of them, Jesus contradicts his own message that he will meet the disciples in Galilee by ascending abruptly from Bethany. However, the last two chapters of John do not appear in the oldest and best manuscripts and even the Catholic church doubts their authenticity, with official Catholic commentary on John stopping at the end of chapter 19. Given the evidence, one is left wondering whether resurrection was actually seen as important during the first fifty years after the crucifixion. Certainly, both Peter and James, two of the inner three, dwell on other aspects of Jesus death – where he went during the three days (c42 hours) from Friday afternoon to Sunday morning. To the extent surviving heretical texts have been recovered, only the Gospel of Peter contains details of the resurrection (some unique) whilst the Gospel of Philip warns people to ignore tales of Jesus resurrection – indicating it may have been seen as a post facto rationalization. Indeed, I have not found any other texts suppressed by the Roman church even refer to Jesus resurrection – it does not seem to have been an important issue for the earliest Christians. This seems very surprising.

5.195 Generally, it seems early Christians mostly believed resurrection was spiritual in nature, with Jesus able to manifest a vision of himself for others to recognize him. It was in this spiritual form that Jesus then ascended to heaven. For detailed research of the early texts which have come to light from Nag Hammadi and other caches, I recommend two of Bart Ehrman's excellent books *'Lost Scriptures: Books That Did Not Make It Into the New Testament'* and *'Misquoting Jesus: The Story Behind Who Changed the Bible and Why'.*

5.196   The early Christian view was consistent with both the ancient belief of the duality of soul and spirit co-existing in the human body and with the Greco-Roman understanding that the soul was 'imprisoned' during its existence in a body, whilst the spirit was eternal. For both, the creator God was seen as spiritual and having no interest in the revival of dead bodies. Greek culture believed in the survival of the soul after death but not in the soul ever being reunited with the dead body.

5.197   Paul agreed with the tripartite existence of spirit, soul and body – in 1 Thessalonians 5:23 Paul wrote: *"May your whole spirit, soul and body be kept blameless at the coming of our Lord Jesus Christ"*. In Corinth, Paul encountered resistance to his teaching of bodily resurrection – devoting chapter 15 of his 1st epistle to the Corinthians to explaining his belief. Paul based bodily resurrection upon his belief that Jesus had bodily resurrected. Paul gets carried away by his own logic, arguing in 15:12-17 that *"if it is preached that Christ has been raised from the dead, how can some of you say that there is no resurrection of the dead? If there is no resurrection of the dead, then not even Christ has been raised. And if Christ has not been raised, our preaching is useless and so is your faith. More than that, we are then found to be false witnesses about God, for we have testified about God that he raised Christ from the dead. But he did not raise him if in fact the dead are not raised. For if the dead are not raised, then Christ has not been raised either. And if Christ has not been raised, your faith is futile; you are still in your sins."* Paul is arguing that if there is no resurrection of the bodies of the dead, then logically Jesus has not been resurrected. If Jesus has not been resurrected then believers faith is in vain and they remain slaves to sin. He concludes by saying that without resurrection of the body, Jesus death on the cross for our sins provides no salvation for us – it was merely the Roman crucifixion of a false messiah.

5.198   It is clear that Paul is referring to bodily resurrection rather than the resurrection of the soul as referred to by James, Peter and many texts deemed heretical, as Paul uses the Greek term 'soma' meaning physical body when describing resurrection. This reveals the key divergence of Pauline Christianity from the teaching of Jesus and set the Catholic church on a path tangential to truth.

5.199   Paul's theology argued that the human body was a temple to house the spirit and therefore we should strive to avoid sin to become righteous, whereupon our bodies would be ready for sanctification. Paul taught we should regard our bodies as a temple designed to house the holy spirit. Paul deduced that having striven to attain righteousness, the sanctified body would not then be abandoned as waste but be physically resurrected to house the soul and spirit in the afterlife.

5.200   The Catholic Catechism is drawn to make the strange Statement 2301, that *The Church permits cremation, provided that it does not demonstrate a denial of faith in the resurrection of the body*. Yet the same faith delighted in burning the bodies of heretics and wilfully scattering their ashes to specifically exclude the heretics from being resurrected at the end times!

5.201   Irenaeus, a Greek bishop (130 to 202), was a notable early supporter of bodily resurrection, arguing for a literal restoration of the flesh. This assertion clearly required further development as it was patently obvious that those who died, whether devout Christians or not, never seemed to experience bodily resurrection. Hence, the development of dogma that said bodily resurrection occurred after Jesus *second* coming. As an aside, the reference to Jesus telling the criminal next to him on another cross that they would meet again in paradise the same day is often misunderstood. Luke 23:42-43 states: *Then he (the criminal) said, 'Jesus, remember me when you come into your kingdom'. Jesus replied, 'Truly I tell you, today you will be with me in Paradise'*. The Greek word 'paradisio' does not mean heaven but a state of delight, a place where all things are just and fair.

5.202   Story of Lazarus is interesting – beyond the startling claim that a dead person, dead for 3 days, was brought back to life. The name of the person brought back to life, Lazarus, is derived from Osiris, which translates into Greek being El-Azar-Us – a striking similarity which a number of authors have commented upon, including Iris Murdoch in *Christ in Egypt: The Horus-Jesus Connection*. At the very least it would seem that familiarity with the story of Osiris influenced the write up in the gospels. Osiris was the god revered in Egypt as having been brought back to life by his son, Horus, and who was foretold as returning to Earth long after his second death – to resurrect the bodies of the righteous. This led Egyptians to worship a trinity comprising Osiris, his wife Isis and their son Horus (the one with the special eye). And who was the leader of the small minority promoting the concept of a trinity to Emperor Constantine at the Council of Nicaea in 325 – Archbishop Athanasius of Alexandria in Egypt. The story of Lazarus is unique to John (chapter

11), which is itself surprising – surely it is odd that the most astonishing of all Jesus miracles goes unmentioned in the three synoptics? Analysis of John 11 suggests the author combined several unrelated events told in the synoptics not covered elsewhere in John – including the head anointing of Jesus in Bethany by an unnamed woman (Mark 14 & Matthew 26); the sinful woman anointing Jesus' feet and wiping with her hair (Luke 7); Jesus visit to Martha and Mary in an unnamed village (Luke 10) and Jesus parable of the rich man and Lazarus (Luke 10). The only other reference to the raising of Lazarus is in a text ruled heretical – the Secret Gospel of Mark – 3.6(#19). The naming of the resurrected man as Lazarus seems a dead give-away – simply an attempt to co-opt a famous incident to make Jesus more 'competitive' with other gods. Could this story be another late addition added to the original text – as with the more plausible story of the woman caught in adultery (John 8:1-11) and also the 3rd/4th century addition of John 20 & 21? Another give-away of it being a late addition is Martha's supposed statement to Jesus (John 11:27) that "you are the Messiah, the Son of God" – the classic oxymoron invented in the late 2nd century by those ignorant of Judaism. Also, rather worryingly for those believing in bodily resurrection – despite his resurrection by Jesus himself, both Catholic and Eastern Orthodox tradition record Lazarus dying a second time. (For more detail, see also 14.25-14.30 below.)

5.203   As explored in the conclusions to Part One, Jesus' strategy as presented in the bible is rather puzzling. During his ministry, Jesus never hesitated to visit the Temple or confront the high priest. The bible narrative presents Jesus as misunderstood and feared as an insurrectionist by the Jewish leadership, which resulted in his crucifixion. If Jesus mission was to imprint his message into the minds of humanity, then what better than to simply walk back into the Sanhedrin after his resurrection? Instead, we read only that he reappeared to a few close friends. The sparse biblical accounts left for us are confusing, some comments indicate Jesus had a bodily form (he eat fish) whilst other comments indicate a purely spiritual form (walking through walls and disappearing from their midst). If Jesus stayed for 40 days there should be far more records of his appearances – in both religious and, particularly, secular history.

5.204   The main problem with bodily resurrection is the sheer absence of logic. Not only are we all aware that most of us die leaving bodies we definitely would not want to be resurrected with, also many bodies are destroyed at death in accidents or during war, many opt for cremation and all buried bodies soon rot to leave a residue of bones. When pressed, some theologians claim we all get fresh new bodies – so most hope for being reborn as Adonis! Getting a new body is not resurrection, it is called..... However, we are also told that our bodily resurrection will enable us to recognize and be recognized by our loved ones – really? For us to be readily recognisable, we would presumably have to have bodies in a state close to our deaths – for many of us that would be somewhat decrepit – not an exciting idea.

5.205   The idea of retaining physical bodies as housing for our spiritual parts also leads to other problems. Our physical bodies primarily exist for mobility, housing our brains and for reproduction – none of which is required for our spiritual parts. Further, physical bodies presumably still require sustenance to maintain their physical components and thereby also involve cellular reproduction, exposing us to genetic malfunctions and ageing. The more one thinks about it the less sense it makes to have physical bodies in an eternal afterlife. As we shall see, the books which were deemed heretical recorded Jesus explaining our afterlife was purely spiritual – but the Church is stuck in a rut imprisoned by 'tradition' and infallibility!

5.206   Statement 366 of the Catholic Catechism explains: *The Church teaches that every spiritual soul is created immediately by God – it is not "produced" by the parents – and also that it is immortal: it does not perish when it separates from the body at death, and it will be reunited with the body at the final Resurrection.* The sources provided in support of this assertion do not include Jesus, nor even any biblical sources but two Popes and the Lateran Council (Pius XII, Humani generis: DS 3896; Paul VI, CPC # 8; Lateran Council V in 1513: DS 1440). As noted above, the Church is stuck with tradition and infallibility.

5.207   Statement 575 of the Catholic Catechism quotes Matthew 22:23-34 as authority for resurrection, which according to its dogma is bodily resurrection: 575 *"Jesus endorses some of the teachings imparted by this religious elite of God's people: the resurrection of the dead"* but fails to realise Jesus is clearly referring to spiritual resurrection of the soul not of dead bodies.

5.208   Catholic belief in bodily resurrection has led it to completely unsustainable positions, as in Statement 1017 *We believe in the true resurrection of this flesh that we now possess* (Council of Lyons II: DS 854). *We sow a corruptible body in the tomb, but he (God) raises up an incorruptible body, a "spiritual body"* (from Paul's epistle to the Corinthians 1 Cor 15:42-44). Followed by Statement 1018: *As a consequence of original sin, man must suffer "bodily death, from which man would have been immune had he not sinned"* (GS # 18). Thus the church finds itself claiming that prior to eating a piece of fruit, mankind enjoyed bodies that were immortal and after death, if saved, they will regain their old bodies (note – not new ones but the flesh we already possess) which somehow will then last eternally.

5.209　Given the current state of mankind's knowledge, this teaching is completely untenable. One day, it may be noticed that the material realm of matter only comprises c4% of the mass energy of our universe, whilst dark energy comprises 68% – might this represent the constituent realms of the material and spiritual?

J　Mariology

5.210　The earliest recorded references to Jesus mother are in Paul's epistles. Galatians 4:4, believed to have been written by Paul around the year 56, reads *"God sent his Son, born of a woman"*. Here Paul is implying Jesus was already divine at birth, as a Jew, Jesus would come from two human parents and be endowed with a Spirit, from God – Paul is saying Jesus had a special spirit as a Son of God.

5.211　It is noteworthy that Paul's statement in Galatians 4:4 , *born of a woman* directly contradicts Jesus numerous statements of being a Son of Man – signifying that Jesus had come with knowledge of his prior lives, unlike all he preached to, whom Jesus described as 'born of woman'.

5.212　A little further on, in Galatians 4:28-29, Paul wrote *"But just as in those days the son born in nature's course persecuted the one whose birth was in the realm of the spirit, so do we find it now"*. Here Paul makes a rather strained comparison of Hagar's son Ishmael, born naturally, who he states persecuted his brother Isaac, born from divine intervention by a formerly barren Sarah – a conflict he then compares with himself born naturally who had previously persecuted the followers of Jesus, born from spiritual intervention.

5.213　A few years later, c58, Paul writes of the dual nature of Jesus in Romans 1:3-4 *"the gospel regarding his Son, who as to his human nature was a descendant of*

David, and who through the spirit of holiness was declared with power to be the Son of God". In Romans 9:5, Paul writes *"Theirs are the patriarchs, and from them is traced the human ancestry of Christ, who is God over all".*

5.214   Later, between 61 to 63, Paul makes further oblique reference in Philippians 2:6-8 to Jesus being born in the likeness of man.

5.215   We can only speculate whether these texts remain unaltered from Paul's original. On balance, it would seem Paul's description of Jesus being God's son is substantiated by the record of doctrinal disputes arising between Paul and the Jerusalem church led by James; alternatively it may reflect later edits arising during the tussles over Christology. From these quotes, Paul is definitely not stating that Jesus was born of a virgin nor that he was without a human biological father. Paul refers to *"James, the Lord's brother"* in Galatians 1:19; and Jesus human side being descended from David in Romans 1:3 (Paul would be referring only to the male line) and again in Romans 9:5 to the patriarchs (all male) from whom the human ancestry of Jesus is traced. Finally, Paul's comparison of himself with Hagar's son Ishmael does not suggest Abraham was not the human father of Isaac, nor that Joseph was not the human father of Jesus.

5.216   The earliest known prayer referring to Mary as 'Theotokos' is the hymn *Sub tuum praesidium* (Beneath thy protection). The earliest manuscript of this hymn was found in a Coptic Christmas liturgy dated by one papyrologist to the 3rd century and by another to the 4th century. Theotokos was a widely used term to describe Isis, the virgin mother of the god Horus. The Egyptian goddess Isis was worshipped extensively across the Roman empire, becoming the most revered female goddess with large temples in many cities including Londinium and York. Thus the foundations were in place for Mary to assume the religious role of Isis as the virgin mother of the new god.

5.217   Epiphanius, bishop of Salamis from 365 to 403, wrote of his search for reliable traditions describing the fate of Mary – and his inability to discover any. He noted there were three beliefs held at that time: that she had died a normal death, she died a martyr and that she did not die – concluding that no one knows her end. The idea that Mary was bodily taken up to heaven first appeared in to texts from sources regarded as heretical: *Liber Requiei Mariae* and the *Six Books Dormition Apocryphon*.

5.218   The Third Ecumenical Council, the Council of Ephesus in 431, again chaired by a Roman Emperor, Theodosius II, debated whether Mary should be described as *Theokotos* (meaning God-bearer or Mother of God) implying Jesus is both God and man in one; or as *Christotokos* (meaning Mother of the Messiah). The Nestorians, who argued for *Christotokos*, were not denying Jesus divinity but that as God the Son, Jesus existed before Mary and calling her Mother of God was confusing and possibly heretical. They argued that Mary was mother of Jesus only as a human. The majority supported the pope's position that denying Mary the title *Theokotos* would imply Jesus was not divine or that Jesus had two separate personhoods – a Christology already ruled heretical. The debate over the title of Mary was less about Mary than the Christological argument over the nature of Jesus.

5.219   A Second Council of Ephesus in 449 overturned the definition of the nature of Jesus, adopting a position known as Monophysitism which held that the person of the Word incarnate was of purely divine nature.

5.220   This was challenged by the Emperor Marcian, who called another Council, the Council of Chalcedon in 451, which issued the Chalcedonian Definition that Jesus is perfect both in deity and in humanness, his self-same person being actually God and actually man – at the same time. The Council was informed by St Juvenal, bishop of Jerusalem (based elsewhere) that Mary died in the presence of all the Apostles, but that her tomb, when opened upon the request of Thomas, was found empty; wherefrom the Apostles concluded that the body was taken up to heaven. This theory is surely highly suspect as Mary is generally believed to have been looked after by John for many years, probably in Ephesus, whilst the other ten remaining apostles soon scattered to spread the gospel – Thomas in particular is believed to have gone east and would have been far away when Mary died. But, the Chalcedonian Definition and the 'guess' of an assumption was enough to see Mary granted the status of deity and worthy of worship. This led to thousands of churches being dedicated to her – firmly establishing Mariology as a central tenet of Catholicism.

5.221   In 600, Emperor Maurice instituted an annual celebration of the Assumption of Mary but it seems to be John of Damascus, 675 to 749, who is recognised widely as the authority. John, an accomplished civil servant to the Caliph of Damascus who later became a monk, repeated the dodgy story giving it further credence, writing that: *"Mary died in the presence of the Apostles, but that her tomb, when opened, upon the request of St Thomas, was found empty; wherefrom the Apostles concluded that the body was taken up to heaven*". This repetition of a highly dubious story seems to have influenced Pope Leo XIII declaring John of Damascus a 'Doctor of the Church' in 1890.

5.222   Pope Leo IV (790 to 855) confirmed the Assumption of Mary as an official feast.

5.223   Another amazing Marian dogma, the Immaculate Conception has a similar origin, a rumour circulating the eastern provinces of the church got picked up and 'theologicalised'. Edmer (c1060 to c1126) a Benedictine monk and biographer of St Anselm, Archbishop of Canterbury (1033 to 1109), wrote a text that converted the previous celebration of Mary's conception into an immaculate conception. Meanwhile Mary's role in the church grew steadily. Bernard of Clairvaux (1090–1153) a highly regarded monk consulted by popes and monarchs, theorised about Mary's power of intercession and her role in redemption in his *Praises on the Virgin Mother*. But the idea of an immaculate conception was dismissed by many theologians for years, until the influential Thomas Aquinas (1225 to 1274) gave it legs, stating that whilst he had reservations he would accept the ruling of the church.

5.224   Typical theological debate arose over when Mary might have become sinless in preparation for her immaculate conception of Jesus. On the one hand, how could she be redeemed prior to Jesus resurrection, on the other she was held to be free even of original sin prior to conception. Duns Scotus, 1265 to 1308, a noted Scottish Franciscan friar and university professor, devised a formula which satisfied the church. Scotus formula was that Mary had been cleansed of original sin at her own conception and had remained sinless throughout her life, simply on the basis *'potuit, decuit ergo fecit'* – God could do it. Scotus asserted that Mary had been redeemed in *anticipation* of Jesus death on the Cross. Neat!

5.225   The search for theological support for Mary being sinless found evidence in a text previously declared heretical, the Proto-Evangelium of James (3.6 #14). This text claimed that Mary was conceived by divine intervention rather than the sexual union of her parents. Her mother, Ann had remained a virgin and 'therefore' Mary had not inherited Original Sin. This issue was debated at the Council of Basle, 1431, which concluded that *"Mary's immaculate conception is a pious opinion consistent with scripture"* – omitting any reference to the only source being heretical!!

5.226   The Rosary, was developed as a system of prayer to Mary and Jesus, after an apparition of Mary appeared to Saint Dominic in 1214. It came to form a central part of Catholic worship. The Rosary comprises a set of beads that enable the prayerful to keep track of their progress in the recitation. The arrangement consists of sets of prayers, ten Hail Marys, called a 'decade', preceded by one Lord's Prayer and followed by one Glory Be. During recitation of each set, thought should be given to one of the Mysteries of the Rosary – events in the lives of Jesus and Mary linked to specific aspects of righteousness. Pope Pius V (1566 to 1572) established a standard of 15 Mysteries, grouping them into three sets: the Joyful, the Sorrowful and the Glorious. In 1716 an annual feast to celebrate the Rosary was introduced. Pope John Paul II (1978 to 2005), placed the rosary at the very center of Christian spirituality and called it *"among the finest and most praiseworthy traditions of Christian contemplation"*. John Paul added a fourth set of five Mysteries he named the Luminous Mysteries. The Glorious mysteries are prayed on Sunday and Wednesday, the Joyful on Monday and Saturday, the Sorrowful on Tuesday and Friday, and the Luminous on Thursday. Usually five decades are recited in a session.

5.227   Unsurprisingly, with the Protestant focus on sola scriptura, Mariology came under attack from leaders such as Martin Luther (1483 to 1546) and John Calvin (1509 to 1564) as being sacrilegious and superstitious whilst equating widespread Marian iconography as idolatry which led to the destruction of much church art in strongly Protestant regions. Nevertheless, the Council of Trent (1545 to 1563) confirmed the appropriateness of Marian artworks in churches.

5.228   Mariology continued to receive strong papal support. The 1571 edition of the Breviary incorporated an elaborate service for the celebration of the Immaculate Conception on December 8. I find no source for the explanation of the date chosen. It may have been based upon the Nativity of Mary on September 8, celebrated by the Byzantine church since the 7th century – by simply deducting nine months. One might speculate whether this date was a relic of earlier knowledge of Jesus birthday – which as we saw in 5.174-178 above would have been close to this time.

5.229 Despite the incredibly weak origins of its theological basis, Pope Paul V confirmed the immaculate conception in 1617 and ruled it inadmissible to deny it. This presumably raised some dissenting voices as Pope Gregory XV had to repeat the ruling in 1622. In 1661, Pope Alexandre VII ruled that the soul of Mary had never been tainted with original sin.

5.230 During these centuries, the Immaculate Conception of Mary was a tradition rather than a defined dogma and pressure grew from Catholic leaders for a papal ruling. Although immaculate conception had been endorsed as doctrine by the Council of Basel (1431 to 1449) this was later ruled not to have been an official Council. So, Pope Pius IX, 1846-1878, asked the bishops for their views and finding 90% supporting the idea, in 1854 he issued the bull *Ineffabilis Deus* declaring Mary had been born free from the stain of original sin. *Ineffabilis Deus* identifies theological support as '*seen*' in various scriptural passages, including the statement by God to the serpent in the Garden of Eden, in Noah's Ark, Jacob's Ladder and even the Burning Bush. (Having consulted these passages, this author has made a note that he must visit SpecSavers.)

5.231 The official description of the long journey that Catholic theology took to discover this miraculous aspect of Mary is described masterfully in statement 491 of the Catholic Catechism: *Through the centuries the Church has become ever more aware that Mary, "full of grace" through God, was redeemed from the moment of her conception. That is what the dogma of the Immaculate Conception confesses, as Pope Pius IX proclaimed in 1854: "The most Blessed Virgin Mary was, from the first moment of her conception, by a singular grace and privilege of almighty God and by virtue of the merits of Jesus, preserved immune from all stain of original sin."* What this statement omits is that the sole source of this assertion is a text that the Vatican declared heretical in 405 and tried hard to destroy all copies of – the The Proto-Evangelium of James.

5.232 In 1950, yes 1950, Pope Pius XII, invoking papal infallibility, issued 'Munificentissimus Deus' which stated *"We proclaim and define it to be a dogma revealed by God that the immaculate Mother of God, Mary ever virgin, when the course of her earthly life was finished, was taken up body and soul into the glory of heaven"*. This formulation leaves open whether or not Mary died before being taken up to heaven. You will note the claim that Mary remained a lifelong virgin, a direct contradiction of numerous biblical statements including:

- Matthew 1:25 stating that Joseph did not consummate his wedding to Mary until Jesus had been born;

- Paul's specific statement naming James as Jesus brother in Galatians 1:19.

- Matthew 13:55 and Mark 6:3 both state that Jesus had four brothers: James, Joses, Judas and Simon. The name Joses was a common abbreviation of Joseph, an obvious device to differentiate from his father, whilst Judas has conventionally been translated to English as Jude – no doubt to differentiate from the other Judas.

5.233   Pope John Paul II, who promoted Marian devotions and reorientated the church towards renewal of Marian veneration, at the same time admitted that *"Many centuries were necessary to arrive at the explicit definition of the revealed truths concerning Mary"*. Nowadays Mary is viewed by many Catholics as Mother of the Church as well as Queen of Heaven. Sites dedicated to Mary have become the most popular pilgrimages – the Basilica of Aparecida in Brazil and the Basilica of Guadalupe in Mexico each receive more than 5 million pilgrims annually. However, Catholic debate during the 20th century has recognized that the elevated veneration of Mary by Catholics has implications for ecumenical unity.

5.234   To conclude, it is easy for others to underestimate the central importance of Mary within the Catholic faith.

K   Church services exclusively in Latin until 1965

5.235   Another barrier between the congregation and the church was that the Mass, and all other services, were only said in Latin – which few could understand. Indeed, many priests were believed to know the service by heart rather than hold any knowledge of Latin. For most attendees the unintelligible service, given by elaborately dressed clerics in awesome surroundings, was tempting to view as magic.

5.236   The logic behind all services being conducted in Latin was simply control. Latin was hardly the lingua franca – that was Greek. Latin was a minority language across the empire. Even the church in Rome celebrated in Greek, until AD190 when Pope Victor started using Latin, but it is believed that it took around another century before Latin was adopted as standard, even in Rome itself. Greek remained the principal language of the church until AD395 when the Roman Empire split – and the Western Empire based in Rome adopted Latin. Latin was regarded as a vulgar language lacking the sophistication of Greek which was associated with culture, philosophy and science. Hence the new translation of the bible into Latin by Jerome, a few years before the split, is still known as the Vulgate.

5.237 During the period between 395 and 1474, the content and prayers for each service gradually developed. The invention of printing allowed the content to be proscribed for all churches to follow, although initially there were regional variations – some 14 versions were known to be used during the hundred years leading up to the Council of Trent (1545-1563). The long sessions of the Council of Trent in many ways represent the Catholic response to the Protestant Reformation. Efforts were made to establish higher standards of priestly education and behaviour, standardised services and in effect tighter central control. In 1570, the Tridentine Mass was published following approval by the Council of Trent. This established a fixed service to be followed by every Catholic church. This version mandated the priest to celebrate mass with his back to the congregation – who prayed silently, with very few able to follow the Latin in books referred to as missals.

5.238 The exclusive use of Latin in all services was only relaxed by the Second Vatican Council (1962-1965), which allowed the use of vernacular languages. The result was unexpected – with virtually all priests abandoning use of the Latin for services. Further reforms were announced by Pope Paul VI in 1969 – including the officiating priest turning to face the congregation, simplified rituals and use of more scriptural readings.

5.239 The printing press facilitated greater control, allowing the imposition of standardised text for all services and leading to the tradition of papal homilies to even standardize the weekly sermon. The level of central control would impress any military dictatorship.

5.240 The adoption of seemingly mechanical repetition of standard texts and the exclusive use of a language that hardly anyone in any congregation could understand clearly bears no relationship to Jesus example or his Great Commission. Jesus almost definitely spoke Aramaic and Greek, indeed Judah was definitely bi-lingual at that time. Jesus is also recorded as speaking with Roman centurions and the Roman Governor – which would certainly have been in Greek or Latin. One might assume that Jesus may have been able to understand and discourse in any language.

5.241   At Pentecost, as described in Acts chapter 2, the great gift of the Holy Spirit was to enable the apostles to speak in tongues so that all could understand the gospel message. Jesus did not instruct his disciples to only use Greek when preaching the gospel to the world.

5.242   So, the Catholic requirement for all services to comprise rote repetition celebrated solely in Latin was surely a perversion, simply control-freakery.

L   Control of clergy through celibacy

5.243   With a few tightly controlled exceptions, the Catholic church maintains a strict rule that ordained priests, bishops and therefore popes should remain celibate. When asked why, most Catholics apparently refer to Jesus remaining unmarried. Many others challenge this assumption on a number of grounds. If Jesus acted as a pious Jew, he would have seen it as an obligation to marry by age 30 and to have children. Some point to odd features of his earliest reported miracle, the marriage at Cana. That Jesus mother managed the refreshments and asked her son to take care as the wine was running low is suggestive of Mary managing the celebration as mother of the groom. Observant Jews were betrothed at 12 (when Jesus happened to visit the Temple) and married at 30 – just before his ministry is recorded as starting. There are also many references to Mary Magdalene being particularly close to Jesus.

5.244   However, led by Paul, proto-Catholicism concluded sex was basically sinful, and women, being in the mould of Eve, were designed to tempt men to sin. Therefore, to remain righteous, ideally, men should abstain from all sex. Augustine of Hippo, who embellished Paul's ideas on Original Sin also emphasized the association of sex with sin – declaring that women were used by evil spirits to deceive men.

5.245   Clerical celibacy was not originally a Christian dogma, it resulted primarily from persistent clerical abuse. References indicate that most of Jesus' apostles were married – including Peter, seen as the first pope. However, reflecting ancient Jewish customs about cleanliness, the Council of Elvira, in 306, decreed that a priest must not sleep with his wife and then celebrate Mass the next day. In 325 the Nicaean Council decreed no priest may be married and in 385 a new pope, Siricius, left his wife when elected and declared any married priests could no longer sleep with their wives. In 567, the 2nd Council of Tours ruled that "any cleric found in bed with his wife would be excommunicated for a year and defrocked".

5.246 These edicts seem to have had little effect as church documents from the 7th Century state most clergy in France were married and in the 8th Century, Boniface, the Archbishop of Mainz, reported to Pope Gregory III that the majority of clergy in Germany were married. At the Council of Aix-la-Chapelle in 836, discussion of abortions and infanticide being common in convents and monasteries to cover up un-celibate activities of the clerics led to calls to permit marriage. In 1045, Pope Benedict IX, an extraordinary chap first elected when only 20 and thrown out for 'vile adulteries' then recovered the papacy by force of arms before deciding to abdicate in order to marry his cousin. Later he managed to secure a third brief period as pope. At least five popes were married and had children whilst pope. During the first millennium, no less than nine popes were children of ordained clerics.

5.247 This sorry state of affairs led the Vatican to assert itself on celibacy. One concern had been potential leakage of church assets, the massive wealth of bishops passed on death (or election as pope) to the Vatican. However, if clergy had wives and also children such assets might 'leak' outside the church. In 580, Pope Pelagius II issued a decree to this effect preventing spouses or children from inheriting any assets of the clergy.

5.248 The acceptance of married clergy in the See of Constantine was a contributory factor in Leo IX excommunicating the Patriarch in 1054. In 1074, Pope Gregory VII decreed that, before anyone could be ordained, they must renounce their wives and pledge celibacy. In 1095, Pope Urban II decreed all priest's wives be seized and sold into slavery!! In 1123, the 1st Lateran Council declared all clerical marriages were invalid. It was not until the end of the 20th Century, when certain Anglican and other protestant denominations voted to accept homosexual laity which then led to a few 'high church' pastors seeking admittance to the Catholic priesthood – that married priests from certain denominations were admitted by certain Catholic diocese.

5.249 To conclude, it seems more like a preference than a strict doctrine and certainly not founded upon apostolic teaching. The real reason probably lies in control – ensuring the undivided attention and loyalty of clergy to church hierarchy, unchallenged by spousal considerations or influence.

The Catholic Catechism

5.250   The Catholic Catechism is a remarkable document. Its primary role is to define and explain doctrine both in arcane theological terms and as a basis to teach followers. It is a huge document, the current English translation covers 814 pages and bears the marks of being frequently updated to keep abreast of social and cultural developments – it even includes counselling concerning the pitfalls of social media.

5.251   The Catechism is masterful in defining and justifying doctrines, assembling a huge number of sources to support every phrase set out. Whilst scripture is heavily quoted, it is often reliant upon interpretation by the church, either papal or by ecclesiastical councils. Tradition also plays a very important role:- 'Tradition' (with a capital T) is said to come from progressive guidance by the Holy Spirit whilst 'tradition' is 'sanctified' by the long standing 'profession' of such a view by the church. As a reference work, the Catechism does suffer from lugubrious repetitious titling and subtitling and from convoluted sentence structures – but it does contain some very good teaching on how man should act towards his fellow man and how those with power and wealth should act towards those with less or none – including clear principles for good government.

5.252   The contents are relatively limited in scope, setting out the Catholic view of what constitutes scripture and how it is to be interpreted together with the key importance for the church of the inheritance of apostolic authority through the pope to his bishops and clergy. This is followed by an extremely detailed examination of the Creeds and the Sacraments. Part Three comprises a very enlightened exposition of how mankind may prosper through lives led by virtues (which it classifies as human and theological), defining mortal and venial sins, espousing charity, justice and freedom for all. It contains a powerful exposition of why state authorities should promote human dignity, freedom of expression and avoid discrimination. The Catechism also extends its teaching to cover respect for private property, legal contracts that humans and their businesses enter into and identifies where communism and totalitarianism deny fundamental human rights, freedoms and dignity.

The Catechism concludes analysing the Ten Commandments and a few prayers. A number of doctrines, not covered earlier, stand out as worthy of note:

5.253 Divine revelation was completed by Jesus, but the work of the Church to understand and explain revelation still continues. Statement 65: *In giving us his Son, his only Word (for he possesses no other), he spoke everything to us at once in this sole Word – and he has no more to say. . . because what he spoke before to the prophets in parts, he has now spoken all at once by giving us the All Who is His Son* (Non-biblical sources). Statement 66: *Yet even if Revelation is already complete, it has not been made completely explicit; it remains for Christian faith gradually to grasp its full significance over the course of the centuries* (Not attributed) and Statement 73: *God has revealed himself fully by sending his own Son, in whom he has established his covenant for ever. The Son is his Father's definitive Word; so there will be no further Revelation after him* (Not attributed). The sole author of these expressions is presumed to be the Editorial Board of the Catechism!

5.254 Interpretation of the Bible is entrusted solely to the Pope. Statement 100: The task of interpreting the Word of God authentically has been entrusted solely to the Magisterium of the Church, i.e. to the Pope and to the bishops in communion with him. Statements 105: *The books of the Bible were written under the inspiration of the Holy Spirit, they have God as their author.* And 106: *"To compose the sacred books, God chose certain men who, all the while he employed them in this task, made full use of their own faculties and powers so that, though he acted in them and by them, it was as true authors that they consigned to writing whatever he wanted written, and no more."* (Source DV11). Er?, whilst making 'full use of their own faculties' they only wrote what God wanted written and no more!

5.255 The relationship of the Holy Spirit to other parts of the Trinity, Statement 246 *The Holy Spirit is eternally from Father and Son; its nature and subsistence simultaneously from the Father and the Son – a status known as the filioque* was first defined by Leo I in 447. The filioque has remained disputed by the Orthodox church which maintains that Holy Spirit only emanates from the Father.

5.256 The Catechism addresses the 'evolution' of the doctrine of the Trinity in Statements 250-252: *During the first centuries the Church sought to clarify her Trinitarian faith, both to deepen her own understanding of the faith and to defend it against the errors that were deforming it. This clarification was the work of the early councils, aided by Church Fathers and sustained by faith. In order to articulate the dogma of the Trinity, the Church had to develop her own terminology with the help of philosophy: 'substance', 'person' or 'hypostasis', 'relation' and so on. In doing this, she did not submit the faith to human wisdom, but gave a new and unprecedented meaning to these terms, which from then on would be used to signify an ineffable mystery, 'infinitely beyond all that we can humanly understand'.* Wondrous glossing!!

5.257   Lots of circular logic arises with the definition of the Trinity, as in Statement 262: *The Incarnation of God's Son reveals that God is the eternal Father and that the Son is consubstantial with the Father, which means that, in the Father and with the Father the Son is one and the same God.* Actually, the 'incarnation' of Jesus does not in any way prove God has a son; nor that God is Jesus father, nor that God is eternal, nor that the Son is consubstantial; nor that the father and Son are one and the same, nor that both are God!

5.258   The prayers of the Church to the Trinity result in a convoluted definition, as in 1553 *The prayer and offering of the Church are inseparable from the prayer and offering of Christ, her head; it is always the case that Christ worships in and through his Church. The whole Church, the Body of Christ, prays and offers herself "through him, with him, in him," in the unity of the Holy Spirit, to God the Father. (i.e. The Church is Jesus praying and worshipping, in the unity of the Holy Spirit, to God the Father.).* Conceptually, one might argue that when Jesus was 'out on a limb' being incarnate in human form on Earth, he might pray to his divine Father back at base – but after the ascension, seated at the right hand of Himself – why would he continue to pray to Himself??

5.259   The Catechism makes bold assertions to proclaim its control, as in: Statements 181 *No one can have God as Father who does not have the Church as Mother;* 454 *To be a Christian, one must believe that Jesus Christ is the Son of God;* and as noted earlier, according to the church, if you don't believe in Original Sin you can't really believe in Jesus: Statement 389: *The Church, which has the mind of Christ, knows very well that we cannot tamper with the revelation of original sin without undermining the mystery of Christ.* 891 thou shalt obey the Church: *When the Church through its supreme Magisterium proposes a doctrine "for belief as being divinely revealed", and as the teaching of Christ, the definitions "must be adhered to with the obedience of faith".* 1778 *Conscience is the aboriginal Vicar of Christ.* 2089 *Heresy is the obstinate post-baptismal denial of some truth which must be believed with divine and catholic faith, or it is likewise an obstinate doubt concerning the same; apostasy is the total repudiation of the Christian faith; schism is the refusal of submission to the Roman Pontiff.*

5.260   Biblical 'veneration' of Gentiles. Statement 58: *The Bible venerates several great figures among the Gentiles: Abel the Just, the king-priest Melchizedek and the upright 'Noah, Daniel, and Job'.* This strikes me as a rather odd definition of 'Gentile' – Abel was the son of Adam murdered by Cain; Melchizedek was the king priest of Jerusalem but who is also viewed as a prior incarnation of Jesus; Noah was held to be 'righteous'; Job and Daniel were surely Jewish?

5.261   The elevation of Mary over the two millennia following Jesus birth is recognised as being a journey: Statement 491 describes: *Through the centuries the Church has become ever more aware that Mary, 'full of grace' through God, was redeemed from the moment of her conception. That is what the dogma of the Immaculate Conception confesses, as Pope Pius IX proclaimed in 1854: "The most Blessed Virgin Mary was, from the first moment of her conception, by a singular grace and privilege of almighty God and by virtue of the merits of Jesus, preserved immune from all stain of original sin."* – the sole source of this was a text declared heretical in 405 – The Proto-Evangelium of James. Statement 500: *Against this doctrine (perpetual virginity) the objection is sometimes raised that the Bible mentions brothers and sisters of Jesus. The Church* **has always understood** *these passages as not referring to other children of the Virgin Mary. In fact, James and Joseph, "brothers of Jesus", are the sons of another Mary, a disciple of Christ, whom St. Matthew significantly calls "the other Mary".* Top marks for creative writing skills, but less credible than the older idea that the brothers and sister were offspring of Joseph from a previous marriage. Statement 966 *"Finally the Immaculate Virgin, preserved free from all stain of original sin, when the course of her earthly life was finished, was taken up body and soul into heavenly glory, and exalted by the Lord as Queen over all things, so that she might be the more fully conformed to her Son, the Lord of lords and conqueror of sin and death."* (Pius XII, Munificentissimus Deus, 1950)

5.262   The challenge of what, to many, is seen as Catholic worship of idols is cleverly treated, turning back the apparent prohibition (in Deuteronomy 4:15-16) against God's own actions in the Old Testament. In Statement 2130: *Nevertheless, already in the Old Testament, God ordained or permitted the making of images that pointed symbolically toward salvation by the incarnate Word: so it was with the bronze serpent, the ark of the covenant, and the cherubim;* and Statement 2131: Basing itself on the mystery of the incarnate Word, the seventh ecumenical council at Nicaea (787*) justified against the iconoclasts the* *veneration of icons – of Christ, but also of the Mother of God, the angels, and all the saints. By becoming incarnate, the Son of God introduced a new 'economy' of images.*

5.263   Some Statements are breath-taking in terms of human arrogance, I just have to share:

- 299. *Talking of Creation, by God out of nothing: "for God willed creation as a gift addressed to man, an inheritance destined for and entrusted to him".*

- 324. *The **fact** that God permits physical and even moral evil is a **mystery** that God **illuminates** by his Son Jesus Christ who died and rose to vanquish evil. **Faith gives us the certainty** that God would not permit an evil if he did not cause a good to come from that very evil, by ways that we shall fully know only in eternal life.* (my emphasis)

- 328. *The existence of the spiritual, non-corporeal beings that Sacred Scripture usually calls 'angels' is **a truth of faith**, the witness of Scripture is as clear as the **unanimity of Tradition**.* (my emphasis)

- 343. *Man is the summit of the Creator's work, as the inspired account expresses by clearly distinguishing the creation of man from that of the other creatures.*

- 358. *God created everything for man, but man in turn was created to serve and love God and **to offer all creation back to him**: Man is that great and wonderful living creature, **more precious** in the eyes of God than all other creatures! **For him the heavens and the earth, the sea and all the rest of creation exist**. God attached so much importance to his salvation that he did not spare his own Son for the sake of man.* (my emphasis)

- 446. *In the Greek translation of the Old Testament, the ineffable Hebrew name YHWH, by which God revealed himself to Moses, is rendered as Kyrios, 'Lord'. From then on, 'Lord' becomes the more usual name by which to indicate the divinity of Israel's God. The New Testament uses this full sense of the title 'Lord' both for the Father and – what is new – for Jesus, who **is thereby recognized** as God Himself. (This is a wonderful glossing – because YHWH is usually translated into Greek as 'Lord' and the New Testament passages frequently describe Jesus as Lord – **this is proof** that Jesus is the eternally existing God –* kerpow!! Catholic officials need to get out a bit more, many in positions of earthly power have for centuries been addressed as Lord but no one thinks that is proof that they are God.

- Statements 464 to 469 give a stout defence of Jesus being wholly God and wholly man simultaneously, even referring to the many heresies which the church vigorously attacked!! One has to admire the textual dexterity – truly marvellous to read!! 470 *Because 'human nature was assumed, not absorbed', in the mysterious union of the Incarnation, the* **Church was led over the course of centuries to confess** *the full reality of Christ's human soul, with its operations of intellect and will, and of his human body.* **In parallel fashion, she had to recall on each occasion** *that Christ's human nature belongs, as his own, to the divine person of the Son of God, who assumed it. Everything that Christ is and does in this nature derives from "one of the Trinity".*

5.264 The role and organisation of Government is addressed at length in some excellent Statements:

- 1885 *The principle of subsidiarity is opposed to all forms of collectivism. It sets limits for state intervention. It aims at harmonizing the relationships between individuals and societies. It tends toward the establishment of a true international order.*

- 1902 *Authority does not derive its moral legitimacy from itself. It must not behave in a despotic manner, but must act for the common good as a "moral force based on freedom and a sense of responsibility". A human law has the character of law to the extent that it accords with right reason, and thus derives from the eternal law. Insofar as it falls short of right reason it is said to be an unjust law, and thus has not so much the nature of law as of a kind of violence.*

- 2499 *Moral judgment must condemn the plague of totalitarian states which systematically falsify the truth, exercise political control of opinion through the media, manipulate defendants and witnesses at public trials, and imagine that they secure their tyranny by strangling and repressing everything they consider "thought crimes".*

Conclusions

5.265 It seems many of the core beliefs were developed with the aim of cementing church power. Catholic beliefs were, and still are, justified by the three pillars of scripture, 'tradition' and papal authority. Immediately, one realises that at least two of the three sources are from purely human sources. Moreover, it does not require much study to conclude that scripture is also wholly man made. The twelve core elements of Catholicism described in this chapter bear little or no relationship even with the edited versions of the scriptures. With the church having ruthlessly destroyed the vast majority of early texts, many likely to have been written by contemporaries of Jesus, our record of his statements and teaching is thereby restricted to the few that were canonised. Amongst the surviving few that were canonised we see scribal enthusiasm to combat ideas contradicting official dogma by wholesale editing to establish conformity – leaving few remains of Jesus original message.

5.266   Indeed, let's ask what we suppose Jesus might think of Catholic doctrines? Jesus message is very difficult to follow consistently but in essence is quite simple – love others as you look after yourself. As for praying, Jesus only referred to praying to God (not to himself and certainly not to his mother). Jesus described his yoke as 'light', angered by the Jewish priesthood who had concocted 613 mitzvot tightly proscribing what people could do. It is worth pondering what Jesus might find most offensive. I would suggest the assumption of papal authority, even infallibility, and its abuse to claim powers of forgiveness which it then ruthlessly monetised. The system of indulgences whereby people collect air miles (for prayers, pilgrimages and cash) to whisk themselves (and for some periods, anyone else they favoured) through Purgatory would surely enrage Jesus – who was upset by people selling chickens in the temple courtyard for sacrifices. If he saw the current versions of scripture he would question the sanity of people claiming belief in original sin and bodily resurrection. I'm sure Jesus would question the content of the sacraments and ask why his church persisted in using a dead language for so many centuries, understand by so few.

5.267   How can the Catholic church defend any of the doctrines discussed in this chapter? Faced with the Catholic church's actions and teaching, Jesus might well turn back to the Pharisees for help!

6

Role of the Bible in Catholic faith

6.1 The fundamental difference in beliefs between Catholics and Protestants relates to the accepted basis of faith. Protestants prioritize the Bible, for many it is *sola scriptura*, 'only scripture' as providing the foundation of dogma and the belief system. Protestant churches and pastors may explain and interpret scripture but not contradict or overrule it. For Catholics, it is quite different, scripture is only one source of church authority alongside 'tradition' and papal authority. Upholding and revering 'tradition' covers a multitude of problems – useful for matters unsupported by scripture or identifiable papal edicts, anything that has been proclaimed or undertaken previously may be later acknowledged as tradition. Tradition is of course particularly helpful when defending dogma not found anywhere in scripture.

6.2 Until as recently as 1943, the Catholic leadership believed ownership, reading and interpretation of the bible should be the sole preserve of the clergy – lay people could not be trusted to understand scripture without guidance. Before the printing press was invented in 1439, the copying by hand of bibles was laborious and largely confined to monasteries. The church only used Latin bibles and indeed all services were conducted only in Latin. Translation to vernacular languages did occur but was limited to one off copies and never available to the general public. In England, half a dozen translations into Saxon occurred between c700 and c1000 – including by the Venerable Bede, Alfred the Great and Aelfric.

6.3   However, the Church was sufficiently concerned at the risk of
       translations making the bible accessible to lay people to make a series
       of rulings prohibiting access by the laity and specifically prohibiting
       translations:

   •   1229 Council of Toulouse decreed: 'We prohibit the laity be
       permitted to have the books of the Old or the New Testament, and
       most strictly forbid their having any translation of these books.'

   •   In 1234 Council of Tarragona ruled: 'No one may possess the books
       of the Old and New Testaments in Latin, and if anyone possess
       such shall deliver the same to their local bishop within 8 days of this
       promulgation, so that they may be burned.'

   •   In 1414 Council of Constance decreed: 'John Wycliffe (deceased),
       Oxford professor and theologian, who had committed heresy by
       translating the New Testament into English, shall have his bones
       exhumed and publicly burned and his ashes thrown into a river.'

   •   In 1440 Gutenberg constructed the first printing press in Strasbourg.

   •   In 1515 Fifth Lateran Council enacted a decree that all books (on
       any subject) were subject to a pre-approval process to be undertaken
       by the local bishop before any were to be printed.

   •   1536 William Tyndale was burned at the stake for translating the
       Bible into English.

   •   1545 to 1564 Council of Trent took the extraordinary step of adding
       the Bible to its list of prohibited books. Despite the practice of most
       churches containing a copy of the Latin Vulgate, chained up to
       prevent theft, laity were forbidden to read the Bible without a written
       license from a Catholic bishop or Inquisitor. The Council added
       these words: *"That if any one shall dare to read or keep in his possession that
       book, without such a license, he shall not receive absolution till he has given it up
       to his ordinary"*.

6.4   The prohibition on Catholic laity reading the Bible continued until quite
       recently:

   •   Pope Pius VII (1800-1823) denounced the Bible Society and expressed shock at the circulation of the Scriptures. Pius VII said, *"It is evidence from experience, that the Holy Scriptures, when circulated in the vulgar tongue, have, through the temerity of men, produced more harm than benefit"*.

• In an encyclical of 1824, Pope Leo XII called the Protestant Bible the 'Gospel of the Devil'.

• In 1850, Leo XII further condemned Bible Societies, admitting the fact that the distribution of scripture has "long been condemned by the holy chair".

6.5 Change only came much later. In 1943, Pius XII issued *Divino Afflante Spiritu* permitting Catholics to study scripture for the first time, even encouraging study. But, it was only the ruling of the Second Vatican Council (1962 to 1965) that permitted the celebration of Mass to be read in the vernacular.

6.6 The obvious question which arises, particularly for Protestants, is why did the Catholic Church ever try to prevent believers from reading the Bible? Today, many find this difficult to believe let alone understand. The original reason was probably the general dislike that Romans had for Jews. Almost from the beginning, it was Pauline Christianity which spread across the core of the Roman Empire whilst the original Nazarene faith spread on the fringes and outside the Empire – across today's Iraq, Iran to India and across North Africa and on the trade routes along the coast of Portugal and France to Cornwall and particularly, Ireland. The original Nazarene Christian Jews retained many Jewish beliefs and continued to attend the Synagogues – which attracted much criticism from early Church writers, such as St John of Chrysostom and the Archbishop of Constantinople. Jews were accused of using Christian babies to conduct ritualistic blood sacrifices and other demonic practices to whip up hatred of Jews. The Catholic Church rulings on usury contributed to persecution of Jews. As early as the 4th century, the Church prohibited clergy from accepting interest and this was extended to the laity in the 5th century. In the 8th century the charging of interest by one Christian to another was declared to be a criminal offense and in 1311, Pope Clement V made the ban on usury absolute and all secular legislation permitting interest to be null and void. The only exception allowed was interest charged by Jews to Christians – hence, with many jurisdictions prohibiting Jews from practicing most trades, the growth of Jewish owned jewellery, money lending and eventually banking businesses flourished.

6.7   Both Bernard Starr of City University, New York, in his book *"Jesus Uncensored: Restoring the authentic Jew"* and Jean Guitton in *"Great Heresies and Church Councils"* point to Catholic concern at the embarrassment of Christians reading the Bible which reports their religion entirely as a Jewish tradition – with no reference to Christianity.

6.8   Whilst Catholic teaching and homilies have always included some biblical references, these rarely include any reference to the Old Testament. Indeed, a dear friend who was educated entirely in institutions run by the Jesuits, told me he could never remember any reference at all being made to the Old Testament throughout his schooling. Despite attending a Jesuit religious school in Italy from 1959 to 1967, he was never given a bible to study. Indeed religious education was limited to teaching Catholic dogma, using the Catechism (described in 5.241 to 5.255 above), with biblical passages predominantly from Paul's epistles. The highlight from his religious lessons was when, as schoolboys of around 15, they had a lesson on the perpetual virginity of Mary – replete with anatomical diagrams!! It is noteworthy that whilst profoundly interested in the divine and in theology, and living in a very Catholic country until aged around 35, my friend shook his head in disbelief when I asked whether any of his friends and relations might have a bible at home – he finally admitted to buying a bible c2007 and then finding the text quite extraordinary. Other friends of a similar age, brought up in a convent school had drilled into them that they should never read the bible – which made such an impression that 50 years later, when given a copy of one of the books in this series in 2019, they politely returned it unread saying they had flipped through and seen that it contained verses quoted from the bible. Even more extraordinary is that these friends, eloquent and highly educated, admitted that they were lapsed Catholics and had not been to confession for a long time – but it seems the 'fear' (?) drilled into them when they were young meant they still avoided reading any scripture whatsoever. I was stunned.

6.9   The other main concern over laity reading the Bible was undoubtedly the realization by learned clerics that the Bible was devoid of evidence supporting most key features of Catholic dogma – there is no basis for papal authority, nor that grace flowed from the pope through the seven sacraments or of the Church holding its own reserves of grace that popes could dispense as indulgences, no reference to relics, to confession, purgatory or excommunication. There was simply too much at stake to allow lay people access to the supposed source of authority.

6.10   I can relate to the majority of Protestants, Muslims and adherents of Judaism who, having read this chapter, ponder whether to throw this book in the bin as 'fake news'. Except for Catholics, all 'Peoples of the Book' have always regarded personal study of scripture as enlightening, righteous and an important duty. I too was stunned when I found reputable sources explain that for over a thousand years simple possession of even a part of the bible by a lay Christian put them in mortal danger, whilst translating even part of the bible from Latin resulted in being excommunicated and fast tracked to eternal hell by being burnt at the stake.

6.11   I wonder what Jesus would make of this – on hearing about it he might smile and conclude it was some kind of alien human joke. He would surely find it completely bizarre that the church he tasked Peter with founding would not only ban his followers from reading scripture but threaten them with an irreversible penalty of eternal damnation.

7

The state of the Catholic Church
on the eve of the Reformation

7.1   By 1300, the Church was in a strong position – it had no competition and enjoyed huge financial resources. Congregations were acquiescent and much progress had been achieved in remedying the worst excesses – the convulsions of rogue popes in the 8th to 10th centuries had faded from memory whilst some monasteries had been reformed.

7.2   However, the church soon suffered from a fresh wave of leadership challenges. Political rivalry between the French monarchy and the Holy Roman Emperor created a papal crisis. Short of money, Philip IV, the French king eyed the enormous wealth of the Templars, by then headquartered in Paris. A papal edict had banned clergy from financially supporting lay authorities (Clericis Laicos). Philip IV campaigned for the appointment of more French bishops and in the papal election of 1305, secured a French Pope, Clement V, whom he then persuaded to base his papacy in France at Avignon. Philip IV moved against the Templars, notoriously on Friday 13th October 1307, seizing their wealth and forcing Clement V to support his charges of heresy against the Templars. When the German Emperor died, Clement V cited the Donation of Constantine as authority to rule the German lands in Italy and appointed the King of Naples 'imperial vicar of Italy'. Clement V openly favoured his relatives and was posthumously charged with simony – the crime of selling church lands and pocketing the proceeds.

7.3   With a substantial number of French bishops, the next few popes were also French and continued to rule from Avignon. The consequences for Rome were severe – following the collapse of Rome as the imperial capital, its population had fallen precipitously. Rome became totally dependent upon the papal administration in the Vatican and the wealth brought by collections and numerous pilgrimages. With the Pope based in Avignon, in what became known as the 'Babylonian captivity' (1309 – 1377), the population of Rome fell further, to a mere 15,000 by 1377. That year Pope Gregory XI had travelled to Rome to consolidate the church land holdings, known as the Papal States, across the middle of the Italian peninsula.

7.4   Conveniently for Rome, Gregory XI died there the following year and his cardinals decided to elect the next Pope whilst in Rome. The Avignon papacy had packed the college of cardinals with Frenchmen – 17 out of 23 were French and 11 of these were with Gregory XI in Rome so they were relaxed about holding their conclave there. However, a Roman mob besieged the cardinals demanding a proper Roman pope be elected. The cardinals complied but soon regretted their decision as the new Pope, Urban VI, tried to impose radical change – ruling that no gratuities or gifts would be accepted by the Church and forbidding cardinals from accepting monies or holding other offices or bishoprics – thereby threatening their luxurious lifestyles. Urban VI also refused to take up residence in Avignon.

7.5   The overwhelming French contingent of cardinals concluded that the election of Urban VI was void as made under duress – and elected another French Pope. However, Urban VI refused to step down – resulting in the church having two competing popes, issuing edicts against each other. Different rulers supported each side: the German Emperor disputed French designs on Naples so supported the Roman Pope, the English likewise would support anyone against the French and so on. Eventually, in 1407 a Church Council was convened which claimed higher authority than a pope – thereby challenging papal infallibility. The Council of Pisa duly appointed a third pope, John XXIII, and ruled the two competing popes should step down. But both refused, leaving the Church with three popes. Eventually, in 1414, the Emperor convened the Council of Constance which immediately deposed John XXIII and eventually secured the resignation of the Roman pope whilst dismissing the claims of the Avignon pope. Finally, in late 1417, the papacy was reunified under a single pope – Martin V. Doubtless, the chaotic 40 year period of multiple popes, which became known as the Western Schism, and brought to a close by a Church Council which dismissed three popes, had undermined the authority of the pope as God's representative on earth.

7.6   The absence of the papal See since 1305 had seen Rome fall into decline, the arrival of Renaissance popes spurred rebuilding and renovation by leading artists to remake Rome as the glittering centre of Christendom. St Peter's Basilica was rebuilt and the Sistine Chapel decorated by Michelangelo. However, the financial costs were huge and triggered a drive to raise funds from the faithful by any means that worked – more and more relics appeared and offers of indulgences diversified. Greed and money raising seemed to become the focal point of papal effort.

8

The Protestant Reformation

Clerical behaviour undermined Catholic dogma

8.1   During the century prior to the Reformation, the reputation of the
        pope and the church had been undermined. The vast majority of the
        population had little understanding of church services which were
        only conducted in Latin – the church presented people with a mystery
        played out in magnificent surroundings. Only their confession to their
        priest was conducted in the vernacular and that included an unsettling
        explanation of the punishments awaiting them and what they had to do
        to even partially reduce what would be meted out to them in purgatory.
        The majority of the population lived miserable lives, food was seasonal
        and meat reserved for festivals. Housing for the majority was a mud
        and wattle hut, only merchants and craftsmen in towns could afford
        a building with multiple rooms. But the clergy occupied comfortable
        dwellings competitive with local landowners whilst the senior clerics,
        bishops, abbots, etc., literally enjoyed palaces. Generally, the churches
        which everyone attended were magnificent palatial buildings compared
        with what most people lived in.

8.2   For most of the 14th century the tales circulating from pilgrims and
        traders returning from Rome (or Avignon) would have been dominated
        by salacious details of two lines of popes competing for authority,
        widespread corruption and immoral behaviour – whilst direct experience
        would be coloured by rapacious campaigns to sell indulgences. These
        traits prepared the ground for the devastating developments which

became known as the Reformation.

8.3   Whilst conventionally, the Reformation is associated with Luther nailing his 95 theses to the church door – in fact two other events had already set in train momentous change. The first was the printing of an English translation of the Latin Vulgate bible by John Wycliffe in 1382 which became widely copied (even today, 150 odd copies are preserved) and distributed, even outside England. The second was the posthumous publication of a critical comparison of the Latin Vulgate against Greek manuscripts by Lorenzo Valla – suggesting some church dogma was based upon poor translations. Awkwardly, these revelations came after a period when papal infallibility had been questioned by the Western Schism and the Donation, the key foundation of the Pope's secular power, being proved to be a fraud.

8.4   **John Wycliffe (1324-1384)**, an ordained priest who became an Oxford professor, launched attacks on the luxury and lavish livings of the clergy, and sparked outrage in denying transubstantiation, rejecting purgatory and disapproving of clerical celibacy and the selling of indulgences. In 1377, Pope Gregory XI issued a bull for Wycliffe's arrest but when appearing at the Palace of Lambeth, Wycliffe's highly placed friends prevented his sentence from being pronounced. In 1378, news came that the church now had two competing popes, both presenting ambassadors in London for accreditation and shortly after followed news of the lewd behaviour of the newly installed Roman pope – which further undermined papal authority. Wycliffe wrote that he would treat the bible as authoritative not the pope. In retirement, he completed a translation of the Bible into Middle English in 1382 which sparked the Lollard movement which adopted his teaching and evolved to dismiss the veneration of saints, the system of sacraments and even the role of the papacy itself. The Vatican's reaction was to declare Wycliffe a heretic but, as he had died before the Church could burn him, ordered his body disinterred and burned with his ashes thrown into a river. The debate Wycliffe and his followers had started was that the Bible, withheld from the people, was not the source of many Catholic tenets of faith.

8.5   **Jan Hus (1372-1415)**, an ordained priest in Bohemia (Czech Republic) was also a follower of Wycliffe and the views he preached quickly attracted the ire of the Vatican. Heavy marketing of indulgences blatantly described as financing wars by the pope to extend the Papal

States in Italy, aggravated the situation and boosted support for Hus. So much so that, after Hus was sentenced as a heretic and executed at the Council of Constance in 1415, many priests and congregations deserted and founded an independent church in Bohemia. Such was the support for Hus that four papal crusades against Bohemia between 1419 and 1434 were all defeated and at the Council of Basel in 1436, the Vatican agreed to allow Bohemia to practise its own Hussite form of Christianity.

8.6 **Lorenzo Valla (1407-1457)** was the son of a papal lawyer who was admitted to the priesthood and lectured at the University of Pavia. In 1435, Valla became royal secretary to the court of the King of Naples. In 1440, he produced a critique of the Donation of Constantine, *Declamatio*, which identified the Latin as too crude for such an important document. Valla noted that the Donation was badly drafted, switching tense many times, and identified a number of terms (such as 'satrap' and 'fief') in the Donation which dated only from the 8th century. Valla's dating corresponds with academic research establishing the first recorded usage of the Donation by a Pope to the year 778. The Donation of Constantine purported to be an Imperial Roman decree by Emperor Constantine legally transferring sovereignty over the Western Roman Empire to the Papacy, in perpetuity. Valla's demolition of the Donation was useful for his employer as the Pope was then at war with the Kingdom of Naples. But, Valla's treatise removed, at a stroke, the entire basis of the papal secular authority and the papal authorities desperately suppressed the document. For 77 years it was blocked and it was not until 1517 that Valla's analysis was finally published.

8.7 Valla also undertook a critique of the Apostles' Creed disputing the church's assertion that it had been composed by the 12 Apostles. Valla was investigated by the Inquisition and found heretical on eight counts but saved from the stake by the personal intervention of the King of Naples. Valla was ahead of his time, modern theologians agree the Apostles' Creed originated in baptismal rites in Rome during the 3rd and 4th centuries, was developed in south western France during the 7th century and officially adopted by Pope Innocent III only in 1206.

8.8 But, Valla's most devastating work went unpublished in his own lifetime, his notes entitled 'Annotations on the New Testament' identified a series of errors in the Vulgate's Latin translation from the original Greek.

8.9 **Erasmus Roterodamus, aka Erasmus of Rotterdam (1466-1536)**. Erasmus, a Dutch philosopher generally regarded as the greatest scholar of the Reformation, was trained as a Catholic priest and remained committed to the Catholic Church all his life. Erasmus discovered Lorenzo Valla's unpublished papers and posthumously published his work '*Annotations on the New Testament*'. Whilst Erasmus was highly critical of abuses, he campaigned for reform. Erasmus produced a Greek version of the New Testament with his new Latin translation alongside, incorporating Valla's Annotations. Erasmus never intended harm to the Catholic faith, dedicating his work to the Pope and receiving a glowing commendation from Pope Leo X.

8.10 The delay in publishing Valla's work until, by coincidence it appeared only months before Luther's Theses, and the fact that it was published in Germany rather than Italy was fortuitous. In 1517 Valla's analysis fell on very fertile ground. Reading Erasmus new translation identified deep problems in Catholic dogma – for example the Vulgate maintained that Matthew 4:17 recorded Jesus as directing believers to "do penance" but the new translation showed the Greek meaning as being that sinners should "repent", explained as expressing regret for their actions and to turn away from sin. This contradicted one of the seven sacraments which demanded physical works, prayers and lucrative payments. Other key elements of dogma seemed similarly adrift of biblical teaching. The first two editions ran to 3,300 copies, ensuring wide circulation across Europe.

8.11 **Martin Luther (1483-1546).** Luther trained as a lawyer but when he was struck by lightning, he vowed to become a monk. He became so devout that when, in 1507, Luther was tasked to lead his first Mass, he was terrified at the prospect of his first direct communication with God – having previously prayed only to intermediaries (Mary and various saints) to plead on his behalf. Luther was obsessed by how he could achieve salvation and begun to study the bible whenever he could. Even monks were not permitted private study of the bible but he found a quiet spot in the monastic library where he accumulated very detailed knowledge.

8.12 In 1510, Luther was sent to Rome on monastic business – he wrote that he was the luckiest man in Christendom. Excited to be in the vicinity of so many places of pilgrimages and holy relics, he noted that it was a shame his parents were still alive – otherwise he could have accumulated so much merit that he could have earned them remission from purgatory.

Luther witnessed the blatant monetisation of spiritual activity, he saw the payment for so many masses to be said for departed loved ones that priests would sing at double speed and even two priests say mass at the same alter. This begun to sow doubt in his mind. Upon his return from Rome, Luther was transferred to a monastery at Wittenberg and appointed lecturer of theology at the new university – resulting in him being required to study and teach the bible – a decision Rome would soon regret!!

8.13   Wittenberg may have been small but its ruler, the Elector of Saxony, had amassed an amazing collection of more than 19,000 holy relics – meaning that if one carefully gazed at each one, you secured 1.9 million days remission from purgatory. It was against this formative background that Luther encountered Johann Tetzel's travelling indulgences marketing show. Tetzel excelled at volume sales of indulgences – from which he earned good commission. His infamous straplines included: "When the coin in the coffer rings, the soul from purgatory springs" and "Place your penny on the drum, the pearly gates open and in strolls Mum". Luther was incensed that all references to the confession of sins and requests for forgiveness had fallen away, one only had to pay money and buy so many days off purgatory for whatever sins you had done, or might commit in future.

8.14   Hence, Martin Luther's main issue concerned the abuse of Indulgences. Initially it seems Luther thought that these abuses were mainly instigated by over incentivised clerical salesmen, acting without the pope's knowledge.

8.15   Conventionally, the Reformation is associated with Martin Luther famously nailing his 95 theses to the church door in Wittenberg on 31st October 1517.

8.16   In response, the pope engaged Johann Eck, professor of theology at the University of Ingolstadt, to bring Luther to heel. Eck invited Luther to a debate in Leipzig in July 1519 at which Eck sought to trick Luther by focusing on authority. Eck proposed that even scripture draws its power and authority from the pope – which subsequently can be seen as a fatal mistake, as it focused debate on to whether one should follow the bible or the pope. Luther retorted that he could understand scripture despite the pope and even against the pope – which led to Eck asserting that Luther was no better than John Wycliffe or Jan Hus. Luther initially rebutted the comparison and the slur that he was a heretic. However, after further consideration, Luther saw that he was indeed on the same page as Hus. Eck had all he needed and returned to Rome to draft a bull denouncing Luther as a heretic.

8.17   Initially, Luther was depressed, if Rome held that the pope had higher authority than the bible then the papacy was unlikely to be reformed by reference to biblical statements. Soon however, Luther was fired up, publishing a blizzard of profound texts in German during 1520. In his *"Christian Nobility of the German Nation"*, Luther attacked the three principles of papal authority:- that the pope was the highest authority on Earth; that only the pope may interpret scripture; and, that only the pope could summon a church council – the mechanism through which any reform would be determined. In his "Babylonian Captivity of the Church", he attacked the church's teaching that the grace of God flowed only through the sacraments controlled by the priests. According to Luther, Paul was clear that grace flowed directly from God to believers and that the only basis for sacraments to be found in the bible was for baptism and the Eucharist.

8.18   By 3 January 1521, Pope Leo X declared 41 of the 95 theses heretical, excommunicating Luther and ordering his ruler, the Holy Roman Emperor Charles V, to arrest and burn him to death. When hauled before the imperial assembly, the Diet of Worms, in 1521, Luther refused to recant the texts he had written and challenged the court to show where he had contradicted Scripture, and if proven then he would recant.

8.19   Luther's initial protest, the 95 theses, had focused on the system of indulgences, which he believed was being exploited by clergy without the Pope's full knowledge – hence as a good Catholic monk, Luther appealed to the Pope to take action. As a monk, Luther had access to the Vulgate Latin bible, his study led him to conclude that the Christian idea of repentance was an inner struggle with sin and not an external system of sacramental confession. Luther concluded that the Pope can only forgive sinners from the Church's own system of penance and not from the guilt of sin itself. Even more radically, Luther denied that the Pope has any knowledge of purgatory nor any power over what happens to those in purgatory. Accordingly, Luther dismissed the idea that, immediately upon payment, the Pope can release one's loved one from purgatory – stating that only God can forgive punishments in purgatory. Moreover, Luther asserted that indulgences were superfluous – indulgences were intended for those truly repentant, but who could determine that – if someone was truly repentant then they would be forgiven by God and an indulgence was worthless. Jesus had died to forgive our sins but buying indulgences was intended to avoid punishment – which for the truly repentant were already forgiven.

8.20   Further, Luther criticized indulgences as discouraging charity, asserting that giving to the poor is much more valuable than buying indulgences. Indeed, buying indulgences invites God's wrath, as it diverts funds which might otherwise be used to support the poor. A common practice was for dedicated indulgence preachers to tour church domains, collecting funds for Rome – with local bishops being instructed to give priority to such persons in addressing congregations – a practice Luther abhorred.

8.21   Luther also attacked the fundamental basis of indulgences. The dogma was based upon the argument that the saints were so righteous that they skipped purgatory and had gone straight to heaven, donating their "surplus" righteousness to the Vatican on their elevation. This "treasury of merit" was what the Pope could then award to deserving sinners to mitigate their own period of purgatory required to purge themselves of sin prior to entry to heaven. Luther actually presented his concerns with the way indulgences were being marketed as something which would concern the Pope and therefore the Pope should act upon Luther's concerns. Luther noted that people were very misled by the way indulgences were preached, giving examples of claims that indulgences could forgive even a sinner who had raped the Virgin Mary; he noted lay concerns that with such a treasury the Pope could simply release all in purgatory; why should further anniversary masses be required for those already released through indulgences?

8.22   So, initially, Luther was not even refuting the concept of indulgences or relics – merely the extreme way they were marketed. But, his continued study of the bible led his progressive discovery that none of the key aspects of Catholic dogma appeared to be supported by Scripture. Faced by a host of treatises that Luther and others begun to publish, the Church reacted with hostility to any level of criticism. However, growing circulation of critical texts combined with the emergence of local vernacular editions of the Bible, steadily shifted opinion ever further towards belief that Catholic doctrine found little basis in biblical texts.

8.23   The reaction to Luther only caused him to think harder. Soon he identified from the bible the issue that undid the entire fabric of Catholic dogma described above. Luther found that Paul had written that justification came from faith alone – the bible made no mention of papal authority to dispense grace through sacraments or indulgences; nor confessions, penance, relics; nor the need for praying to intermediaries such as the Saints or Mary and no concept of excommunication. Luther concluded that Christianity should be *sola scriptura* – solely based upon the bible.

8.24   Luther concluded the best route to reform was to teach the content of the bible and encourage others to study it. He identified Catholic sacraments as keeping the bible hidden – so he wrote books of sermons for priests to use as bible teaching. In Catholic services, congregations were very passive, the priest spoke and sung whilst they basically just watched (very few understood Latin) repeating "amen" at numerous points. So, Luther sought to engage congregations more by introducing hymns incorporating biblical teaching – and wrote hymnals full of biblical phrases.

8.25   **Huldrich Zwingli (1484-1531)**, was another key reformer, an ordained Swiss priest who was inspired by getting a copy of Erasmus translation of the New Testament. Zwingli wrote of his excitement at being able to read the very words of God, written by the Apostles inspired by the Holy Spirit. Zwingli's beliefs evolved slowly but in 1523 he published his devastating 67 Articles. Unlike Luther's attack on merely abuses associated with indulgences and relics, Zwingli's attack was far broader. Zwingli penned a comprehensive Reformation text:

(i)   Jesus was the true head of the Church and rules his church through his word, not through the pope. This cut straight to the authority and power of the papacy;

(ii)   Jesus' death on the cross was a complete sacrifice, and did not need to be repeated endlessly on the alter in Mass – challenging the primary purpose of the priesthood;

(iii) We are saved through belief in Jesus;

(iv) Only Jesus can remit sin – penance, indulgences and relics are all ineffective;

(v) Purgatory does not exist;

(vi) Priestly celibacy is non-biblical; and,

(vii) Praying to saints is pointless as Jesus taught that only he is the intermediary between us and God.

8.26 **Jean Cauvin, later known as John Calvin, 1509-1564**, the son of a cathedral lawyer, by the age of 12 was a clerk to a bishop, with his head shaved into a priestly tonsure. Studying as a contemporary of Erasmus at the same university, Calvin was absorbed by reformation activities. At just 26, Calvin published the first edition of his life's work, the Institutes of the Christian Religion – which he dedicated to the French king, Francis I. Calvin had the opportunity to explain to the young and progressive king that the Lutherans were not dangerous heretics but promoting true Christian religion that the king had sworn to uphold.

8.27 As with other leading theologians of the time, the exposure to bible study led Calvin's initial focus on reforming abuses in the Catholic church to evolve into rejection of key planks of dogma. Whereas Luther's main theological conclusion came from Paul's teaching that justification came solely from faith, as set out in Romans; the followers of Calvin focused on Jesus sacrificial of atonement for mankind's sins – concluding that this was a complete work. Indeed, Catholic belief stated that upon Jesus relinquishing his human body, the excess merit released (back to the papacy for redistribution) was "unlimited". Therefore, followers, concluded further repeated priestly services of Jesus sacrifice (i.e. the Mass) was superfluous and, as with other acts of atonement, were actually insulting to Jesus – suggesting his sacrifice was insufficient.

8.28 Calvin's theology came to be succinctly set out in response to a letter from Cardinal Sadoleto. Calvin had stayed in Geneva for a few years leading the reformation there but the authorities there felt he was too radical and expelled him in 1538. This led the church in Rome to believe the Genevois could be tempted back into allegiance to Rome. Cardinal Sadoleto was given the task and wrote a carefully drafted invitation, remarkably agreeing with the extent of clerical abuses and even the concept of justification by faith – before explaining that such belief would lead to people abandoning efforts to be righteous as all their future sins were already forgiven. The Council of Geneva invited Calvin to respond and his reply provides a succinct summary of his belief: *sola gratia, solus Christos, sola fide, sola Scriptura*. By this, Calvin stated that salvation is solely a gift of God's grace, found in Jesus alone, received only through faith and we know this only from scripture. Calvin's argument, based upon Paul's Epistle to the Romans, unequivocally attributes salvation to faith in Jesus, granted as a gift, and there is nothing we can do to earn it. Therefore, much of the Catholic church sacraments and its system of penances, indulgences and relics are superfluous as salvation cannot be earned and much less be bought.

8.29   Calvin went on to establish an education centre to develop a cadre of protestant pastors to preach biblical theology to reformist congregations across Europe. He established a college which eventually became the College Calvin, one of the leading Grammar schools of Geneva, and an 'academie' which became the University of Geneva. Soon there were 1200 students in the college studying Greek and Hebrew amongst other subjects and 300 in the *academie* studying the detailed commentaries that Calvin had written on almost every book in the bible. The graduates were despatched as fully trained pastors to spread the reformist teaching across Europe.

8.30   **Henry VIII, king of England, 1491-1547**. The breach between England and Rome was triggered not by theological issues but Henry VIII's marriage problems. In his efforts to get rid of his first wife, Catherine, in order to marry Anne Boleyn, in 1532 Henry VIII's lawyers developed the argument that the Church in England was founded by Joseph of Arimathea (possibly with Jesus – see Part Three) in Glastonbury, decades prior to their being any church in Rome. Therefore, the Church in England was headed by the king and independent of Rome – but this did not mean Henry had any dispute with Catholic dogma. England continued to witness leading theologians burned at the stake for bible translation, such as Thomas Bilney in 1531 and William Tyndale in 1535. But gradually evangelicals started to take more important positions in the administration – including Thomas Cromwell and Sir Thomas More. When discussions about clerical laxity and abuses started circulating from continental debates, the wealth of the monastic estates begun to appeal to Henry as combining easy source of funds for his treasury and a way of imposing his will in a popular cause.

8.31 Henry, generally held to be a staunch Catholic really wanted an English Catholicism rather than a Roman one, he wanted control and he wanted the loyalty of the church in England to be to the English king rather than the Roman pope. But his use of arguments against clerical excess, wealth and indulgences chimed with reformation thinking, leading to pressure for further change. He agreed an English Church headed by the English king needed an English bible and, only 3 years after sentencing Tyndale to burning at the stake, in 1538 Henry declared that no man should be discouraged from reading the bible and every person should be exhorted to study the word of God. In 1539, Henry authorised publication of the Great Bible, ironically based heavily upon Tyndale's translation, with copies placed in every church. Henry's move proved very popular with his subjects and once the dam was breached there was no going back.

Key theological message of the Reformation

8.32 The theological reputation of Luther is based upon his identification that in Romans it is written that righteousness is granted to men as an entirely unmerited gift. Luther wrote that *'even if heaven and earth are destroyed, this is the belief upon which the church stands or falls'*. For those who believed that God freely makes sinners righteous, the new doctrine of justification was a source of comfort and joy. Few of the other leading reformers seized upon justification as Luther did.

8.33 However, one Cardinal had also realised the implication of Romans but Contarini failed to see it destroyed the basis for the Catholic Mass, purgatory and all the efforts to earn relief from the torture of purgatory. Surprisingly, it was Cardinal Contarini whom Rome sent as head of the delegation to the Colloquy of Ratisbon convened at Regensburg in Bavaria by the Holy Roman Emperor Charles V in 1541 to seek to restore religious unity. The negotiations made good progress in hammering out agreed definitions for most of the 23 draft articles but Justification was the most difficult. The Protestant team knew they needed Luther's consent and sent the drafts to him for comment. However, whilst awaiting a response, Contarini's draft on Justification was flatly rejected by the Vatican. The chance for restoring unity passed and the Catholic authorities convened the Council of Trent in response.

8.34 Standing back, the Reformation was a movement led by Catholic priests who initially were horrified by the blatant abuse of indulgences to raise revenue and then begun to focus on the lack of biblical support for most aspects of Catholic doctrine. Until Barach Spinoza, 1632 – 1677, a Dutch Jew and one of the most revered philosophers, no one really challenged the bible or the conventional idea of God.

8.35 Spinoza's beliefs were way ahead of his time, he was prescient in trying to describe the fabric of the universe. For Spinoza, God must be the sum of all the attributes (essences) of all the substances (close to a definition of all the elements) in the universe. Spinoza held that God is not a person but exists everywhere – very similar to Hinduism. Applying modern terminology, Spinoza might have been saying God is present in every element of visible matter. Whereas, personally, I see God as designer of the algebra that creates different elements and the attributes exhibited by every combination of elements, with God more likely to be dark energy than being matter (whether visible or dark).

8.36 Spinoza describes the human mind as part of the infinite intellect of God – who Spinoza explains is not a person but the Universe. Again, I concur, I see humans as housing a chip off God's block of Spirit, providing us with the freewill to conceive of any thought or action, so yes we are a part of the infinite intellect of God, and for me God is not a person but a type of energy force.

8.37 Spinoza has a special definition of "Blessedness" – meaning salvation or freedom, consisting of the constant and eternal love of God and in particular God's love of man. Blessedness he defines as the most elevated and desirable state one can attain. Freedom comes from searching and finding the truth. For Spinoza, as humans become more rational (scientific) we will understand God better, this makes us better humans so we become more blessed.

8.38 Spinoza's world view defined knowledge as truth or fiction. Spinoza saw rational knowledge, reason, science and philosophy, as the source of truth – with truth providing us with knowledge of God. The first few chapters of Part One of this series attest to this concept. By contrast, Spinoza said that religion is useful in interpreting God in a way people can understand. The aim of religion is not to tell the truth but to make people believe and to behave well. Religion is a 'fiction' (i.e. not truth), but an organising principle promoting peace and harmony by which society can prosper. The role of religion is to manage people – through images and feelings. For Spinoza, religion and politics are the same – using fictions (not outright truths) to create systems of governance, laws and punishments to keep people in check. He saw that eventually, humans may become sufficiently rational for truth to overcome fictions and the need for religion will pass away.

8.39   As one can imagine, church authorities were apoplectic. But legally there was not much that could be done, as Spinoza was a Jew and had been thrown out by his synagogue – he could not be excommunicated as he had never been baptised a Christian. So, the church labelled him an atheist, probably to avoid any discussion of his heretical views about God – but no one reading his works could doubt for a moment that he believed in a divine creator. For example, Spinoza described Jesus as manifesting the eternal wisdom of God in our human minds – without which no one can come to a state of blessedness, inasmuch as it is God's wisdom alone that teaches what is true or false, good or evil. Despite views like these, even today, many commentators still follow the Catholic position that Spinoza was an atheist!!

8.40   Spinoza is in amazing company. According to Beth Lord, a Professor at University of Dundee, Richard Dworkins talks of Einstein's God as being very similar to Spinoza's and that Einstein was a great fan of Spinoza. Beth advises her students that dislike using the word 'God' to use the word 'energy' – she got to the truth before I did. Spinoza himself compared his view of God as similar to the great polymath Maimonides.

9

The Catholic Counter-reformation

9.1 Luther's original intention, when posting his Theses in 1517, was focused on papal reform of indulgences. But such was the widespread anger over indulgences and the sharp analysis provided by Luther, that the debate rapidly expanded into a far wider criticism of the blatant luxury and corruption practised by the clergy, the veneration of relics, the use of saints as mediators to obtain salvation and the absolute power abused by popes. Ten years later, an unpaid army of the Holy Roman Empire, mainly German soldiery outraged by papal excesses, marched on Rome to secure recompense. The resulting 'Sack of Rome' by 34,000 soldiers in 1527, which looted many valuables and destroyed around 2/3rds of all the buildings in Rome, led to widespread sympathy flowing back in favour of the church.

9.2 A new pope, Paul III, 1534 to 1549, seized on the more sympathetic feelings towards the papacy by focusing on rebuilding work and efforts to complete the new St Pater's. Paul III reconciled with the Holy Roman Emperor and in 1545 convened the Council of Trent to revitalise and renew the church transforming it from its medieval ways into a modern church. Paul III sought to restore Christian morality and reunify all Christians. However, the addressing the key issue of the sale of indulgences was left until the final session in 1563.

9.3 Whilst the Council of Trent was regarded by Catholics as a successful counter-reformation, in retrospect it resembled more a doubling down on dogma thoroughly discredited in the minds of Protestant reformers.

9.4   Growing trade brought prosperity to large parts of Europe, which led to improved education, raising literacy when copies of the bible in everyday languages started to become plentiful. In the 16th century, those who translated the official Latin Vulgate bible were declared heretics and burnt at the stake. The Council of Trent backed this and ruled none could even read the Latin Vulgate in church except they had obtained a written license from a bishop and were supervised by their priest. Those found to possess a copy of even any part of the bible were to surrender it to the church for burning and absolution would be withheld until they complied – i.e. their sins would accumulate and their time in purgatory would increase. As late as 1850, Leo XII condemned bible distribution by Protestants and called bibles in the vernacular the 'Gospel of the Devil'. It was only in 1943 that Pius XII announced that henceforth Catholics were permitted to read the bible; and only the Second Vatican Council (1962-1965) that decided that the sacraments could be said in the vernacular so congregations could understand the services they attended!

9.5   However, the long standing Catholic prohibition on the laity reading the bible persists even today. This was brought home to me when writing this booklet. The two examples I referred to in section 6.8 above show Catholic institutions continued to resist the idea of laity reading the bible. In Italy, 25 years after Pope Pius XII issued *Divino Afflante Spiritu* encouraging bible study by laity, Jesuit schools did not permit students to read the bible. After leaving college and emigrating from Italy, my friend took 40 years to summon courage to buy a copy of the bible – and found its content extraordinary. Other friends, taught elsewhere in a Catholic school in the 1960's, whilst self-described as 'lapsed' still averred to even reading biblical quotes six decades later. They explained they had never opened a bible and would never do so, they had only listened to short sections read out by a priest. Such was the lasting impact of Catholic teaching – no doubt the overhang of earlier rules proscribing excommunication or death.

9.6   With the benefit of hindsight, we can see the most fundamental issue of Protestant theology is justification by faith. Some strands of reformers took this to be a license to continue sinning, as all sins would be forgiven. Others pointed to James – faith without (good) works achieves nothing. The Catholic theology rejects *Sola Scriptura* in favour of a combination of *Papal guidance, Scripture and Tradition*. Tradition being defined as oral and written traditions handed down from Jesus Apostles through successive church leaders and therefore of equal value. This provided an effective way of maintaining papal authority by emphasising its heritage. The core tenet of belief being confirmed as a need for love combined with faith to secure salvation. Increased 'love', good works, charity, penance, etc., earning merit to gradually increase one's righteousness. To Protestants, this appeared to say that Jesus sacrifice was insufficient to save us.

9.7   Looked at objectively, the position advanced by each side is simply contradictory. Protestants asserting *Sola Scriptura* cannot reconcile Paul's undeserved free gift of salvation with James statement that faith without good works has no benefit. Catholics continue to assert good works earn merit, providing a palliative reducing the punishment for sins committed – seemingly, unless one is Mother Teresa, no amount of faith plus good works guarantees to secure salvation.

9.8   For me, this raises an important question. For Luther, drawn from the Book of Romans, justification by faith was his most important discovery. But, consider a moment – where did Paul get this idea from?

9.9   Luther's enthusiasm for Paul's salvation simply based upon faith sits uncomfortably beside James writing that 'faith without works' is pointless and Matthew's quotation from Jesus of his teaching in 25:31-47 which sets out in some detail the works which it claims Jesus will base one's salvation upon.

10

Heresies that believers died for

10.1   Now let's turn back to heresy. The Roman church defined heresy as virtually any belief which contradicted its own dogma.

10.2   The notion of heresy dates back to the origins of Christianity. Marcion (AD85 to 160) is generally regarded as the first heretic for preaching his views that the god of the Old Testament was not the Creator but a secondary god who had fallen from righteousness causing Jesus to be sent by the true God to rescue the world from sin. It is easy to see the Marcion view growing from the then contemporary understanding of John 1:1 – that Jesus was the divine intermediary, sent by the Creator God to convey his directions to humanity via the spoken word. In AD144, Marcion presented his views to the church leaders in Rome, horrified they excommunicated him but his teaching became very popular across the Roman Empire – where the idea that the supreme god was Jewish was an anathema.

10.3   Those who knew Jesus from direct experience of hearing him preach referred to him as a rabbi, a teacher. His message was clear, but dangerous to the clerical hierarchy – he pointed out the hypocrisy and the tangle of detailed rules and interpretations which acted to constrain Jewish daily life. Whilst Jesus never claimed to be divine himself, he repeatedly stated he was acting on behalf of his spiritual father, carrying out his father's wishes and had been granted authority by his father. As discussed in Part Three, I do not think that Jesus references to 'father' were meant to be understood literally but to convey parental guidance and obedience to a higher power. There is also evidence that when Jesus referred to his 'father' he was not referring to God – as explored later in chapter 15. And in chapter 15 we shall also find there is another stunning explanation – hidden within plain sight. I also wonder if Jesus was really pointing to 'love' as the power he was serving and obedient to. During his ministry and probably throughout the rest of the first century, Jesus was believed to have been born a natural man and brought up in a family with several siblings – four brothers and at least one sister.

10.4   Originally, Jesus divine powers were believed to have been granted at his baptism by John the Baptist, with the dove alighting on him and the voice from above declaring that *today* you have become my (adopted) son – as recorded in the oldest gospel manuscripts. Two contemporary factors strongly contributed to Jesus being acclaimed a messiah:

•   Firstly, the contemporary belief in Judah's religious and political redemption being signified by the birth of two messiahs, a priest messiah and a king messiah – as found in key texts discovered amongst the Dead Sea Scrolls but edited in Christian bibles to refer to only a single messiah – e.g. Malachi 3:1-2; and,

•   Secondly, the idea of Jesus descent from a line of the Davidic house. Some dismiss the claim of Davidic descent because the record keeping necessary to maintain this knowledge for a millennium through wars and destruction is not credible and that such records were only kept for royalty. But, consider Judaism's record in maintaining its calendar from the coronation of Etana, described as the first fully human king of Sumeria, in 3760BC – over nearly six millennia – with this year AD2022, being year 5782 in the Jewish calendar. Consider then, that Temple records did show Jesus was a descendant of the House of David. The genealogies in Matthew and Luke also provide indirect proof – written after the Temple was utterly destroyed by the Romans in AD70, the precious records were lost. The genealogies in Matthew and Luke were desperate attempts to recreate the record to 'prove' Jesus was a messiah – but, as we found earlier, these are obviously fake (see Part Three), and were even denounced as such by Paul.

10.5   The claim that Jesus was a messiah does have very long legs. Many Judaic texts of the 2nd and 1st centuries BC spoke about the coming of two messiahs, including the *Testament of the Twelve Patriarchs*, the *Testament of Simon 7:2*, the *Testament of Judah*, the *Book of Jubilees*, and *Malachi*. Malachi got revised in both the early Christian versions of the Old Testament and in the 9th century Masoretic Jewish scriptures to refer only to a single expected messiah. Against this cultural background and the possibility that Joseph's lineage was maintained in the Temple records, imagine the excitement when his wife produced surviving twin brothers. One of Jesus brothers is openly referred to as "Thomas, also called Didymus" (John 20:24). What is never explained by the church is that 'thomas' means twin in Aramaic and 'didymus' means twin in Greek – so this brother of Jesus is referred to as the "Twin called Twin" – seems like his being a twin is the most salient thing about him. A number of books banned by the church also referred to Jesus having a twin brother, including the *Gospel of Thomas*, the *Acts of Thomas* and the *Gospel of St Bartholomew* – which has Jesus himself stating that Judas was his brother, his twin and also a messiah: *Jesus, approaching Simon Peter and Judas Thomas, addresses them "Greetings my venerable guardian Peter, greetings twin, my second Messiah"*.

10.6   Of course without the gnosis, the overwhelming majority of Christians have been misled. Hiding truth in plain sight is highly effective, Rome did not want have a text referred to as *"Evangelium enim Geminae"*, so Thomas was left in Aramaic rather than have anyone refer to the *"Gospel of the Twin"* – which would have led to many uncomfortable questions.

10.7   The Proto-Evangelium of James is the source of much Catholic doctrine rejected by Protestants – which is somewhat ironic as Rome banned the text as heretical. Some of its teaching also found its way into the Koran.

10.8   The Gospel of Peter, the Gospel of Thomas and the Testimony of Truth are probably the most important rediscovered texts and also seem to be judged highly authentic early first century.

10.9   The idea that Jesus had a twin brother is the most significant and most persistent 'heresy' and has persisted right through to the 20th century despite desperate efforts by the Roman church to suppress it. For more details please refer to Part Three chapter 13 – The Sign.

10.10   In the canonised gospels, the role of Thomas is minimal but it now appears that his missionary work was on a par with Paul – even the Roman church now agrees that Thomas preached across modern Syria, Iraq, Iran, Pakistan and India converting substantial numbers and establishing churches across India found by Portuguese explorers in the 15th century who proceeded to impose the Latin rites.

10.11   It seems that there were far more books about Thomas and references to Thomas in books that were banned by the church – perhaps indicating one reason that such works were deemed heretical.

10.12   Based primarily upon Pauline theology, the 2nd and 3rd centuries saw church theologians develop early dogma which sought to elevate Jesus into something quite different from what was believed in the 1st century. The Johannine belief that Jesus was the Word incarnate, created by God and sent to do his work was one tradition which led to belief that a divine spirit had entered a man to undertake God's work on Earth and then depart, maybe on the Cross – *"why has thou deserted me"*.

10.13   Another strand of belief, ultimately successful, was designed to make Jesus more competitive with other contemporary divine beings. Every self-respecting king claimed the right to rule was based upon his divine ancestry, usually he was the son of a god, often as a result of a union with an earthly woman. Of all the books canonised in the New Testament, only Matthew and Luke refer to Jesus conception being the work of the Holy Spirit, i.e. God. However, the coverage of the early life of Jesus in both gospels is highly suspect. As explored in Part Three, many aspects of the story around the birth of Jesus not only lack credibility but seem to draw extensively from the then highly popular story of Isis, her conception and birth of her babe Horus. Further, as examined in Part Three, the two accounts in Matthew and Luke directly contradict each other in many basic details.

10.14   Once it was decided that Jesus originated from a union between God and Mary, various consequences followed. Joseph was positioned as an accepting cuckold and scribes begun to rephrase descriptions – references to 'Jesus parents' became 'Jesus mother and her husband', etc. Despite clear references in Paul's epistles to Jesus having brothers (using the correct Greek term rather than 'cousins' used to refer to other relationships by Paul) the Roman church begun to describe Mary as having conceived as a virgin, and of having been chosen as a pure vessel by God, she then became described as perpetually virgin untouched by mortal men. Logically, this meant Jesus could not be permitted a twin brother nor any siblings at all. This must have created a huge challenge

– Jesus brother James succeeded him after the ascension as head of the Nazarene church, other brothers also played key roles. The descendants of Jesus and his brothers were known as 'Desposyni', eight were recorded as visiting Rome in AD318. Therefore many texts used by the early church in the first centuries would have made references to Jesus siblings and their descendants – but according to the Roman church none had ever existed. Therefore all texts containing references to Jesus family members had to be 'interpreted' or destroyed – the thoroughness and the scale of the destruction was immense – see chapter 3 earlier for more details. The Roman church developed the theory that those described as Jesus brothers and sisters in canon were actually referring to half siblings, being the issue of Joseph from a former marriage.

10.15   In addition to removing any record of Jesus having siblings, there may have been a further aspect to edit out from history. Much speculation arose from the Dan Brown book and film based around Jesus spawning a bloodline – but church doctrine is counter intuitive. The Roman church decided that sex is sinful, being misogynist, the priesthood blame women for tempting man to sin, whilst pure men abstain from sex. This is hard to reconcile with the teaching that God came to Earth incarnate as a real man, laying aside his divine powers to experience what human life is really like. How can such a plan to experience what man encounters in life be credible if sex is omitted? Jesus teaching is all about relationships – so excluding marriage and sex makes no sense. Culturally, by age 30 when starting his ministry, a God-fearing Jew would definitely have to be married and obliged to have children. Some have questioned whether the wedding at Cana (John 2:1-11), with Jesus mother seemingly in charge, was actually Jesus marriage.

10.16   Another major early controversy arose from efforts to suppress the ancient idea of humans living with a spiritual duality – a soul containing our individual memories which normally went to a dark place at death cut off from God and for all eternity; and a spirit, our freewill which returned to God. This was a near universal understanding and referred to in many early Christian texts but introduced the dangerous idea of multiple chances at salvation and of salvation lying in our own hands (rather than being controlled by the church). The origin of these ideas and its place in Jesus ministry is discussed in detail in chapter 15. The issue represented a huge challenge to the monopoly power of the church over salvation and needed to be ruthlessly suppressed.

10.17   Valentinus (c100 to c160), an early church father who openly taught reincarnation, travelled to Rome c135 and became very popular, he narrowly missed being elected pope. Later, Valentinus and all his works were declared heretical. The First Council of Constantinople in 381, approved teaching that a human is comprised of three parts – body, spirit and soul.

10.18   However, the Catechism of the Catholic Church suppresses the idea of both a Spirit and a Soul. Clause 366 states "*The Church teaches that every spiritual soul is created immediately by God – it is not 'produced' by the parents – and also that it is immortal: it does not perish when it separates from the body at death, and it will be reunited with the body at the final Resurrection.*" However, the authority for this doctrine is not Jesus or even any biblical source but two popes and a Council: the Lateran Council V in 1513, a ruling by Pope Paul VI and *Humani Generis* issued in 1950 by Pope Pius XII.

10.19   Clause 367 of the Catechism admits Paul, the real founder of the Catholic doctrine, actually said something clearly different. However, even Paul falls foul of papal reinterpretation. "*Sometimes the soul is distinguished from the spirit: St. Paul for instance prays that God may sanctify his people 'wholly', with 'spirit and soul and body' kept sound and blameless at the Lord's coming*". (1 Thessalonians 5:23) This contradiction is explained away by (i) The Fourth Council of Constantinople ruling in 870 that of Church teaches that this distinction does not introduce a duality into the soul; whilst (ii) the *Humani Generis* issued in 1950 by Pope Pius XII declared that "'*Spirit' signifies that from creation man is ordered to a supernatural end and that his soul can gratuitously be raised beyond all it deserves to communion with God.*" This glossing just tries to merge the two by inventing a 'spiritual soul'.

10.20   Under ecclesiastical law, any deviation from the Nicaean Creed constitutes heresy – so anyone stating and not subsequently recanting anything contradicting dogma, or harbouring any text that did so in written form, was guilty of heresy for which there was only one remedy – excommunication. The key heresies included numerous statements that are far more likely to be true than false:

•   Joseph was the biological father of Jesus

•   Mary did not remain a virgin for her entire life

•   Jesus had any siblings

- Jesus married or had children

- Jesus was not an incarnation of God himself

- Jesus was not simultaneously wholly human and wholly God

- Jesus had not bodily resurrected

- Jesus had not bodily ascended to heaven

- Jesus had taught man could save himself, independently of the church

- Denied papal authority as God's representative and dispenser of grace

- Denied the effectiveness of the sacraments

- Denied the universal stain on humanity of Original Sin

- Heresies arising from scientific discoveries, e.g. of Earth not being the centre of the universe

10.21 Heresy then came to be the product of Ecclesiastical Councils of the church making determinations concerning fundamental aspects of dogma – starting with trying to define Jesus relation to God and then the nature of Jesus – divine or man or both? Starting with the Council of Nicaea in 325, those such as the Arians who disagreed with the Council's conclusion were ruled to be heretics and excommunicated.

10.22 The Edict of Thessalonica, issued by Emperor Theodosius I in 380, granted the church authority to carry out executions of heretics itself rather than have to hand heretics over to Roman civil authorities for carrying out sentences. This power remained in force until gradually withdrawn by individual countries after the Reformation but persisting in Spain until 1834. The first heretic killed by the church was a Spanish bishop, Priscillian, in 385 and the last was a Spanish schoolmaster, following a 2 year trial under the Inquisition, in 1826. The standard form of punishment for heretics was excommunication – cut off from the sacraments by papal authority such a person became destined for eternal damnation in hell. Often the process was accelerated by sentence of immediate death to prevent any further dissemination of heretical ideas and to speed the individual into hell. Theodosius II, emperor of the Eastern Roman Empire following the spilt, issued an edict in 435 providing severe punishment for those promoting the heresy of Nestorianism and death for those found with any written material on Nestorianism. The enthusiasm for punishing those expressing or even harbouring texts incorporating views deemed heretical also extended to the families of those found to be heretics.

10.23   The concept of excommunication drew from Old Testament practice of outcasts being cut off from the community. Excommunication could only apply to those who had been baptised, into the faith, and therefore did not impact those of other faiths or none.

10.24   In 1553, Michael Servetus, an early textual analyst of scripture, was burned at the stake in Geneva – with Calvin in attendance for refusing to believe in the Trinity.

11

Christians martyred on the orders of the Roman Church

11.1   This is one aspect of history that has really surprised me. I was under the impression, both from historical accounts and, no doubt bolstered by Hollywood, that the Roman Empire had killed very large numbers of Christians prior to the Empire adopting Christianity. So, it was surprising to discover that, whilst there would appear to have been strong reasons for the Roman authorities to discourage the spread of Christianity by persecuting believers, actually the consensus is that the numbers of those martyred was actually quite low. As discussed in Chapter 4, the total number of those martyred by the Roman state is now believed to be around 5,000 to 6,000. Whilst still a huge number, it represents a rate of only 20 per year across the whole Empire over the three centuries between the Crucifixion and the Council of Nicaea. Given that in AD68 there were 36 provinces within the Roman Empire, the frequency of martyrdom in each province averaged around one martyr every two years. Moreover, as the majority of killings resulted from specific Edicts, it becomes clear that the practise of Christianity continued without any persecution for centuries in most Roman provinces.

11.2   At the conclusion of the Council of Nicaea in 325, Emperor Constantine banished Arius (who had led opposition to making Jesus equal to, and part of, God) and ordering the death penalty for all those who did not conform to the opinion approved at Nicaea.

11.3   Constantine also ordered the seizure and burning of all texts (and their owners) that did not support the new Duality of God and Jesus (it took a few more church councils to incorporate the Holy Spirit). This initial exclusion of the Holy Spirit echoed down the centuries and led to the failure of the efforts to reunite the Roman and Orthodox churches in the 15th century. Rome insisted that the Spirit could be commanded to go forth by God and Jesus but the Orthodox could not accept that Jesus could command the Spirit. (To me, both views seem a bit strange if one is claiming there is a Trinity!)

11.4   Ironically, in 337, when Constantine was dying, he relented and summoned Eusebius (an Arian) to baptise him at the same time Constantine recanted the notion that Jesus was God and adopted the Arian creed.

11.5   It has been estimated by the historian Will Durant that more Christians were slaughtered by fellow Christians in the *two* years following Nicaea than by the persecutions of Christians by pagans in the entire history of Rome (*The Story of Civilisation, Vol4, The Age of Faith 1950*).

11.6   55 years after Nicaea, Emperor Theodosius I issued the Edict of Thessalonica in 380, adopting Christianity as the state religion. The Edict granted the church power to enforce judgments, including the death sentence, against heretics, a power previously reserved for the state. Whilst the civil authorities would not be terribly exercised by what the church deemed to be heretical views, the church viewed all such deviations as threats to its monopoly power.

11.7   The most famous early case was the Spanish bishop, Priscillian, who with five followers was executed in 386. Such was the widespread popularity of Priscillian that it is believed Compostela de Santiago in north west Spain was built as his shrine and became the second most popular place of pilgrimage after the Vatican itself.

11.8   What followed during the next few centuries appears to have been a fire-storm of book burning and massacring of those judged to be heretics.

11.9   How can we judge the numbers killed in those first two centuries after Nicaea:- the church clearly did not venerate those it killed in the way it venerated those who had been martyred prior to 311 when Christianity had become legally permitted. Will Durant equates the number with 5,000 to 6,000 in just the first two years when only Roman secular powers were carrying out the eradication program.

11.10 We can judge the numbers of texts that we know were all but completely eradicated, see chapter 3. Most of these texts were have been carefully copied and distributed between the various churches – so we are definitely talking of thousands. In addition, whole communities of believers, followers of those priests declared to be heretics, were also hunted down. It was common practise to kill entire households when a banned text was found during a search of a home.

11.11 When the church needed secular muscle to combat what it saw as persisting heresies, it seems to have called upon the Emperor for reinforcements. For example, an edict of Theodosius II issued in 435, sentenced to death all those who possessed writings by either Arius or Nestorius.

11.12 This merging of state and religion was made even more explicit under Emperor Justinian. Justinian identified that the empire's legal system needed an overhaul as it had become a mass of often outdated and conflicting laws. The commission he appointed produced an initial codex in 529 but it was then decided that a more extensive project was required – which led to the publication of the twelve part set of the *Codex Repetitae Praelectionis*, aka *The Codex Justinianus*, in 534. Book 1 contained Ecclesiastical Law, indicating both priorities and the firm embrace of the state, and all its organs of power, for enforcement. Clause 5:12 of Book 1 baldly defines as a heretic *"everyone who is not devoted to the Catholic Church and to our orthodox holy Faith"*.

11.13 Such was the popularity of the concept of declaring those not subscribing to Roman dogma as heretics that Gregory I (pope from 590 to 604) combined the hatred of the Jews with heresy, claiming that all heresy was 'Jewish', in effect licensing ethnic persecutions of Jewish communities across Europe.

11.14 John of Damascus (676 to 749) tried something similar for Muslims. Known as something of an intellectual in mathematics, music and philosophy, John was an early promoter of Mariology and defended idolatry but was so harsh about the Qur'an that he described Islam as the "heresy of the Ishmaelites". This standpoint remained popular for many centuries – again providing a religious cover for slaughtering those holding different beliefs.

11.15 Various sects which had spread widely were pursued rigorously, including

Arianism, Pelagianism, Donatism, Mancheanism, Marcionism and Montanism. Surprisingly, many early Christian beliefs persisted, resisting the harshest attempts to eradicate them:- particularly issues around the nature of Jesus and whether he had a twin brother together with antipathy towards bishops driven by popular observation of the extreme secular power and wealth they displayed. The 11th and 12th centuries saw many hostile campaigns carried out by Rome against deviant churches – against the Bogomils (modern Bulgaria), the Cathars of southern France, the Dulcinians, Patarini, Paulicians and Waldensians.

11.16   Details of the barbarities carried out against the Cathars have come down to us. The Cathars were the longest lasting branch of the original Nazarene church and their 'sins' included belief in spiritual duality of soul and spirit, and thus of reincarnation. They believed Jesus, as a devout Jew, was betrothed at 12 and married to Mary Magdalene at 30 in Cana. The campaigns against the Cathars lasted sporadically over a couple of centuries as the extreme measures drove surviving adherents underground. The campaigns were largely contracted out by the Vatican to the French crown – which was incentivised by the award of both captured territory and any looting they could carry out. The Albigensian Crusade 1209 to 1229, declared by Pope Innocent III (ironic name) was notorious for its practice of herding entire communities into their village church, bolting the doors and setting fire to the church – claiming that any innocent souls would be known to God and rescued from eternal damnation.

11.17   Many who know of the Inquisition believe it started as the Spanish Inquisition. Actually, it was formed on the instruction of Pope Gregory IX in 1233, under his direct control to exterminate the remaining French Cathars. Using the Dominican order of Black Friars, inquisition councils were set up in numerous towns throughout the ancient Pays D'Oc. Some, like Raymond VII of Toulouse used his commission from the Inquisition to arrest owners of attractive plots of land, accuse them of heresy, burn them at the stake and seize their assets. Those accused were neither able to get legal assistance nor even face towards their accusers. Those who confessed readily and were judged redeemable were forced to sew large yellow crosses on their clothes so they would be readily identifiable – maybe the inspiration for the Nazi's adornment of Jews.

11.18   Inquisitors were used by the French crown to launch the mass arrest and torture of around 15,000 Knights Templar on Black Friday, 13 October 1307. The numbers actually executed are disputed but the charges against the Templars were later revealed to be entirely trumped up by the French Crown. The real reason for the attack on the Templars was to seize their headquarters in Paris, their considerable wealth and to cancel the huge loans the French king had borrowed from the Templars.

11.19 Joan of Arc is another famous injustice by the Inquisition. Having led a French army to victory over the invading English, she was later captured by a Burgundian force allied to the English and tried by an Inquisitor under charges of witchcraft and heresy. At only 19, she was burned at the stake in 1431.

11.20 In Spain, ancient Jewish communities which had been reinforced by exiles fleeing the genocidal Roman campaigns in the 1st and 2nd centuries in Judea, had been forced to convert to Christianity in the pogroms of 1391 and became known as Conversos. However, they continued to be viewed with suspicion and were easy targets for blame when plagues occurred. They were accused of poisoning water supplies and of abducting Christian boys for barbaric rituals. Jealousy was a key driver, as Rome had forbidden usury, the Jews were the only people allowed to lend money and therefore as all money was gold or silver, Jews monopolised the trade in gold and jewellery – generating considerable wealth. This attracted the attention of King Ferdinand II and Queen Isabella who needed funds to finance a crusade against Grenada. The solution was to accuse the Jews as being responsible for the highly visible corruption within the Spanish church. His solution was to appoint an Inquisition in 1480, led by the infamous Tomas de Torquemada to investigate. For Torquemada the only acceptable response to an accusation was the confession of guilt – which resulted in death and confiscation of wealth. In 1481, over 20,000 Conversos confessed to heresy but each was also required to identify another heretic – and by the end of the year hundreds had been burnt at the stake. Naturally, this led to a mass migration from the Jewish communities – with disastrous long term consequences for the Spanish economy.

11.21 Having established the Inquisition in Spain, under Philip II (king from 1556 to 1598) it put down roots and expanded into Spanish territories conquered in north Africa – full of Muslims (all heretics) and into South America (also full of heretics). The Inquisition was established in Mexico in 1570 and by 1574 was burning Lutherans at the stake. Soon it was established in Peru and begun burning Protestants alive there. In 1580, Philip II conquered Portugal, allowing the Inquisition to arrest and kill Jews that had fled to Portugal from Spain – their flight alone being deemed to prove their guilt – and to arrest Moors who were either killed or sold into slavery.

11.22   After his death, Philip II's son, Philip III, organised large scale expulsions of Moors, Muslims who had already been forced to convert to Christianity. It is estimated that 150,000 were expelled between 1609 and 1615. From this time, the Inquisition had made life so oppressive across Spanish domains that Protestants avoided such territories altogether. This acted to isolate the Spanish empire from much of the benefits that international trade, particularly with the predominant English and Dutch traders distributing the merchandise from the start of the industrial revolution and their more open colonial developments. Spain suffered from the importation of vast amounts of gold from South America inflating its monetary base and stifling political and religious bureaucracy which killed enterprise, leading inevitably to a stultified economy which persisted for centuries.

11.23   In Rome, Pope Paul III decided that an Inquisition was the response required to deal with Protestantism and in 1542 established the *Supreme Sacred Congregation of the Roman and Universal Inquisition*. This still exists today, but in 1965 its name changed to the *Congregation for the Doctrine of the Faith*. It was this body which seized Galileo in 1633 for his heresy of stating that the Earth revolved around the Sun. Galileo had been warned in 1616 that his writings appeared to state that the Earth was not stationary but moved around the Sun – at that time, he had promised not to publicise his views on heliocentricity – a point he maintained under examination in 1633. For recanting his view before the Inquisition, Galileo escaped torture but was charged with being "vehemently suspect of heresy" and committed to life imprisonment (later commuted to house arrest) and prohibited from ever publishing any work.

11.24   After conquering Spain, Napoleon abolished the Spanish Inquisition in 1808 but after his defeat it was re-established although much weakened – ceding its authority to carry out killings to the state. Its last death sentence was of a school teacher, Cayetano Ripoll in 1826. Despite his sentence to be burned at the stake, the civil authorities hung him instead.

His 'crime' was to assert that reason and observation of the natural world are sufficient to establish the existence of a Supreme Creator – the Bible, which as a Catholic he was banned from reading, he viewed as superfluous.

11.25 The successor to the Inquisition, the *Congregation for the Doctrine of the Faith*, remains active and continues to excommunicate Catholics for heresy – e.g. the excommunication of Father Tissa Balasuriya on 5 January 1997, referred to in paragraph 5.67 above. Even in 2020, three Catholics living on Westray in the Orkneys, a priest and monk and a lay doctor, were excommunicated for posting an online declaration which claimed the leadership of the church remained silent, failing to respond to calls for urgently needed reforms. For a Catholic, the sentencing power of the modern Inquisition is barely reduced – excommunication separates you from the church for the remainder of your earthly life, cutting you off from the supply of grace and puts you on track for eternal damnation in the everlasting torment of hell once you die. Catholic doctrine asserts that once served with excommunication under papal authority not even God will intervene to save you.

11.26 If one attempts to estimate the numbers killed by the church, yes by the church, in the 1500 years between Nicaea, 325, and the last person executed by the Inquisition in 1826, the scale of the total number is likely to exceed a million. It appears credible that at least 100,000 Cathars were killed, and some estimates indicate more than 200,000, in the most bloodthirsty of the numerous campaigns against the Cathars. In one attack, on Béziers in 1209, the papal legate Cistercian Abbot Arnaud Amairic reported to the Vatican that over 20,000 men, women and children had been massacred without regard to sex, age or rank and, to remove the stain of heresy, the city had been utterly destroyed. Many other campaigns against alleged heretical tendencies must have killed tens of thousands each. Estimates of the numbers killed by the Spanish branch of the Inquisition range from 30,000 to 300,000, although some historians are convinced many millions died. Some estimates claim 10 million and even multiples of that number but objective judgment of the size of populations and resourcing of the Inquisition organisations suggests that would be an exaggeration. So, I would judge that globally across territories controlled by Catholic states somewhere between 1 and 2 million were killed. Born under the sway of thinking that heresy deserved death, many Protestant countries also executed heretics but the total numbers were very small by comparison.

11.27   According to Juan Antonio Llorente (1756-1823), Secretary-General
to the Spanish Inquisition, in his *'Histoire critique de l'Inquisition espagnole'*
the institution had recorded 31,912 were burned at the stake by the
Inquisition in Spain and another 291,450 condemned to serve penances.
Unfortunately, his immense cache of records in Madrid was later
consumed in a fire but according to the *Encyclopaedia Britannica*, Llorente
made honest use of the documents he had. It has been estimated by 21st
century historians, Perez and Rummel, that a further 100,000 to 125,000
died in Spanish prisons as a result of torture and maltreatment which
were not recorded as death penalties in the Inquisition records.

11.28   Alert to the poor image created by the Inquisition, a Catholic historian,
Professor Agostino Borromeo of Sapienza University, published a 783
page volume in June 2004 which concluded only 1,250 of his estimate of
the 125,000 tried by the Spanish Inquisition were executed or burned to
death. This smacks of a cover-up given the numbers published, shown
above, by the Secretary-General of the organisation using its original
records, even although subsequently lost. Indeed, it was reported that the
explanations put forward generated wry smiles amongst the audience of
journalists at the launch event. The excuses put forward included:

- "Many of the thousands of executions for heresy conventionally
  attributed to the church were in fact carried out by non-church
  tribunals" (so they don't count!!)

- The church initiated a strictly regulated process, in which torture was
  allowed for only 15 minutes and in the presence of a doctor, although
  they sometimes got out of hand when other parties were present
  (really?)

11.29   Even the Catholic Catechism is drawn to make a half-hearted apology
for the for the brutal actions carried out by church officials, whom it
claims were forbidden to shed blood(!!) – in Statement 2298: *Pastors of the
Church, who themselves adopted in their own tribunals the prescriptions of Roman
law concerning torture. Regrettable as these facts are, the Church always taught the
duty of clemency and mercy. She forbade clerics to shed blood. In recent times it has
become evident that these cruel practices were neither necessary for public order, nor in
conformity with the legitimate rights of the human person.*

12

Evidence of meaningful edits to New Testament texts

Phrases used in canon which jar when read in the context of when supposedly written

12.1   When one starts to understand the meanings of biblical terms used in the context of the contemporary culture at the time texts were originally written, later editing can easily be detected. Certain phrases in text jump out as inconsistent or, at a minimum, examples of poor translation. Two similar cases came to my attention on successive days. In his sermon, my own pastor quoted John 20.31, which paraphrasing various orthodox English translations, refers to "the Messiah, Jesus Christ, the Son of God". Most Christians, would see this as utterly unremarkable, 'Christ' has come to be used almost as though it is seen as Jesus family surname.

12.2   However, this phrase would be an extraordinary one for John to have written in his gospel. Firstly, for any Jew, the phrase contains two mutually exclusive concepts – 'Christ', being the Greek 'Kristos', meaning 'Messiah' a title defined as a male descendant from either Aaron (Moses' brother) or from King David who would be eligible to be anointed a messiah. But as set out in the Torah, it is a grave sin to claim to be a messiah before being anointed with a specific blend of oils and incense by the officiating High Priest. As examined previously, there are strong indications in the record of Jesus life that he was eligible to become a messiah, but there is no evidence that he was anointed by any High Priest. However, the very definition of a messiah means Jesus could not be divine, as a messiah by definition had a human male father –

excluding, for Jewish understanding, the revolutionary and blasphemous idea of God having a son.

12.3 Moreover, both concepts – 'Messiah' and 'Son of God' clearly contradict the statements in the opening verse of John's gospel – that Jesus is the Word, the Logos. Nowadays, the concept of Jesus being the Word is understood in the context of the Word being the Sword of Truth, a term used to explain the power of Jesus teaching. However, to John's contemporaries the term was very familiar and had a very specific meaning. John stated his gospel was written in Ephesus, then a major centre of Greek culture, on the western side of modern Turkey. The Greeks believed that the ultimate creator God deployed another entity to convey his intentions and teachings to humanity – this divinity, charged with teaching humanity on behalf of the ultimate creator, was known as the Logos, in English, the 'Word'. Therefore, in the context of when it was written, John 1.1 constitutes a flat denial that Jesus was either a messiah or a son of God.

12.4 In Greek, the pervasive cultural and lingua franca of the time, John opens his gospel by stating that Jesus is the Logos. The meaning was crystal clear at the time – Jesus had been created by God to convey God's will and teach humanity. John's adoption of Logos to identify Jesus fitted contemporary beliefs perfectly. Accordingly, in his opening statement, John is describing Jesus as created by God and sent to teach humanity on behalf of God – the actions, teachings and descriptions John records of Jesus in his gospel are entirely consistent with Jesus being what people understood of the Logos. John writes of Jesus categorizing God as his 'father' who he prayed to, obeyed and who had granted him tasks and authority also meshed with contemporary culture where powerful men took the brightest youngsters into their household would bestow inheritance rights and accordingly (Roman) citizenship – which rich men would usually have purchased, if not themselves of Roman descent.

12.5 So, given the clarity of John 1:1, I was surprised to read John later writing in verse 20:31 that Jesus was a mere messiah (a purely human descendant of Jewish patriarchs) and also that Jesus was a Son of God – which also contradicts the many times Jesus is quoted as described himself as a Son of Man. Then I started to dig and found a number of academic articles claiming the last two chapters of John's gospel (20 and 21) are not found in the earliest and most credible manuscripts suggesting they are late additions and not part of the original text. Even some commentaries of John published by the Catholic Church stop at the end of chapter 19. Pope Benedict XVI, in his book *Jesus of Nazareth*, refers in p276 to John 21:15-17 as being in the 'appendix' to John's gospel – a delicate way of saying it was not original. So, it seems that the verse that jumped out at me may well be part of a late addition grafted on the John's gospel and containing orthodox phrases complying with dogma created by the church centuries after Jesus life on earth.

12.6   The very next day, for an upcoming bible study class, I was working on Paul's first letter to the Corinthians. There again, in 1 Corinthians 1:9, is embedded almost the same text: 'the Lord Jesus Christ, the Son of God'. This struck me as both a coincidence and out of place for other reasons. Paul, as a highly educated Pharisee, an expert in the Law (probably able to recite most of the Torah from memory), would instinctively know the two terms 'messiah' and 'Son of God' were mutually exclusive. Most of Paul's writing reads like a legal brief, each point Paul makes is buttressed by definitions and verbal proofs. For Paul, words have precise meanings – so it seems very unlikely Paul would ever have described Jesus as a messiah, and, at the same time as the 'Son of God'. It also seems unlikely that Paul would have described Jesus as the Son of God – Paul himself frequently describes how upon reaching a city he would go to the Jewish community and preach in the synagogue – describing Jesus as the 'Son of God' in a synagogue would have been seen as very blasphemous and led swiftly to his extrajudicial killing. His views on kosher food were enough to get Paul hounded out of many cities!

12.7   The nature of Jesus is a very fertile ground in which to identify scribal editing. The synoptics are littered with examples of texts where differences arise from the earliest manuscripts. The earliest and best manuscripts originally stated Jesus was adopted to sonship at his baptism in the Jordan. Luke describes Jesus' baptism followed by 40 days in the wilderness and when he returns to Galilee *"in the power of the spirit"* (Luke 4:18) he begins his first sermon by quoting Isaiah 61:1 *"The spirit of the Lord is upon me because he anointed me"*. So, when did God anoint Jesus – the original answer was in the previous chapter, 3:22 when Jesus was adopted *today* by God as his Son.

12.8   Even the current versions of Paul's letter to the Romans state clearly that Jesus was only promoted to sonship *after* his resurrection. Romans 1:3-4:

"who as to his earthly life was a descendant of David, and who through the Spirit of holiness was appointed the Son of God in power by his resurrection from the dead" *(NIV)*. Not only does Paul write that Jesus was a descendant of David but that he was only promoted to sonship by his resurrection. The survival of this wording is surprising, maybe it is an example where the text of the earliest manuscripts has been restored as more authentic.

12.9 If Jesus had been conceived from the Holy Spirit, why would he need to be anointed at any point? In Acts 10:37-38 the text has not been finessed, leaving the reader with the clear impression that God anointed Jesus with power and Spirit **after** his baptism by John: *You know what has happened throughout the province of Judea, beginning in Galilee **after** the baptism that John preached how God anointed Jesus of Nazareth with the Holy Spirit and power, and how he went around doing good and healing all who were under the power of the devil, because God was with him.* Some manuscripts show the text changed from *"after the baptism that John preached"* to *"after the preaching of John"* to avoid the linkage of adoption with the baptism by John.

12.10 The Nicaean Creed dictated that Jesus had always existed as a facet of God, "begotten not made", but the early manuscripts of Hebrews 3:2 read *he was faithful to the one who **made** him*, which then became *he was faithful to the one who had **appointed** him.* Quite how the three elements within the Trinity can appoint each other to roles and send each other on missions whilst remaining a single monotheism is a challenge equalled only by the intellectual powerhouse that is the Catholic hierarchy.

12.11 Luke's coverage of the Transfiguration is also indicative. Modern translations revive speculation, with Luke 9:35 in the NIV stating: *A voice came from the cloud, saying, "This is my Son, whom I have chosen; listen to him".* From a Trinitarian perspective this must be baffling – if Jesus is God, how can Jesus be 'chosen'. Nine of the earliest and best manuscripts read "my Son, the one who has been chosen" – surely from a doctrinal standpoint, and from an orthodox perspective, if anyone was chosen it was Mary not Jesus?

Christology (defining the nature of Jesus)

12.12 This is a subject that caused endless debate in the early centuries of the church. It was eventually settled within Christendom by the Roman church killing anyone who did not accept their idea of a Trinity and the chosen definition as set out in their Creed.

12.13   The issue arose from the evolution of the descriptions of Jesus. Jesus taught how to achieve immortality, stories circulated that he had performed miracles and forgiven sins. Surely, it was said, only God has such powers. By the end of the 1st Century, writers were replacing Son of Man, Jesus favourite description of himself, with Son of God. Those seeking to spread Jesus teaching to the Gentiles saw that to be competitive, Jesus not only had to be divine but at least one parent had to be divine. In Judaism, only one God is available but it was quite normal for a god to be born of a human mother but fathered by a deity. Jewish beliefs made it difficult to introduce multiple Gods so this led to the adoption of a useful pagan motif of a Trinity.

12.14   As described in Chapter 4, there were a multitude of explanations of what Jesus had been when on earth. Academic analysis has adopted the categories defined by Roman apologists to defend orthodox doctrine:

- 'anti-adoptionist' – arguing that Jesus was not adopted by God but Mary conceived from the Holy Spirit;

- 'anti-separationist' – arguing that Jesus was not a man temporarily inhabited by the divine but actually both fully man and fully God at the same time, throughout his time on Earth;

- 'anti-docetic' – arguing against Jesus being a spiritual being who just appeared clothed in a body without human feelings but did actually experience pain and human feelings;

- 'anti-patripassianist' – arguing that Jesus was not God converted into human form but a real human.

12.15   All the categories above could be supported by verses even from texts accepted as orthodox, so many examples exist of texts being tweaked to try to block their use to support any of these ideas. The first two would seem to be the earliest ideas and the second pair came from attempts to enhance the Jesus brand against pagan gods. The four categories were thwarted by scribal edits when copying texts to combat phrases that supported the original belief. One of the earliest glaring edits in the canonised gospels was the change to the words spoken by the voice from heaven at Jesus baptism – clearly it was embarrassing to have key texts which state that the God adopted Jesus at baptism when you are trying to argue he was fathered by the Holy Spirit.

12.16 Paragraphs 5.72 to 5.74 above provide another example of Christological editing to promote Jesus to God in order to claim divine powers had been devolved onto Peter and thence passed down the line of elected popes.

12.17 Numerous other edits, seeking to undermine beliefs contrary to Roman doctrine, have been identified by simply comparing the oldest autographs with later canonised variants. Yet others, such as *"Jesus Christ, Son of God"*, stand out as oxymorons committed by Europeans totally unaware of the meaning of the word 'messiah'. Sometimes attempts to block use of a phrase to support one view deemed heretical would later be seen as helpful to support a different heresy.

12.18 There is no evidence that doctrinally inspired edits to texts being copied were undertaken on an organised basis but it seems that earnest scribes, finding phrases which clashed with contemporary doctrine or were ambiguous, simply 'improved' the text – leading to the vast number of textual variations we have today.

12.19 For an erudite exposition of this complex subject there is none better than Bart Ehrman's authoritative work: *The Orthodox Corruption of Scripture.*

Pontius Pilate trial of Jesus

12.20 Pontius Pilate was a Roman Prefect with almost unlimited powers in military and policing matters. Pilate was known to view the Jews with contempt, despising their traditions and religion. As a Prefect, he had the 'Ius gladiis' which was the authority to condemn people to death. He was recalled to Rome following his ferocious repression of a Samaritan revolt. It is absolutely unbelievable that such a man would entertain the idea of having a public debate about the fate of Jesus. This would constitute a precedent that no Roman authority would want to contemplate.

12.21 To render justice, Pilate had to sit on the 'sella curulis' which represented the judicial authority he was vested with, and this chair was usually placed inside the Praetorium. There are no Roman records of the biblically claimed 'tradition' to free one prisoner at Passover. The only record we have is for a different situation in another province, in AD86 the governor of Egypt, Settimio Vegeto, declared to a defendant Fibione that he would release him to 'the crowd'.

12.22 Moreover, under no circumstances he could free a prisoner accused of insurrection and murder (as per Mark 15:7). Waiver of such accusations was way above his paygrade. If Barabbas had been so accused and Pilate had released him, Pilate would have been accused of dereliction of duties and sent to Rome to answer to the Emperor (Lex Iulia De Vi). So, the story of Pilate entering into a debate with the crowd is very dubious. Pilate would certainly not hesitate to order a crucifixion because he was a cruel, insensitive individual concerned with his own personal position but indifferent as to the life or death of one he would have regarded as an insignificant peasant from Galilee.

12.23 Another aspect of the story of Pilate offering the people a choice of who was to die reveals both original efforts to craft a religiously significant story and also of early attempts to edit early texts to 'protect' orthodoxy. Again, it is instructive to try to recall what you learned as a child in school – I suspect, like mine, your learning was that Pilate offered the crowd the choice of freeing a criminal (based on the description in Mark 15:7) or freeing Jesus and that the sinful crowd then chose to free the criminal. Does that ring a bell? Now, try to remember the name of that criminal – it was Barabbas. Bar Abbas may be translated as 'Son of the Father' and by some as 'Son of God'. Surprised? Well, all the early codex of Matthew named Barabbas as 'Jesus Barabbas'. So, it seems the original text has Pilate asking the crowd whether to free Jesus the Son of God or Jesus whom you call the Messiah? Wow, that would be difficult for the Roman church to explain! So, lets delete the name Jesus from Barabbas and the Gentiles will be unaware what Barabbas means, and to make sure we will describe the man freed by Pilate as a criminal, add a few words to Mark – after all Barabbas had been arrested by the authorities!! The fact the record was changed is acknowledged by Pope Benedict XVI, p41 of his book *Jesus of Nazareth* states *"Up to the 4th century most manuscripts of the Gospels referred to the criminal offered against Jesus as Jesus Barabbas"*. But, Ratzinger offers no comment about *why* the gospels were changed.

12.24 But, what led to the original story? The most plausible explanation is that the author of Matthew was describing events in a way immediately recognizable to Jewish readers as the perfect offering of the sacrificial lamb. The Mosaic Law required two perfect specimens to be brought before the High Priest to take on the sins of the Jewish people, both took place in the ceremony – one was sacrificed on the alter and the other, the scapegoat, was released to wander off unharmed.

12.25   Some commentary even indicates that the *'well-known'* Barabbas was a priest. Given the then contemporary discussion of there being two messiahs, the Jesus we know was clearly the King Messiah, welcomed the previous week entering Jerusalem as king, was the other, the twin, would have been the Priest Messiah? The Priest Messiah was the more senior and therefore in Jewish terms, offered the choice, the people would logically free the priest messiah. Might this be the original truth?

12.26   The speculation that Jesus had a twin brother, Judas, *Didymus Judas Thomas (translating as: Twin Judas Twin)*, provides a perfect subject for a potential scapegoat to illustrate the dual sacrificial offering for the Jewish audience.

12.27   Later when the first doctrinal dispute arose between the Jerusalem church headed by Jesus' brother James and the church founded in Antioch (3rd city of the Roman empire at that time) it is noteworthy that the Jerusalem church decided to send two of the most senior brothers to Antioch, Judas Barsabbas and Silas – Acts 15.22. Could Judas Barabbas, Judas Barsabbas and Judas the Thomas actually all be the same person?

12.28   Maybe what happened was the Temple Guard, under orders from the Sanhedrin, arrested two troublemakers, unsure which twin was which, and both were brought to Pilate. The accusations did not amount to a crime under Roman law and Pilate would have been delighted at the chance to annoy the Pharisees – so he might have concluded only one could be claiming to be 'king of the Jews' and therefore the other was innocent. Obviously, the messiah named as the king of the Jews would have been the 'king messiah' and the priest released would have been the 'priest messiah'. Mark writing to a Roman audience, wanted to show the Romans as just and sympathetic to Jesus whilst making sure the Jews were blamed for killing a Messiah – hence Barabbas may have been portrayed as a murderer to emphasize how cold hearted the Jews behaved. There even seems to be a parallel: just as possibly Jesus twin brother was repurposed as a terrorist, so too was Mary Magdalene changed from being Jesus betrothed (maybe wife) to be described as a prostitute. If two were arrested and cross examined by Pilate with one being released – it would also explain how a transcript found its way into the gospels!

12.29   Another odd feature of Jesus trial is how to explain the people of Jerusalem warmly welcoming Jesus as the King Messiah on Sunday only to vote for his death barely 5 days later? This has always been a mystery.

I have come across two possible explanations:

- Jesus was arrested quietly at night so news did not spread and he was judged in camara by the Sanhedrin before being taken to Pilate with only civil servants (Pharisees and Sadducees) allowed in;

- When Jesus and his twin brother were both arrested and brought before Pilate, Pilate sought confirmation of which was the King of the Jews, the King Messiah, as that one was the troublemaker. If Jesus twin, named in the oldest texts as Jesus Barabbas, was believed to be the Priest Messiah it is obvious why the crowd selected him to be released. In Judaism, the Priest Messiah has seniority.

Both the above explanations are surely more credible than the version canonized by the Catholic Church.

12.30   When the Roman church decided Jesus had to be God, then a chain of consequences flowed – Mary had to conceive courtesy of the Holy Spirit, Mary had to be and remain a virgin as whilst God could have a Son, it was not appropriate that he have half-brothers – and a twin brother was simply out of the question – all references had to be excised. Perhaps some scribes adopted the use of a code or nickname to protect the truth when copying texts they knew would be seen as heretical?

12.31   And finally, I admit it is possible that reading this, you are now thinking the author is just making this all up. The good news is that there is plenty of good honest work being done to restore more authentic wording to biblical texts – the extract below is from the latest NIV, no less, I too was surprised by the current text of Matthew 27:15-18, 20, 22: *Now it was the governor's custom at the festival to release a prisoner chosen by the crowd. At that time they had a well-known prisoner whose name was Jesus Barabbas. So when the crowd had gathered, Pilate asked them, "Which one do you want me to release to you: Jesus Barabbas, or Jesus who is called the Messiah?" For he knew it was out of self-interest that they had handed Jesus over to him. But the chief priests and the elders persuaded the crowd to ask for Barabbas and to have Jesus executed. "What shall I do, then, with Jesus who is called the Messiah?" Pilate asked.*

Evidence the 'Western' tradition edited texts to promote Roman sympathy and Jewish hatred towards Jesus

12.32   Just as Mark wrote a text addressing a Roman audience and painting the

Roman authorities as fairly neutral towards Jesus, there is strong evidence that the Book of Acts was also subject to widespread editing in a strongly anti-Judaic fashion. In his work entitled '*The Theological Tendency of Codex Bezae Cantabrigiensis in Acts*', Eldon Epp examined all the significant textual variants in the Book of Acts. Comparing the oldest Greek manuscripts with translations into Latin in the early centuries and found a full 40% of the significant edits introduced changes which could be described as anti-Jewish.

Rampant textual variations arose in early Greek texts

12.33   We are generally led to believe that the texts of the New Testament have come down to us with their original text and meaning intact. We understand different translations have attempted to convey original meanings more closely and are often seeking to bring the texts alive by using contemporary language.

12.34   However, over three centuries ago, John Mill, a learned English theologian undertook a comparison of 100 early Greek manuscripts of the New Testament. Mill, spent most of his career at Oxford, as Chaplain to Charles II and then as Principal of St Edmund Hall. He published his monumental work *Testamentum Graecum, cum lectionibus variantibus* (Variations in Greek NT texts) in 1707. In comparing these texts, Mill identified over 30,000 variations. Clearly some were more significant than others, many appear to be simple copying errors, others the common practice of adopting overwritten margin notes to "improve" the text but also differences in wording which resulted in changes in meaning – removing uncomfortable phrases or adapting them to conform to accepted dogma.

12.35   Bart Ehrman also comments on the scale of variations, stating that over the succeeding 100 years, the study of further manuscripts increased the volume of scriptural variations identified five-fold to over 150,000.

12.36   The latest analysis of written manuscripts of the NT in Greek, numbering 5778 different documents, has identified over 400,000 variations – which far exceeds the total number of words in the NT – which is only 139,000.

12.37   Textual analysts agree at least 90% of these variations are clearly scribal copying errors, spelling mistakes and other differences of no consequence

– but that leaves around 40,000 variations that are of some consequence.

Subtle edits may also be found

12.38   A good example that I came across is Romans 9:5. Current texts read:
        "Theirs are the patriarchs, and from them is traced the human ancestry of the
        Messiah, who is God overall, forever praised! Amen." But the oldest and best
        manuscripts differ in an important respect, variously as:

        "human ancestry of the Messiah, who is over all. God be forever praised!" and,

        "human ancestry of the Messiah. God who is over all be forever praised."

        NOTE the inclusion of the full stop. Thus when Paul wrote, he DID
        write Jesus had human ancestors, but DID NOT say Jesus was God.
        Hence we come across yet another 5th century edit trying to make Jesus
        into God.

Biblical apologists try to draw teeth by openly acknowledging inconsequential edits

12.39   Most apologists and many bibles accept that the story of the woman
        caught in adultery (John 7:53 to 8:11) is a late edition a few centuries
        after John was originally written. However, this admission is of no
        consequence regarding the doctrine of any denomination and reads
        as absolutely typical of a real life incident that Jesus might have been
        involved in.

12.40   By comparison, apologists refuse to acknowledge that Matthew 28:19 has
        been corrupted, in a rather clumsy fashion, to try to support the doctrine
        of the Trinity – despite overwhelming evidence of its corruption (see Part
        Three chapter 20).

12.41   One must also wonder how very detailed verbatim conversations are
        included in the gospels concerning events when no one was there to
        record the words spoken. It seems highly unlikely various detailed
        conversations would ever have been recorded:

        • the temptation of Jesus in the desert – would Jesus have bragged to
          the disciples how he bested the Devil?

- Jesus conversation with the Samaritan woman at the well recorded as only the two of them being present – did one of the apostles stay behind and do a careful follow up interview with that woman?

- Jesus prayers in Gethsemane just before his arrest – when could Jesus have briefed any of the disciples about the exact words that he prayed during the period that they were asleep? Particularly as very soon afterwards Jesus was arrested.

12.42 The traditional Christian answer falls back on the idea that the bible is the inspired Word of God, that God put thoughts into each author's mind. But this idea is extraordinarily weak – as it then places the blame on God for all the multiple errors and inconsistencies in the Bible. It would seem ridiculous to claim certain passages are divinely inspired but many others originate simply from human authorship and are therefore subject to human vagaries in terms of accuracy.

12.43 The Inerrants position to resolve this is quite interesting, they assert that it is only the original autographs, i.e. the original texts of each book, that were divinely inspired. Which, as everybody agrees we do not have a single original autograph of any book in the Bible, lets the Inerrants off the hook. But it also means that no Christian in the world has an accurate copy of the Bible. I have not found any assessment by Inerrantists of whether the original autographs of any books deemed heretical by Rome might also have been divinely inspired.

Conclusions on authenticity of current NT texts

12.44 Given the evidence of numerous edits made during the early centuries to conform texts with newly dominant dogma and to remove text which supported gnostic or other heretical beliefs, it is indeed quite surprising that so many suggestive phrases have survived.

12.45 That there is widespread agreement within the leading established churches that certain sections of the gospels were added sometime later by other authors, e.g. John chapters 20 and 21; the tale of the woman Jesus saved from stoning (John 7.53 to 8:11); and the last few chapters of Acts. And, of course, the blatantly fake genealogies in Luke and Matthew.

12.46 Serious academic analysis of a number of fundamental doctrinal tenets indicates they were simply invented – including the 'virgin birth' and the bodily resurrection were later additions devoid of factual foundation – if so, then why was Jesus teaching so successful – the revelations will surprise you!!

12.47 One has to conclude that these scriptures cannot be texts written by man but fully inspired by God – even if some parts may be inspired, why would a deity bother to patiently inspire an author but then allow his message to then be corrupted by every copyist, and allow the corrupted versions to dominate?

13

What Jesus did between Crucifixion and Resurrection

13.1   The apostle Peter offers an intriguing explanation of what Jesus did during the period between his crucifixion and his resurrection – he visited Sheol, to give news to the souls of the dead – and following his resurrection he was awarded a promotion from his Father.

13.2   In 1 Peter 3:18-20 Peter describes Jesus activity after death but before resurrection in these terms: *"He was put to death in the body but made alive in the Spirit. After being made alive, he went and made proclamation to the imprisoned spirits, to those who were disobedient long ago."* It would seem likely that Peter's contemporaries would interpret these words as meaning Jesus had descended to Sheol to bring good news to the souls of the dead. The next chapter, 1 Peter 4:6 again refers to the dead having been given the good news *"For this is the reason the gospel was preached even to those who are now dead, so that they might be judged according to human standards in regard to the body, but live according to God in regard to the spirit."*

13.3   The Gospel of the Saviour also refers to Jesus visiting Sheol, with v7 translated as '*Since I have healed those of the world, I must go down to Hades on account of the others who are bound there*'.

13.4   The Second Treatise of the Great Seth similarly describes Jesus descending to Sheol to resurrect the Souls that were there: *The veil of his temple he tore with his hands. There was a trembling that overcame the chaos of the Earth, for the souls that were in the sleep below were released, and they were resurrected.*

13.5   The efforts of conventional theologians to explain why Jesus would visit Sheol are simply risible, and I quote: *most common interpretation takes "the spirits in prison" to be evil angels who were "disobedient in the days of Noah" in that they cohabited with women on earth and fathered a race of giants by them in the days before the Flood (Genesis 6:1-4). For this they were confined by God in a place of punishment, awaiting final judgment in the end times. The other major line of interpretation understands "the spirits in prison" to be unrighteous humans, now dead and confined in hell, who lived in the days of Noah. In the spiritual realm, Christ went to those and preached to them a message of repentance through Noah, a preacher of righteousness (2 Peter 2:5). But they resisted God's longsuffering mercy during the building of the ark and were destroyed in the Flood. This interpretation also fits the wording and immediate context of the passage very well. The reference to human disobedience leading right up to the judgment of the Flood is consistent with the emphasis of Genesis 6. Two factors favour the reference to Christ's preaching through Noah. One is the Greek participle of verse 20, translated "who disobeyed" in the NIV. The grammatical characteristics of this construction (participle in predicate position to an articular noun) indicate that the participle is adverbial in sense rather than adjectival (not "who disobeyed," but "as they disobeyed") and that it describes the time of the main verbal idea, "he preached" in verse 19. The sense then is "Christ went and preached to them, as they long ago disobeyed when God's patience waited in the days of Noah while the ark was being built." This strongly supports the reference to Christ's preaching **through** Noah.* Seriously, this sounds more like a doctoral thesis than a credible explanation. Moreover, it constructs a huge edifice on the highly unlikely assumption it is accessing the authors original text.

13.6   This passage in Peter has provoked much theological debate. Tyrannius Rufinus (340 to 410), a monk, wrote a commentary on the Apostles Creed in which he added "ad inferna" to the description of Jesus 'descent' – effectively changing the meaning from Sheol to the Catholic idea of Hell. This description became popular and was added to the Creed some centuries later.

13.7   Augustine of Hippo (354 to 430) argued that the reference to Jesus descent was more allegory than fact. He claimed that Jesus had spoken 'through' Noah to those who were dead but also said that the question of whom, exactly, Jesus preached to after his death "disturbs me profoundly".

13.8   The development of Catholic doctrine added additional compartments to the afterlife – hades, purgatory and limbo – for details see section

5.162-185. Thomas Aquinas pondered which realm Jesus had visited
and whom he had saved. Martin Luther and John Calvin argued over
whether Jesus had visited hell in order to fully experience the human
condition.

13.9   The Catholic Catechism includes some interesting statements. Clause
630: *During Christ's period in the tomb, his divine person continued to assume both
his soul and his body, although they were separated from each other by death. For
this reason the dead Christ's body "saw no corruption".* This statement is rather
baffling, perhaps the addition of the word 'human' before 'soul' might
clarify it to mean that Jesus divine nature maintained his human nature
(body and soul) so that his body did not decay. The meaning is made
more obscure by Rome's efforts to suppress reference to the concept
that humans contain a binary soul and spirit. This Catholic dogma also
points to a more intriguing suggestion – that Jesus spirit did not leave his
human body after the crucifixion – if his divine spirit was retained with
the body, can we even say that Jesus died? Such is the confusion created
by fake dogma – the Catholic concept that Jesus was fully divine, nay
God himself, as well as fully human. So, what exactly did Jesus present –
a human body, a human soul, a divine soul, a human spirit and a divine
spirit – it must have been a complex economy to manage day to day?

13.10 Clause 632 of the Catechism gives more recognition to Jewish beliefs:
*The frequent New Testament affirmations that Jesus was 'raised from the dead'
presuppose that the crucified one sojourned in the realm of the dead prior to his
resurrection. This was the first meaning given in the apostolic preaching to Christ's
descent into hell: that Jesus, like all men, experienced death and in his soul joined
the others in the realm of the dead. But he descended there as Saviour, proclaiming
the Good News to the spirits imprisoned there.* One can spot deliberate sowing
of confusion here – any Jew would point out that the imprisoned are
the souls, not the spirits – the souls are imprisoned but the spirits have
returned to God. Actually, the above statement acknowledges that Jesus
soul descended to Sheol to give the Good News to the **spirits** (originally
this must have been written as 'souls'). Again, this suggests that Jesus
spirit remained with his body, maybe in a coma, whilst it was his Soul
that descended to Sheol? Again, technically Jesus would not have died
– and for Trinitarians the embarrassment of God 'dying' would also be
avoided.

13.11 Wayne Grudem, a former president of the Evangelical Theological

Society, says the confusion and arguments could be ended by correcting the Apostles' Creed 'once and for all' and excising the line about the descent. However, this would require a new papal Bull of at least 500 pages to explain how a string of former popes had been totally correct but had been misquoted and misunderstood.

Did Jesus gain a promotion upon completing his mission

13.12   Peter's writing indicated that Jesus was promoted after completing his mission on Earth. The early Greek texts of 1 Peter 3:22 imply that only after the resurrection was Jesus granted authority over 'angels, authorities and powers'. Even the Catholic CEI (Italia Episcopal Conference), part of the Vatican, confirms this. It has major implications for the nature of Jesus if he was granted a major promotion after his resurrection on the basis 'mission accomplished' – what was his status beforehand? If Jesus was already God, what was he promoted to? Modern translations finesse this awkward relic away, the authors of the KJV were specifically instructed to deal with such 'problems' by redrafting to align with dogma – so the verse becomes "*Who is gone into heaven, and is on the right hand of God; angels and authorities and powers being made subject unto him.*"

13.13   In addition, the author of the Epistle to the Hebrews (1:3-5), appears to indicate that God created Jesus after the angels and Jesus was only promoted above angels after completion of his mission to Earth. *After he had provided purification for sins, he sat down at the right hand of the Majesty in heaven. So he became as much superior to the angels as the name he has inherited is superior to theirs. For to which of the angels did God ever say, "You are my Son; today I have become your Father"?*

13.14   The above statement from Hebrews appears to indicate that Jesus became 'much superior' to the angels after he had provided purification for sins, i.e. his crucifixion. Moreover, the next verse repeats the heretical reference to Jesus being adopted as a Son 'today' at his baptism. Many attribute the Epistle to the Hebrews to Paul but others questions this. My question is:- how would any author be aware of the details of any promotion Jesus received after his mission?

13.15   At least eight of Jesus apostles (Andrew, Bartholomew, James, John, Judas, Peter, Philip and Thomas) are known to have written texts about his teaching or their missionary works but only a few texts from just three of these were accepted by the Roman church and accepted into the bible. However, whilst most of the Apostles should have witnessed the ascension (if it happened) none of them wrote about it. For the ascension we only have Mark and Luke – neither of whom ever met Jesus.

14

Resurrection or Reincarnation?

14.1   The concept of bodily resurrection contradicts everything we know about the physical realm – ageing and death is a definition of life. Whilst we know resuscitation can happen, either naturally or by medical intervention – this is usually a quick return of a dead body to life and usually for their natural term or less. By contrast, resurrection is held to be the re-clothing of a long dead skeleton with either the body it lost (in Zoroastrianism) so as to enable recognition by friends or even with a shiny new body – in both cases for potentially eternal life. Christian symbolism (and some Christians) believe long buried bodies will literally rise up from cemeteries in an End Times mass resurrection. Catholic treatment of heretics was to purposely burn their bodies and scatter their ashes outside sanctified ground to prevent resurrection, although oddly the Catholic Catechism quaintly reassures readers that cremation will not hinder your bodily resurrection. Quite apart from whether many of us would actually like to return to live in the body we died in, it is not just the biology that makes no sense but the theology too.

14.2   The conventional theology has been driven by two factors – humans prefer to think in anthropomorphic terms and the Catholic desire for control over people's lives. It is more familiar and more comforting to think we will meet our loved ones again in the afterlife and recognise them in the form that we remember them in the prime of *our* lives – we think of our grandparents as grandparents and of our grandchildren as grandchildren. But, unless they had died young, our grandparents would presumably prefer to appear as they did in the prime of their life, similarly our grandchildren would presumably prefer to appear as mature adults, recognisable to their own children – not as young children. So, being physically recognisable is pure fallacy. People imagine paradise as a beautiful place somewhere like Earth – with delicious food freely available. There is no squalor, no poverty and no war. Deep inside we should recognise this is all nonsense – it literally makes no sense!

14.3   In theological terms, the Roman church sought to place itself in a pivotal position – reincarnation of a human spirit into a new body was seen as a threat to its power: if people knew they might return again in a subsequent life, why bother with the church in this life? Therefore any and all texts which referred to reincarnation were destroyed and references in canonised books generally excised or edited.

References to reincarnation by the disciples

14.4   But even the canonised gospels show the clear contemporary acceptance of reincarnation. When Jesus asked his disciples who they thought he was, the answers reveal what most people would have thought at that time: *When Jesus came to the region of Caesarea Philippi, he asked his disciples, "Who do people say the Son of Man is?" They replied, "Some say John the Baptist; others say Elijah; and still others, Jeremiah or one of the prophets." "But what about you?" he asked. "Who do you say I am?" Simon Peter answered, "You are the Messiah, the Son of the living God."* Matthew 16:13-16.

Please note the following:

- Jesus prefaced his question by telling them whom he was, a Son of Man – which means he was reincarnated with full knowledge of his previous life (or lives), the soul of his 'father' (i.e. his previous incarnation) was alive and conscious within his mind;

- All four recorded answers state that Jesus is a reincarnation – of variously John the Baptist, Elijah, Jeremiah or one of the other prophets;

- One, Simon Peter, said he was a Messiah, again we see text edited to create an oxymoron – Peter would never have said Jesus was "the" Messiah, but "a" Messiah – and, if he had, he would not have said "and the Son of God" – because Simon believed in one God and that a messiah could never be born from God.

14.5   Read carefully, even the canonised texts clearly point to Jesus teaching that he came to show us how to save our souls but if we failed and lost them, our souls *not our bodies* would eventually be restored to us at Judgement. But despite Jesus teaching and the force of cold logic, the Roman church decided to claim that belief in reincarnation was a heresy and that our physical bodies faced the chance of bodily resurrection. The church teaches that first, a dead person goes to Purgatory (to be purged of sins) and, if they clean up well, they will be chosen for paradise and a new life including, at some point, resurrection in their own body – but hardened and unrepentant sinners would be consigned to everlasting hell.

14.6   There are numerous references to reincarnation, even in the canonized texts. In John 3:3, Jesus says to Nicodemus: *"Truth, in truth, I say unto you, unless one is born again, he cannot see the kingdom of God."* Nicodemus asked him, *"How can a man be born again when he is already old? Can he re-enter his mother's womb to be regenerated?"*

14.7   Consider the circumstances of this exchange: Jesus and Nicodemus spoke the same language, Aramaic. Nicodemus was not ignorant or illiterate but one of the most cultured religious teachers, a member of the Sanhedrin, the government. Jesus and Nicodemus seemed to have talked at length, maybe John gives us only the most significant passages. Logically, they would have understood each other clearly. The church treats *"being born again"* as merely symbolic, not as pointing to a physical rebirth. However, the text indicates that Nicodemus correctly interprets the meaning as being in a material sense, that he must be born again, after being old, from the womb of a new mother. Jesus then answers Nicodemus: *"You must be begot again"*. The meaning is very clear. The verb "to generate" refers to being born in a physical, carnal sense from the womb, not to moral change. There is no misunderstanding here. And he adds that this *"being born again"*, *"being generated again"* is necessary. Jesus goes on to explain to Nicodemus that the spirit is not born together with the flesh, i.e. in carnal birth (as the Church maintains), but is independent of it, pre-existing before earthly birth and surviving bodily death.

14.8   The interpretation in paragraph 14.7 above is shared by Origen, in his *On Principals* written in 250, refers to the Jewish understanding of the ruah returning to God and the nephesh going to Sheol. Moreover,

Origen wrote of the pre-existence of the soul and that a person's status in their current life would reflect the sins or righteousness in their previous lives. In Origen's view, arguing Jesus and God were of the same substance was heretical. Origen was recognized as a church father but all his works were declared heretical by a Roman Emperor – Justinian in 543, followed by a broader condemnation of reincarnation by the Council of Constantinople in 553.

14.9 Jesus' words in John 3:6 are clear and unequivocal: *"That which is begotten of the flesh is flesh; and what is born of the spirit is spirit. Do not be surprised if I have told you: you must be begot again".* Here too, the words clearly refer to a carnal birth, to generate in a carnal sense, as Nicodemus had perfectly understood, there is no talk of a change in moral outlook, nor of baptism, as the Church teaches. This shows the meaning of Jesus' words has been distorted to support man made dogma. Common sense and logic tell us that the meaning is reincarnation, as understood by the early Christians.

14.10 Another gospel also proves Jesus' apostles knew about reincarnation: *Passing by he saw a man, who was blind from birth. His disciples questioned him, saying, "Master, who has sinned, he or his parents, to be blind from birth?"* (John 9:1-2) The wording of the question reveals the disciples assumed reincarnation:- how could the blind man have already sinned so badly to be born blind? Logically the blindness could only be sins of his parents **or** of the newborn who had sinned *in a prior life existence*. The Torah makes several references to the sins of the father being inherited unto the 3rd and 4th generation – so it was valid to ask if the blind man was blind at birth because his own father or grandfather had sinned. But the reference to "or" for the man himself to have sinned before his birth must point to thinking he was a reincarnation. Conventional Christianity implies God had deliberately made this man blind from birth, to live a miserable life for many decades, purely so that Jesus could come along and do a bit of magic to 'glorify' God? Really?

14.11 Many will also recall an earlier passage in John (5:1-9) where Jesus similarly heals a man blind for 38 years. This passage is suspected as being a late addition. The description of the Bethesda pool building with its colonnade fits a building inaugurated by Emperor Hadrian in 135. Hence it is possible that this passage was only drafted a century after Jesus ministry – which would seem to reduce the weight one might give to the accuracy of the purported conversation. Further it shows evidence of later editing – referring to Jesus claiming he was the Son of God (John 5:25).

14.12 If for the disciples the concept of reincarnation had not been very clear, they would not even have asked this question. Instead they wonder why that man is blind from birth: who has sinned? Him or his parents? Without reincarnation – how could he have sinned in a way to be punished from birth? In order to deny the logical conclusion of reincarnation, Catholic theologians claim this man had sinned in the womb! According to Catholic belief, he had committed such a grave sin in his mother's womb that he had been punished with blindness! So, according to Catholic theology, congenital defects arise from sinning in your mother's womb prior to birth.

14.13 We have another reference in Matthew where Jesus speaks of the prophet Elijah, who according to the prophecies was supposed to be resurrected to prepare the ground for a special messiah. *"Elijah has already come and they have not recognized him; in fact, they did everything they wanted. Then the disciples understood that he had spoken to them about John the Baptist."* (Matthew 17:12-13)

14.14 *"He (John the Baptist) is the Elijah who was to come. Whoever has ears to hear hears."* (Matthew 11:14). The words here too are very clear. Elijah came just before Jesus to prepare the ground for him, but they did not understand that it was him and they killed him. The disciples, on the other hand, who accepted reincarnation, understood perfectly well that Elijah had reincarnated as John the Baptist – the Gospel explains it to us as clearly as possible. Here, too, those who have ears to *indendere intenda* means that not everyone is given to understand it.

14.15 In the Gospel of Thomas, only rediscovered in 1945 and therefore largely exempt from alterations and censorship, it is written: *The disciples said to Jesus, "Tell us how our end will be?" Jesus said "Have you discovered, then, the beginning, that you look for the end? For where the beginning is, there will the end be. Blessed is he that will take his place at the beginning; he will know the end and will not taste death."* Gospel of Thomas 18. Here, Jesus explains that man is caged in the cycle of reincarnations, of rebirths and deaths until he has reached a certain level of awareness, after which his evolution will continue in the spiritual realm, no longer needing to be reincarnated.

14.16   And again, explaining that the resurrection of the flesh is actually reincarnation: *We were passing through an ancient cemetery and one of the disciples asked Jesus: "What remains of these poor dead, besides their bones that go to dust and on what day, those who have died will awaken from their rest and on what day will life and the new world begin again for them?" Jesus then answered: "You have allowed yourselves too distracted by those tombs and bones. What you are waiting for has already happened. But you do not notice it and you continue to say: may the dead rest in peace!"* (Gospel of Thomas 51). Here Jesus is telling his disciples not to wait for these dead to be resurrected – because many will have reincarnated into new bodies already.

14.17   In the Gospel of Mary Magdalene (v.235-236), *Jesus says: It is so, it is necessary to die of many deaths to know the light of birth.* This tells of our experiencing many lives before unifying, whereupon our spirit becomes visible – our light.

14.18   The Gospel of Mary is listed in the Catholic Encyclopaedia from 1904. Large sections of a text were found in the 'Berlin Codex' originally discovered in 1896 but it was only made public in 1983. This may explain the Catholic Encyclopaedia stating there was "no surviving text". Three fragments have also been found – two in Greek (published in 1938 and 1983) and one in Coptic (published 1955).

14.19   Karen King, a professor at Harvard Divinity School, considers the Gospel of Mary provides an intriguing glimpse into a kind of Christianity lost for almost fifteen hundred years...[it] "presents a radical interpretation of Jesus' teachings as a path to inner spiritual knowledge; it rejects His suffering and death as the path to eternal life; it exposes the erroneous view that Mary of Magdala was a prostitute for what it is – a piece of theological fiction; it presents the most straightforward and convincing argument in any early Christian writing for the legitimacy of women's leadership; it offers a sharp critique of illegitimate power and a utopian vision of spiritual perfection; it challenges our rather romantic views about the harmony and unanimity of the first Christians; and it asks us to rethink the basis for church authority" (2003). Explosive stuff!!

References to reincarnation by early Church Fathers

14.20   The 'Church Fathers' of the first centuries shared a clear understanding of reincarnation, including: Justin, Augustine, Herma, Irenaeus, Theophilus of Antioch, Hynesius, Minucius Felix, Hippolytus, Clement of Alexandria, Minucius Felix, Tertullian and Origen.

14.21 In 250, Origen, one of the most important Church Fathers, in the work 'On Principles' explains that souls are assigned to their *"place or region or condition"* according to their actions *"before the present life"*. Origen wrote: *"God organized the universe on the principle of absolutely impartial retribution"*. God did not create *"according to any favouritism"* but *"gave souls a body according to the sins of each one."* This implies one reincarnated life reflects justice based on prior behaviour giving everyone what they deserve, without relying on chance or favouritism.

14.22 Origen asks *"If the soul has not had a pre-existence why are some blind from birth, having not sinned, while others are born without any defect?"* He answers his own question: *"It is clear that some sins existed (that is, they had been committed) before the soul entered a body, and as a result of such sins, each soul receives a reward in proportion to what it deserves."*

14.23 Origen also writes: *"Every soul...she comes into this world strengthened by the victories or weakened by the defeats of her past life."* The reference to reincarnation is obvious and undeniable. The first Christians, the apostles, the Fathers of the Church, firmly believed in reincarnation, consistent with the teachings of Jesus.

14.24 St. Augustine in 'The Confessions', written c400: *"Before that life, O God of my joy, I already existed in some other place or other body"*.

Emergence of denial of reincarnation by the Church

14.25 The historical record shows that the Roman church was well established before it began to deny reincarnation. It was only in 553 that the Byzantine emperor Justinian condemned the theses on reincarnation, three centuries after the death of Origen, proclaiming them heresies at the Second Council of Constantinople – ordering texts supporting it be burnt and those believing to be persecuted. Until then the Christian world had been divided between those who thought the true message of Jesus included reincarnation and those who denied it. From the 2nd Council of Constantinople in 553, the concept of reincarnation was officially banned by the Church and replaced with that of resurrection of dead flesh into the original physical body on the day of the Last Judgment.

14.26   According to the dogma of the Resurrection of the flesh, at the "end of time", after a last judgment, the souls of the good and those of the bad will be reunited with the bodies of the dead and will live forever with these! Thus, the Church forbade the cremation of the dead because otherwise the soul would no longer have a body to which it could be reunited! Later it was realized that, cremated or not, the remains of the deceased will in any case dissolve into dust over time, so now they claim that the bodies of flesh and bones will be recreated from scratch, after the Last Judgment, but they will be incorruptible "flesh" and "bones", destined to last for eternity. This is not the raising (i.e. resurrection) of the old body but clothing the spirit in a new body – which is surely reincarnation, but the Church denies it.

14.27   The concept of reincarnation is rejected by the Catholic Church for obvious reasons. If one were to accept the idea that a soul needs more earthly lives for its spiritual evolution, many dogmas, such as that on eternal damnation, on absolutions made by priests for sins, would be doomed to fail. That is why when the Catholic Church begun to acquire power and control over the ignorant masses, it needed a change of course aimed at excluding this dangerous concept of reincarnation from dogma.

14.28   Denial of reincarnation was reiterated at the 2nd Council of Lyons in 1274 and at the Council of Florence in 1439, condemning the reincarnation as "an ancient pagan idea" and a heresy.

14.29   Having destroyed all early references explaining reincarnation, Catholic denial focused on beliefs of ancient Eastern cultures – that man had been expelled from Heaven and, as a punishment, confined to live eternally on Earth, therefore human life was considered a period of exile. This had led to the belief that man tries to free himself from the ruthless circle of repeated earthly lives that forces him to return to a physical body on earth, a place of pain. Over time, a further distortion arose, of the possibility of reincarnation of a human spirit into an animal body (methempsicosis) as a further punishment for serious shortcomings or sins committed. Thus, Catholic denial rests on denial of two false premises:

- the idea of eternal return as punishment and, consequently, the non-possibility of spiritual evolution

- the idea of reincarnation as a possible fall into an animal species –

methempsicosis

By comparison, the older belief of reincarnation as spiritual evolution relies upon the gradual perfection that takes place by bringing the human spiritual part, to live alternately in the terrestrial and spiritual worlds, to achieve spiritual unity by controlling its freewill.

14.30   The Roman church remains in denial of reincarnation – Statement 1013 of the Catechism states: *Death is the end of man's earthly pilgrimage, of the time of grace and mercy which God offers him so as to work out his earthly life in keeping with the divine plan, and to decide his ultimate destiny. When "the single course of our earthly life" is completed, we shall not return to other earthly lives: "It is appointed for men to die once." There is no "reincarnation" after death.*

14.31   The Church's denial of reincarnation because it insisted mankind has only a single shot at incarnate life and thereby needs the mitigation of the sacraments in order to have any chance of salvation raises a number of theological problems. The Roman teaching is that life is to enable us to grow in righteousness by following the teaching and have faith in eternal life. Whilst sins may be forgiven, flouting the rules and rejecting Catholic dogma will lead to everlasting damnation. Limiting incarnate existence to a single life creates a lottery.

14.32   To grow in faith and righteousness requires a significant lifespan, adequate material resources and a degree of education that trains the brain to think. As a reader of this book, you are part of a tiny minority with the material resources and free time to ponder about the meaning of life and consider how to spiritually evolve. For the mass of mankind, since the beginning, life has been brutal and relatively short struggle – the majority of humanity has always lived in grinding poverty and under authoritative oppression which provides limited education. The absence of social justice undermines the idea of a benevolent God. If a father lavished resources on one child and gave nothing at all to another – all would say he was a bad father. So if God grants a few the time and resources to gain maturity and understanding but most get meagre rations – can we maintain God is benevolent? Church rejection of reincarnation means most humans have little chance to spiritually develop during their single incarnate life. The best option seems to be to die very young, before committing any serious sin – as Jesus said, the young children are pure in heart and easily enter the Kingdom. If so, on this basis, one must question the purpose of having any incarnate life at all?

14.33　By contrast, serial reincarnation seems far more divinely benevolent: even if the soul memories of each life remain inaccessible to those spirits who have failed to graduate, our spirit itself may retain some learning from each incarnation. (This will become clearer after reading the next chapter.)

14.34　The Catechism is convinced that our bodies are resurrected but is unsure how we shall look: Statement 1017 *"We believe in the true resurrection of this flesh that we now possess" (Council of Lyons II: DS 854). We sow a corruptible body in the tomb, but he raises up an incorruptible body, a "spiritual body"* (1Cor 15:42-44).

14.35　As we covered earlier, the Roman church saw a great opportunity for enrichment using its self-proclaimed monopoly on Grace to sell 'indulgences'. These enable you to do a bit of sinning, or prepay on Earth for sinning already done, or indeed pay for prior sins committed by your loved ones currently being tortured in Purgatory. The Catholic church liked the idea of regularly burning people, those it decided were heretics or witches, because as well as accelerating judgment it showed the population just how terrible purgatory would be and how unthinkable the agony of spending eternity in hell. It was a very effective and remunerative marketing strategy.

14.36　Having just read the above, you might be thinking…well, Jesus seems to have resurrected himself? If so, the canonised text also indicates that with resurrection you do get your old body back complete with wounds, etc. That would be a horrific prospect for those who die in war, disasters and accidents. And, again, this makes no sense in biological terms or spiritual terms – why do we need physical bodies in a spiritual afterlife? The Church tries to place the resurrection of Jesus as the central tenet of Christianity – if you do not believe Jesus was resurrected there is no hope.

14.37　Church sermons emphasise the central importance of the resurrection to the faith – so presumably the resurrection is clearly set out in the bible, in the gospels? Well not quite, the most detailed account is in John – two entire chapters, from which the details in many sermons are taken. However, the two last chapters of John (20 and 21) appear to be late additions – the oldest and best manuscripts end at chapter 19. Most Catholic bible commentaries end at chapter 19 – which is really telling. Pope Benedict XVI refers to a verse in John 21 as being "in the appendix" of John's gospel. The author of Acts opens with an executive summary of all he reported concerning the resurrection in the Gospel of Luke – except almost none of the summarised detail is actually in Luke? Indeed, the commentary in Luke and Matthew is meagre and contradictory. Mark originally ended at the discovery of an empty tomb – the body was gone. It is widely acknowledged, including by the NIV, that the last verses Mark 16:9-20 were added in the 5th century. No doubt the additions to John and Mark were well intentioned – but do they reflect truth? It must be salient that, with only two exceptions, I have not found any reference to Jesus resurrection is any of the texts deemed heretical. If one checks two of the most widely used texts in the early church, at least by the number of references to them, the Didache and the Gospel of Thomas, it is noteworthy that neither make any reference at all to the resurrection – a strange omission given the centrality of the redemptive sacrifice in Pauline and later orthodox Christianity? Oh, and the two exceptions are the Gospel of Peter, which gives some unique details of the resurrection, and the Gospel of Philip, which warns readers against believing stories of Jesus resurrection! For most Christians this must be a huge issue.

14.38   By now, I trust the reader is open to consideration of Jesus 'resurrection' as being superfluous to his core message and teaching – the whole idea of the resurrection seems to have been manufactured by the early church (see chapter 4 section I above). The logic of the marketing strategy forced the idea of bodily resurrection: if Jesus was divine he had to be the offspring of God; if Jesus was actually God himself then, even if crucified, he could not really die – as surely God cannot die; therefore Jesus had to be resurrected as visible proof God was still alive.

14.39   Intriguingly, the Catholic Catechism even contains a Statement (630) asserting that Jesus body did not experience decay because *his divine person continued to assume both his soul and his body*. Although it is not internally consistent, as the Catechism tries to argue that humans contain only a single spiritual element which it mainly labels as the 'soul'. In the Statements that follow, the Catechism concurs with the views of James and Peter that whilst his body lay in the tomb, Jesus soul visited Sheol, to bring the gospel message to the souls of those who had already died.

Thus it would seem that Jesus spirit never left his body – if so, then one must consider that Jesus did not die but, maybe whilst in a coma, his soul visited the souls of the dead. (When the body is sleeping, the soul may detach from the body but returns prior to waking, if the spirit departs it causes death and takes the soul with it.) So, what actually happened at the end of the crucifixion?

14.40 Weighing the biblical evidence (we have no other), one is led to conclude that the most likely historical chain of events is that Jesus did not die on the Cross. That must seem an extraordinary claim but let's review what is known concerning the Roman practise of crucifixion.

14.41 Whilst Roman crucifixion was horrifically brutal, people were expected to suffer for up to two days but death was not a foregone conclusion. Roman administration wanted not only to punish but to show how a law breaker would suffer prolonged agony as an object lesson to onlookers. Various contemporary Roman chroniclers wrote describing crucifixion. My dear friend, Alberto Zencanaro, has identified various contemporary sources, including Seneca (1BC-cAD65), Dionysius of Halicarnassus (60BC-7BC), Appian of Alexandria (AD95-165) and Marcus Velleius (c19BC-AD31).

14.42 The writers identified in the paragraph above provide credible contemporary historical detail. In *Consolatio ad Marciam*, Seneca describes in great detail the crucifixion practices of 1st Century Rome. The severest practices were reserved exclusively for slaves. Those condemned to death were required to have a plaque attached identifying the sentencing judge and the title of the section of the legal code condemned under. Dionysius also identified that only condemned slaves were paraded through the town with their arms tied to the crossbar. Appian, a Greek historian wrote in detail describing Roman justice, sentencing, torture and execution during the 1st Century. Marcus Velleius Paterculus was a Roman historian writing of contemporary events whose career after soldiering was as an advocate pleading cases before the courts and who later became a senator.

14.43 These authoritative writings reveal some details that may surprise:

- Pre-crucifixion flogging, carried out with a flagellum (a leather strip with sheep bones and stones set in it) was reserved for use only on slaves;

- The cross upon which convicted were crucified comprised two separate parts – the upright pole (the stipites) set in the ground and reusable, and the cross bar (the patibulum) to which the accused arms were tied with rope;

- The legs of the convicted were normally left to hang – restraining the legs by rope or nails would have provided some relief from the growing pain exerted from the shoulders having to support the body;

- Iron nails were rarely used. Iron was scarce and valuable, its use by the legions carrying out Roman punishments would have been reserved for military purposes – swords, spears, helmets, etc – not wasted on worthless convicts when plentiful supplies of cheap rope would have been available. One exception was the brutal crucifixion of all the rebellious slaves following Spartacus, whose defeat Crassus made a particular spectacle – using nails to further prolong the agony of those crucified.

- Where legs were tied to the stipites, providing a modicum of support to prolong the agony, the legionnaires would break legs after 2 or 3 days to speed up death for those so convicted;

- Those so intended to die would be speared before being cut down – but through the heart to ensure that they were dead, not the side – which would prove nothing;

14.44 The use of crucifixion was **not** primarily a capital punishment but to provide a public spectacle showing prolonged agony could be inflicted in order to deter others from similar crimes. It was noted that those who were cut down after 2 or 3 days always had to be assisted by legionnaires as they could no longer walk. Most then headed for prison although some were released on payment of money.

14.45 To some degree we have all been conditioned by Hollywood (and the church) conflating crucifixion with execution. In reality, crucifixion was not even mainly a capital punishment. Jesus was certainly not a slave and even the gospels are clear that Pontius Pilate did not judge Jesus of being guilty of anything – certainly not serious crimes against the Roman authorities. So, based on the gospel accounts it seems very unlikely that Pilate's sentence of crucifixion was intended as a capital sentence.

14.46   If we then apply Roman custom to gospel accounts of Jesus crucifixion various problems arise:

- Jesus was never said to be a slave – so he would not have been whipped;

- Pilate himself is reported as saying more than once that he saw nothing wrong with Jesus – so any crucifixion sentence would not have been capital punishment;

- Jesus hands would have been tied with rope to a patibulum – so there was no cross to be carried to Golgotha – the stipites would already be there;

- Nails would not have been used in either Jesus hands nor his feet – so no marks would have been visible after his 'resurrection' for Thomas to check;

- If someone had been able to read the plaque affixed to the upright of the cross on which Jesus was crucified, it should have also stated "by the order of Pontius Pilate, under Civil Code # 123 for crime of ???" which surely would have been recorded for posterity?

- The purpose of the spearing was to certify death – so Jesus would not have had a spear in his side;

- Being cut down after only 3 hours, a 33 year old man would certainly not have been dead – it is more likely Jesus had passed out, maybe gone into a coma.

14.47   Roman records show the legion based at Jerusalem at this time was comprised Syriac mercenaries. It is possible that these legionnaires were more susceptible to a bribe by Joseph of Arimaethea to allow Jesus to be cut down 'early' and taken away to Joseph's sepulchre to 'recover'. Maybe not, perhaps Pilate only sentenced Jesus to 3 hours?

14.48   But hang on, why did the gospel writers seem to get so many details wrong and describe Jesus crucifixion the way they did. Surely they would have been familiar with Roman crucifixions and written more accurately? Consider, the three synoptic gospels are generally considered to have been written in the 70's and John maybe in the 90's. This followed the intensifying acts of terrorism against Roman forces by the Zealots which culminated in the Roman campaign from 66 to 70, leading to the destruction of the Temple. Acts of terrorism against the legions may have resulted in crucifixions more like those of Spartacus and his followers – e.g. the use of nails to further prolong the agony. Moreover, it is generally agreed that, apart from John, none of the gospel writers ever met Jesus and certainly were not present at his crucifixion. So, were recent memories of the crucifixion of Zealot terrorists applied to the description of the crucifixion of Jesus which had occurred 40 to 50 years earlier?

14.49   As noted previously, one lie (even an innocent mistake) inevitably leads to other lies to sustain a position. Having described a crucifixion involving nails and a lance through his side, Jesus is then described as appearing with a resurrected body with wounds from nails in his hands and feet and the wound from the lance in his side. Confusingly, Jesus is described as resurrected in his old physical body with the ability to walk, talk; make breakfast and share it with his disciples but also demonstrating the ability to walk through walls – which sounds more like a spiritual manifestation than a person with a body – whether resurrected or not. Luke 24:30-31 also tells us that after Jesus broke bread and gave it to them, he vanished in front of their eyes – however, Luke himself was not present. Likewise, Jesus Ascension is described in a way that sounds spiritual, an ethereal incarnation rising up into the sky – unlike Elijah who boarded a star-ship and ascended in a whirlwind of fire and light. (One is also reminded of *beam me up, Scotty*')

14.50   Does it matter whether Jesus died on the cross? As we have discussed, Jesus told his disciples (and they clearly believed) that he had previously died on Earth and was a reincarnation (see 14.4). The question has been asked, if Jesus did not die, then why did he not go out and start preaching widely again? But actually the same question equally applies if Jesus had been bodily resurrected? One plausible explanation is that Joseph did bribe the officials to get Jesus released and if reports had circulated that Jesus had survived he would have been declared a fugitive from Roman justice and the legions would have been on the look-out for him.

14.51   With limited medical knowledge, those whom Jesus did meet after the crucifixion may have presumed he had been dead when cut down from the cross. The biblical support for Jesus resurrection is actually much weaker than most Christians realise – from an early age the resurrection is described as almost the most important aspect of the faith. Yet, as we have reviewed in 5.189 to 5.194 and in 14.33 above, the coverage in the gospels is sparse and contradictory – and mostly added 4 or 5 centuries later. For those undertaking missionary work, the leader of the faith who had died would surely need to be resurrected – not least in order to be competitive with many other gods being worshipped at that time, who after dying had been resurrected – including Achilles, Hercules, Osiris, Pelops.

14.52   Let's go back to see when and from where the idea of resurrection emerged, as it was not part of Jewish belief until a few centuries after the end of prophetic revelation. It was only around 160 years before Jesus birth, seemingly as a reaction to the harsh rule of Antiochus Epiphanes, that the idea of resurrection became mainstream. Bodily resurrection was a recent idea when Jesus arrived.

14.53   Pre-exilic Judaism held that the role of the body ended at death – dust to dust, whilst the soul continued for eternity in a miserable dark place forever cut off from God. Job, regarded as one of the oldest of all Jewish texts, it states in 7:7-9: *"Remember that my life is a breath; My eye will not again see goodness; a cloud dissolves and it is gone; so is one who descends to Sheol; he will not ascend."*

14.54   However, much later. during the three centuries before Jesus, Judaism was influenced by two alternative belief systems – from Persian Zoroastrianism (which believed in bodily resurrection) and the Greek culture which believed in a joyous afterlife of the soul.

14.55   With roots which may date back as far as 1000BC, Zoroastrianism served as the state religion of Persia from around 600BC until the final defeat by Moslem armies in 654AD. The Zoroastrian view of God is quite appealing. According to Zoroastrianism, God has seven characteristics, being Omniscient, Omnipotent, Omnipresent, Impossible for humans to conceive, Unchanging, the Creator of life and the Source of all goodness and happiness. Zarathustra lived in the 6th century BC and his teaching has clearly influenced Christian beliefs.

14.56   In 539BC, the Persian emperor, Cyrus the Great (Cyrus II) captured Babylon – having already established an empire embracing the whole of modern Turkey, Armenia, Azerbaijan, Iran and most of Pakistan.

Capturing Babylon and its king Nabonidus, brought the entire Neo Babylonian empire under Cyrus control – comprising modern day Iraq, Syria, Lebanon, Jordan and Israel – but not Egypt. With this control over a vast area, the next 200 years (until the rise of Alexander) meant Persian cultural suzerainty. Even so, it was not until long after Alexander had died that Judaism started embracing resurrection and an afterlife – so the causal influence would seem to be very clear.

14.57 The Persian view, which Cyrus shared, seems to have been that the duty of each individual to find the truth, it was not to be imposed. The core belief of Zoroastrianism being the Threefold Path – life's journey should comprise Good Thoughts, Good Words and Good Deeds. There is a heavy emphasis on individuals spreading happiness, being charitable and upholding equality of the genders. Cyrus obviously felt allowing nationalities to worship their own lesser deities spread happiness. In Zoroastrianism, death is followed by bodily resurrection and judgment. Those who, on balance, were found to have been good passing on to pairidáeza (from which we get 'paradise') and the losers going to hell where eventually they are purified in molten metal and reborn cleansed and able to join the good. Apart from a late splinter group in India, influenced no doubt by Buddhism, Zoroastrian beliefs did not embrace reincarnation.

14.58 Zoroastrian belief is that an individual's Soul (*urvan*) exists united with its Spirit (*fravashi*) prior to birth. The fravashi works with the divine Creator and acts as our inspiration, an individual may venerate his ancestral spirits and call upon them for aid during life. Death separates the body, *urvan* and *fravashi* but on the 4th day *urvan* and *fravashi* reunite to assemble the experiences of life in the material world. Thus the binary soul doctrine also sat at the core of Zoroastrianism.

14.59 The Greek concept of the immortal soul which exists without a physical body in another place for eternity, is reflected in the Book of Jubilees and the Wisdom of Solomon – both dated to the 2nd century BC. This concept became part of the beliefs of the Sadducees and the Essenes. Jesus, Peter and James make statements which clarify the distinction between Spirit and Soul (e.g. saving one's soul and avoiding the second death) providing another hint of Jesus potential upbringing in, or later membership of, an Essene community. The possibility of Jesus and his family being part of an Essene community is endorsed by Pope Benedict

XVI in his book *Jesus of Nazareth*, page 14 "*It appears that not only John the Baptist, but possibly Jesus and his family were close to the Qumran community. At any rate, there are numerous points of contact with the Christian message in the Qumran writings. It is a reasonable hypothesis that John the Baptist lived for some time in this community and received part of his religious formation from it.*" By contrast, Paul preaches bodily resurrection, maybe reflecting his beliefs as a Pharisee – and subsequently, the Roman Church inherited the idea of bodily resurrection through Pauline theology.

14.60 It is interesting to trace the evolution in Old Testament scripture of the idea of bodily resurrection. There are three references in post exilic texts and amendments to older texts:

(i) Ezekiel 37 – clearly subject to various later revisions, is interpreted either literally as the resurrection of individuals or of the whole nation of Israel. Annette Evans, University of Pretoria, opined: "The prophetic role played by Ezekiel in his vision of the valley of dry bones in chapter 37 is contentious because he lived at a time when death and an afterlife was not part of the Israelite tradition. It was a long time before Judaism began to explore the concept of resurrection based on the judgments of a person's or nation's conduct". My own view is that Ezekiel is describing the resuscitation of the nation and its faith. After the destruction of Jerusalem and the Temple, the Jews must have concluded Yahweh had died as well. Ezekiel wrote in the immediate aftermath, trying to reassure the Jews. Christians should discount Ezekiel 37 – as regrowing bodies on long dead bones is neither credible nor theologically sound. Why use old bones – would that result in new bodies being recognisable as old people? Would this actually even be resurrection – indeed rather than using old bones in new bodies why not grow new bones as well? Pope Francis was serious in dismissing God as being a magician – nothing we see in the material world operates by magic, so would God 'cheat' by using magic?

(ii) Isaiah 24-26 again seems to refer generally to the restoration of the nation of Israel. Interestingly, the Septuagint translation differs – death is not devoured, "Death, having prevailed, swallowed them up, and God has taken every tear from every face."

(iii)   Daniel 12:2-3 – dated between 167BC and 165BC, contains the only generally accepted clear canonical OT reference to individual bodily resurrection followed by eternal life. In Daniel, the afterlife is firmly on Earth, not celestial or in 'heaven'. Daniel is primarily concerned with the emancipation of Israel from the yoke of oppressive foreign rule under Antiochus Epiphanes who sought to Hellenize Jewish life.

14.61   The Pharisees were the first Jewish sect to believe in bodily resurrection, they were founded in 167BC at a time when various non-canonical works were appearing which referred to bodily resurrection:

(i)   The Book of the Watchers, part of 1 Enoch, dating from 3rd century BC. Enoch describes the souls of the dead waiting in dark chambers for the final judgment. After the final judgment, the Chosen are allowed to eat from the Tree of Life – granting immortality. Clearly, those regaining physical bodies require food. As these physical bodies are not specified as their originals, Enoch may be referring to reincarnation rather than bodily resurrection.

(ii)   The Book of Parables, generally attributed to the reign of Herod or slightly later, talks of the Earth giving back what was entrusted to it (dead bodies) and Sheol likewise giving back the souls of the dead, going on to describe the post mortem life as earthly and physical. It describes the resurrected as the Righteous, who will live in paradise located on Earth, joined by the Son of Man sent by the Lord God of Spirits. Clearly influenced by Persian thought, this may have influenced gospel writers a few decades later.

(iii)   2nd Book of Maccabees, dated to be written between 130BC and 100BC makes a clear reference to bodily resurrection and one may deduce that the resurrected are returned to their old bodies.

(iv)   4th Book of Ezra, dated to around AD100, tells of dead bodies rising from the earth and souls released from the deep, reuniting to live again on Earth.

(v)   2nd Book of Baruch, dated to between AD100 and AD130, tells of similar reuniting of resurrected bodies and souls but specifically states that souls return to bodies with the same appearance as when they died – so they shall be recognizable to all.

14.62　No doubt, during the centuries leading up to the birth of Jesus, the Greek cultural belief in a joyous afterlife for the soul also made the older Jewish idea of Sheol an increasingly difficult sell – it was simply no longer competitive!!

14.63　In the New Testament, Jesus is not the only case of bodily resurrection. The story of Jesus resurrecting the body of Lazarus is the most striking of all the miracles he performed. In fact, it also stands out because it does not fit the narrative taught by Jesus. It may have contributed greatly to the false doctrine of bodily resurrection as a Christian belief. When one starts to dig, it quickly becomes apparent that the story is very closely modelled on the ancient myth of the resurrection of the Egyptian god Osiris.

14.64　The Egyptian 'Book of the Dead' describes the death, entombment and bodily resurrection of Osiris in the ancient city of Anu. Later known by its Greek name, Heliopolis, each year saw the ritual enactment of the death and resurrection of Osiris. Intriguingly, Anu was referred to as the 'place of multiplying bread' whilst Bethlehem means in Hebrew 'the house of bread'. Bethany, were Lazarus was resurrected, means the House of Anu (Beth = house and 'Anu' became 'any').

14.65　The Egyptian story of Osiris was very popular and widely known. Osiris was murdered, living on as a spirit in heaven from where he inseminated his wife, Isis, who gave birth to the great god Horus. Isis managed to gather Osiris body parts and then with Horus proceeded to resurrect his father, Osiris. The three were often considered together, forming a trinity, and are believed to have influenced the Alexandrian school who promoted the idea of the godhead being a trinity to Emperor Constantine at Nicaea.

14.66　The Semitic name for Osiris came from the root Asar – from which is derived the god's name of Ashur, the Assyrian people and the modern country Syria. As Osiris was a god, the Hebrews prefixed Asar with El, and in Greek and Latin the suffix 'us' denoted the individual was male – hence El-Asar-us. In translation the word was run together becoming Lazarus.

14.67　Consequently the raising of Lazarus at Beth-Anu (Bethany) is an obvious copy of Horus raising Osiris (El Asár) at Anu. Two sisters mourned at the resurrection of Lazarus – Isis and Nephthys, guess what:- two sisters mourned for Lazarus – Mary and Martha. **But Jesus did not teach of resurrecting bodies but of resurrecting souls.**

14.68   Thus one might conclude that the story of Lazarus would seem to be a fabrication designed to leverage the story of Jesus miraculous works with a popular contemporary myth. It is surprising that the plagiarism is so blatant. Helmut Koestler, in an article published in the Biblical Archaeology Review in 2009, argues that the story of Lazarus may have been 'developed' from a similar recounting of a resurrection in the Secret Gospel of Mark, which is assessed as written decades prior to the Gospel of John. Given the stunning impact that such a resurrection would have had, it is surprising that all of the synoptic gospels are silent about the event. Whilst John devotes a long section, John 11:1-44, no one is recorded as asking Lazarus the obvious questions that you would ask – what was it like? Tell us what happened during the 4 days you were dead?

14.69   Having revealed crucial elements of Jesus teaching that the church tried very hard, and almost succeeded, in permanently supressing – specifically, that our Spirit may return to live many bodily lives until we learn to listen to and embrace our Soul – many more questions follow. Jesus described those enlightened persons, who managed to 'marry' their Soul, as becoming a Son of Man – to distinguish them from those 'born of woman' whose past life memories are closed, locked away, reviving with their Soul blank, without memories, at the rebirth (reincarnation) of their Spirit.

14.70   The surviving texts indicate that Jesus proclaimed that John the Baptist was a reincarnation of Elijah – see Matthew 11:13-14 and Matthew 17:10-13. With our rediscovered knowledge, Jesus statement in Luke 7:24-28 becomes far more revealing, as verse 28 (NASB) states *"I say to you, among those born of women there is no one greater than John"*. Consciously or not, some translations (e.g. NLB) try to hide this reference by stating *"I tell you, of those who have ever lived..."* – removing the key reference to *"those born of women"*. By referring to John the Baptist as being born of woman rather than as a Son of Man, Jesus is stating that Elijah had not managed to fully embrace his Soul and therefore when the Spirit of Elijah reincarnated as John the Baptist, he had no memory of his prior life as Elijah. If knowledge of Jesus real meaning had been widespread, no doubt such references would have been eradicated by the Church. This issue strikes at the heart of the Roman Church powerbase – namely that saving grace can only be obtained through the church hierarchy – whereas Jesus teaching told of how each of us could save ourselves.

14.71   Today, across the western world, long denial of reincarnation by the church has been followed by the idea being trashed as a concept by wild stories in the popular press. But, historically the belief was widespread across all the earliest civilisations in the Middle East and remains today across much of Asia. Buddhism, Hinduism, Jainism and Sikhism all originated from India and all include belief in reincarnation. The core concept of multiple return missions until achieving enlightenment differs in certain respects from what we can glean from early Christian texts but the fundamental message of multiple reincarnations in pursuit of enlightenment is the same.

Is there any evidence of reincarnation?

14.72   The popular image of reincarnation today, at least in the West, is typically of maybe a social media star claiming to have been, say, Cleopatra, in her former life. We all ridicule such stories but few are aware of serious research that has been conducted to try to establish whether there is any basis for believing in reincarnation? Some of the research undertaken has been extremely rigorous and has identified some intriguing details. For example, work by Professor Ian Stephenson, who was head of the Psychology Department at the University of Virginia for an amazing 50 years – from 1957 until his death in 2007. In 1997, Professor Stevenson's published his Magnum Opus, a massive 2,268 page, two volume work entitled *Reincarnation and Biology* which included over 3,000 case studies he had collected.

14.73   A number of issues stand out from Professor Stephenson's work. Firstly, the sheer volume of detailed case studies – over 3,000 painstakingly researched over 30 years. Secondly, the structured academic approach seeking to avoid unsubstantiated or unproveable claims. The overwhelming majority of these cases involved children, who had casually identified numerous specific details of a previous life – itself cut short in childhood. Although appearing to be totally unconnected with the location and experiences of their current life, they were able to vividly describe many details of people, locations and events in a previous life which were then verified as factually accurate.

14.74   One might speculate that in early life, our relatively innocent Spirits hold close our Souls and information might be shared from a previous incarnation, as we age and our Spirit becomes more assertive, it begins to push away the civilising influence of the Soul and we are led inevitably towards a second death, when our Soul will separate from our Spirit. Thus it may be possible that innocent young children who suffer death or murder at a young age still have Spirits which hold their young Souls close, avoid the second death and return united with, at least, their immediately prior Soul – and thereby retain a vivid memory of their previous short life.

14.75   One unexpected and somewhat disturbing characteristic of many cases which seem to be examples of reincarnation, is the frequency of congenital defects seemingly reproducing prior life accidents or mutilations that had been suffered. It is both very disturbing and very surprising that an injury suffered in one life might be 'inherited' in the next incarnation. Early in his research, Stevenson spotted that many who remember past lives had birthmarks or birth defects that corresponded to wounds, usually fatal, on the person whose life was remembered.

14.76   As a Western medical professional, Stevenson realized that the idea that wounds on a deceased person can influence the embryo of a later-born, and completely unrelated, baby was an outrageous proposition. Yet, he found many such cases and collated photographs to support the claim. I refer anyone wishing to follow this up to the case study published by Stephenson listed in the Bibliography, as well as other books he has published. Stephenson is not alone in publishing material on scientific appraisal of reincarnation – but his work seems the most thorough and therefore the most mentally thought provoking.

14.77   Cases studied by Stephenson suggest that a Spirit whose young body is accidentally injured or whose murder involved mutilation may re-emerge 5 to 10 years later, in the broad vicinity (a number of cases were within 100 miles) with the same defect – missing fingers on the same hand, missing foot from the same leg, etc. This is absolutely not what one would expect occurs in a reincarnation – either spiritually or biologically. It implies that the Spirit may have some control over the material body –

in effect, overruling ones DNA and commanding the body not to grow fingers it had lost in its previous incarnation. This would illustrate the proverbial Mind over Matter. Why, the Spirit might decide to replicate the deformity in its new body is not easy to fathom.

14.78 One must assume that these cases of children returning with defects from a previous incarnation are exceptions to the rule – otherwise most of humanity would have accumulated a horrific collection of debilitating mutilations over millennia of life on this planet.

14.79 If the Spirit can command changes to the DNA coding for the body, it might explain other puzzles. Before I knew better, it always struck me as very disappointing that Jesus was resurrected still retaining the wounds from his crucifixion. When the church teaches of resurrection, it generally implies those resurrected get fresh new bodies – that miraculously do not subsequently age! However, the only example that the Church can provide evidence of is rather depressing – what if we are resurrected with crippled and aged bodies – it doesn't sound very appealing. However, if some Spirit's, i.e. those of great purity, can control their DNA – it might explain how Jesus could affect miraculous healing – through his Spirit entering the subject's body and commanding its DNA to undertake repairs. Of itself, this power does not mean Jesus is God, the Designer of our Universe – but it does make him very special indeed.

15

Truth revealed – what Jesus really taught

15.1 Most readers will find this chapter very surprising, I myself was astonished by what I found – particularly by the fact that this understanding is even available for anyone to find. It will probably take some days for the full import of this radical understanding to fully sink in – it may raise many questions in your mind. Many nights, I lay awake for hours pondering whether it could be true – but the amount of supporting evidence is surprising.

15.2 We have reviewed the thoroughness with which texts deemed 'heretical' were ruthlessly destroyed by the Roman church – to the extent we know of dozens of titles of once revered texts of which not even partial copies now remain. We feel the pain from the destruction of the Library of Alexandria (quoted as holding 500,000 manuscripts) and also the destruction of the ancient Sabian library of Harran and the early Christian library of Caesarea (quoted as holding 30,000 texts). But armed with new understanding, you will be astonished to find unedited traces of the original knowledge in plain sight – buried in the canonical books of the New Testament.

Humans comprise a Trinity, not God

15.3 To understand Jesus revolutionary message to humanity, one has to first study the cultural background 2000 years ago. Sumerians, Egyptians, and subsequently Israelites, had shared the same deep understanding of humanity for many thousands of years. The core belief is that each human contains a spirit, which is immortal and departs the human body at death. The body is transitory and of fleeting existence – very much 'dust to dust'. However, there is a third force, our soul – which contains all our personal memories, our personality, our emotional responses and the essence of what makes us an individual.

15.4   Bodily death releases our spirit and the soul departs with it, however, unless our spirit has embraced and unified with our soul during our life – the two go separate ways. This separation, depriving our spirit of all knowledge of our mortal life, is referred to as the second death. The use of the term 'death' is in relation to our soul, the repository of our personality and memories, which was understood to be lost forever, consigned to silent darkness, a place referred to as Shoel in Judaism. Sheol is mentioned 65 times in the OT, but of course invariably translated as something else: 'pit' (3 times); 'grave' (31 times); and 'hell' (31 times). Psalm 6:5 is typical; *"For in death there is no remembrance of You, in Sheol who can give You thanks?"* (Because in Sheol, you are cut off even from God.) Also, in particular, see Psalms 89:48, Ecclesiastes 9:10 and Isaiah 38:10 and 38:18. It is possible that these translations of Sheol were deliberate – to move away from talking of the Soul to a more general destination of the wicked. Perhaps the Roman church was concerned that believers would feel some comfort knowing whatever happened their Spirit would return to God after death.

15.5   The second death is referred to a number of times even in canonized biblical texts – but all knowledge of its meaning was suppressed. The concept of the second death was well known in Jesus' time, but no one had ever suggested that the effect could be reversed. The Egyptians devoted enormous resources trying to work out and plan to prevent this second death and separation – which they believed to be permanent. This Egyptian belief is most graphically demonstrated in the design of the Giza pyramid. Entering the internal structure of the pyramid there is a declining passageway descending down below the bedrock to a roughly hewn claustrophobic dead-end – illustrating the destination of the body. Before reaching the bedrock, there is an upward sloping passageway illustrating the separation of the spirit and the soul from the dead body. Soon afterwards there is another split representing the second death, the separation of spirit and soul. A gently downward sloping passageway ends in another dead-end, this time expansive and decorated, indicating the destination of the soul, whilst the passageway continuing upwards has enormous fluted ducts reaching up indicating the release of the spirit into the afterlife. The design admits the possibility of escaping the second death and of both *ba* and *ka* ascending to paradise united.

15.6   A number of pharaoh's incorporated the concept of being a reincarnated soul into their throne names. The significance of the ka name being that they had previously united their *ba* and *ka* thereby reincarnating as a Son of Man (to use the title Jesus applied). One example is Pharaoh Senusret I, half-brother to Sarai (Abraham's wife), whose name meant "he whose previous births live". Some pharaohs used the title 'Setekhy' meaning "repeater of births". Other pharaohs adopted throne names or Horus names pointing to their reincarnated soul, e.g. Nebka – meaning Lord of the Ka, the soul reincarnated; Neferkare – meaning the beautiful Ka of Ra, the spirit of Ra reincarnated

15.7   Egyptians, and Chinese, believed that it was possible for individuals to escape the second death thereby immortalizing their memories in the afterlife with the possibility of later reincarnating aware of their past lives. These cultures put enormous emphasis on preparations to help those released from their mortal body to remain united with their Soul.

15.8   The Sumerian epic of Gilgamesh, very popular literature for literally thousands of years, is a dramatic tale of the spirit and soul battling to avoid the second death in order to achieve immortality.

15.9   Other cultures saw the second death as inevitable and focused on their spirit remaining immortal, returning to God. The Hebrew faith shared a similar understanding of having a spirit (*ruah*) and a soul (*nephesh*). However, whilst they believed they were the chosen people of God, after death their personalities and all their memories were cut off, their soul forever committed to Sheol. Sheol was believed to be a place of endless darkness where both the righteous and the evil end up, cut off from God and where they remain for all eternity. This is reflected in the writings of Origen of Alexandria (184 to 253) one of the most prolific and most revered of the early church fathers – Origen believed in the reincarnation of the Spirit but ruled out reincarnation of the Soul, cleaving to the Jewish belief that the Soul is lost forever. Origen was later condemned as heretical because he taught reincarnation of the spirit.

15.10   In India, the cycle of rebirth providing the opportunity to attain perfection has underpinned the culture from time immemorial.

15.11 Now let's look at some key aspects of this understanding, which is often, somewhat confusingly, referred to as the Binary Soul Doctrine. Confusing because we do not have two souls but there can, and ideally should, be a binary relationship between our spirit and our soul.

15.12 Having read this far, you may be beginning to wonder if the author of this book is a crank – so let me electrify you. One of Jesus recorded sayings is *"Your spirit belongs to God, but your souls belong to me"*. What, I can hear you say!! I do not recognize that statement, where does it come from and what does it mean? Let me tease you just a moment longer – the source text was written by Jesus' twin brother.

15.13 You may be thinking what evidence is there for this idea that ancient cultures shared a common belief in people hosting a soul and a spirit. Well, let's start with language – unlike the modern world where the terms soul and spirit are confused and used interchangeably, the concepts were well defined in ancient times:

The Spirit (*aka the light*)	**The Soul** (*aka the image*)
Conscious Spirit	Unconscious Soul (aka Mind)
Left brain	Right brain
Freewill and intellect	Absorbs & emanates Emotions
Is a person's life-force	Contains your Memories
Departure of Spirit = death	Soul can have out of body experiences

15.14 All ancient cultures shared this common understanding:

	The Spirit	**The Soul**
Egyptian	ba	ka
Mesopotamia	napistu	zaqiqu
Canaanite	nps	th
Jewish	ruah	nephesh
Persian	fravashi	urvan
Indian	atman	jiva
Chinese	hun	po
Greek	psyche	thymos

15.15 One aspect which affects understanding is exactly when conception becomes a new individual. For example, Zoroastrian belief is that an individual's Soul (*urvan*) exists united with its Spirit (*fravashi*) just prior to birth, others believe the spirit and soul are drawn to attach during gestation. Some believe the physical body unites with the spiritual after birth – either at the cutting of the placenta or at the point the new born begins to breathe independently – hence a still born baby may be so because it has not received a Spirit or Soul.

15.16   There is some suggestion that the new-born may be initially united, the wide eyed and innocent, which Jesus indicated were able to enter the Kingdom of Heaven more easily. As we grow, we begin to scheme and lie, thus begins the separation of our Soul from our Spirit. The Kingdom of Heaven being a state existing within our minds.

15.17   The Book of the Dead, a collection of ancient Egyptian funerary and ritual texts, copies of which have been dated back to 2400BC, describes in great detail how to meet the challenges of the afterlife. The Egyptian belief was when the body died, its soul known as ka (body double) would dwell in the Fields of Aaru whilst the ba (spiritual personality) would go to the Kingdom of the Dead.

15.18   The Egyptian belief in the immortality of the soul existed millennia before Judaism, Hellenism, Hinduism, Buddhism, Christianity and Islam. According to Herodotus, the Greeks adopted belief in the immortality of the soul from the Egyptians: *"The Egyptians also were the first who asserted the doctrine that the soul of man is immortal . . . This opinion, some among the Greeks have at different periods of time, adopted as their own."* The Greek philosopher Socrates (470-399BC) travelled to Egypt to consult the Egyptians on their teachings on the immortality of the soul. Upon his return to Greece, he imparted this teaching to his most famous pupil, Plato.

15.19   The Israelites believed that their Spirit came from and, after death, reunited with God but their Souls went down to a dark place, Sheol, forever cut off – even from God. This eternal loss of existence, applying equally to the righteous and the wicked seemed unjust and in the Maccabean period (2nd century BC) led to Jewish theologians, no doubt influenced by Persian ideas, developing the notion of an end times revival of the souls of the righteous, with some arguing they gained new bodies. Whilst resurrection was supported by the Pharisees, at least the resurrection of souls if not necessarily of bodies, the Sadducees firmly rejected such new-fangled ideas and maintained that Souls remained in Sheol forever. Greek thinking differed, the Spirit (*psyche*) is permanently frozen at death but the Soul is judged and enjoys options – the wealthy, the famous and the righteous go to the best place, the victorious and courageous warriors who die in glory enjoy the Elysian Fields, etc.

15.20　In his *Original Christianity*, Peter Novak also identifies adherents of the Binary Soul Doctrine amongst the native peoples across the Eurasian landmass, across North and South America and even in Australia.

15.21　For a belief that is absolutely not self-evident, it seems quite extraordinary that it seems to have been culturally adopted, in ancient times, in all corners of the world. Does this evidence indicate that these native peoples were the remnants of an ancient worldwide civilisation that had somehow arrived at this belief in a dual spiritual existence within humans?

15.22　One explanation is that Jesus, or one of his fellow unified soul/spirits, came to Earth in the past, teaching early human civilisations how to live. Perhaps the earlier teaching took place prior to the climatic upheavals of the Younger Dryas Period – that would account for the worldwide memory of the binary soul doctrine. Perhaps a return visit to Earth was justified on the basis that a natural disaster had largely wiped out human civilisation.

15.23　A more extraordinary but theoretically possible origin is the idea that human visitors from elsewhere taught this far from obvious belief. Throughout this series, we have been open minded about the possibility that extra-terrestrial visitors, probably human because of their exploits, engaged with the ancient cultures. The binary soul doctrine seems far too sophisticated to have just emerged and gained a worldwide understanding in hunter gather societies. The doctrine seems more plausible as the knowledge of an advanced technological society. Indeed, it is only in the past century that psychologists have developed theories about the operation of our brains that dovetail very well into the binary soul doctrine of two complementary parts of the mind focused on the same division of tasks as attributed to the soul and the spirit.

15.24　In fact, it is a little unnerving to compare the descriptions of the two spiritual halves of the binary soul doctrine with modern psychoanalytical explanations of the functions of the two halves of our brains – our conscious left brain spirit initiating and leading our actions and our unconscious right brain soul – our conscience defining our morality, counselling us and judging what we do.

Jesus core message

15.25 It was into this cultural context that Jesus came and his teaching was revolutionary. Jesus taught that belief and application of his teaching would provide true freedom and the salvation of the soul. The Good News for the Jewish was, firstly, that by living righteously in this life it was possible to avoid the second death – avoid going to Sheol. And, the power to do so rested in each person. Secondly, if one failed, you got a second chance later – Jesus taught that souls would be resurrected from Sheol.

15.26 This teaching was dynamite for the Jews – death was not the end of their memories, their personalities would become immortal, and, if they followed Jesus teaching closely in this life, they could avoid Sheol entirely. Likewise, within Greek culture, Jesus message was immediately understood and had a dramatic impact on thinking.

15.27 Jesus taught that there was a solution to the problem everyone knew they had – even if they died the second death, now there was a future awaiting them. As Jesus is quoted in John 11:25-26, *Jesus said to her, "I am the resurrection and the life. He who believes in me will still live, even if he dies. Whoever lives and believes in me will never die."* Very clearly, Jesus was not saying that the individual would not suffer a mortal death, but that they could, by following Jesus teaching, avoid the second death and enjoy immortality – they could succeed where Gilgamesh failed. Moreover, even if one fails in this life, Jesus promised the future resurrection of the soul and its reunion with its spirit. Many believed that it was possible to avoid the second death but few believed anything remained if one failed.

15.28 The New Testament has a number of references which suggest there were two teachings, the public message and some teaching that Jesus reserved for his apostles. Mark 4:10-12 records a discussion between Jesus and his disciples in which they question his use of parables and Jesus responds by explaining that some secret knowledge has been imparted to them which many others do not understand: *When he was alone, the Twelve and the others around him asked him about the parables. He told them, "The secret of the kingdom of God has been given to you. But to those on the outside everything is said in parables so that, they may be ever seeing but never perceiving, and ever hearing but never understanding; otherwise they might turn and be forgiven!"* The same discussion is also related in Matthew 13:10-13 and Luke 8:9-10. In the

Gospel of Thomas, Jesus explains he manages the different messages through different 'hands': *Jesus said "I disclose my mysteries to those who are worthy of my mysteries. Do not let your left hand know what your right hand is doing."* Gospel of Thomas 62. Paul also refers to two levels of teaching: milk for the babes and the strong meat for the spiritually mature (e.g. 1 Corinthians 3:1-3).

15.29 The orthodox church saw the secret teaching as undermining its authority, accurately labelling such teaching as gnostic (secret or esoteric) but declaring all such matters heretical.

15.30 In life, the soul is regarded as submissive, feminine, dominated by the masculine spirit exercising freewill. It is your Soul (often referred to as your conscience) that will suggest that you treat your neighbour as you treat yourself. By acting in love towards others, your freewill Spirit is curbing its will and bending to follow the teaching of your Soul, when your Spirit fully embraces your Soul – the Two become One. Once this occurs, you are not only immortal but begin to awaken the memories of all your past lives – i.e. unify with your past life souls. Your spiritual father awakens within your head.

15.31 Jesus taught that the path to unity in this life, to make your spiritual two become one, was to apply his teaching – basically to love your neighbours (all of them) as you love yourself. The extra bonus is that if one achieves this in life, somehow in ways we cannot understand, some force of Jesus himself, maybe his Soul, can permeate any human soul ready to help the process of methodical absorption of our souls from our previous lives. This makes a crucial difference – as it will be very traumatic to discover our memories from a single previous life co-habiting our mind alongside our current personality, relationships, agenda, etc. The fact that we may have hundreds or even thousands of past life souls to absorb suggests a huge challenge awaits us.

15.32 If we achieve unification of Soul and Spirit, our body still dies but we avoid the second death – what happens then is unknown – maybe we come back as Jesus did, as a Son of Man, maybe we have options, maybe we get tasks allocated by the Divine Designer – we will be amazed when we find out.

15.33 Conventional Christianity teaches that after death we wait and after his second coming, Jesus will resurrect the dead for judgment, but his salvation will enable our entry to the Kingdom of Heaven. However, looking closely at the canonized bible texts it seems that Jesus stated a number of times that the Kingdom of Heaven was already here, it arrives the moment we open our Soul to receive it. Jesus taught the Kingdom of Heaven is already present in our hearts. At the beginning of his ministry, Mark 1:14-15 records: *Jesus came into Galilee, preaching the gospel of the kingdom of God, and saying, "The time is fulfilled, and the kingdom of God is at hand: repent ye, and believe the gospel"*. Similarly, in Matthew 4:17 *From that time Jesus began to preach, and to say, Repent: for the kingdom of heaven is at hand.*

15.34   When preaching in the synagogue and reading from Isaiah the prophesy of the coming Kingdom of God, Jesus closes by stating *"This day is this scripture fulfilled in your ears"* Luke 4:21. In Luke 11:20 Jesus is recorded stating: *"But if I with the finger of God cast out devils, no doubt the kingdom of God is come upon you."*

15.35   The Gospel of Thomas states even more plainly that the Kingdom of Heaven has already come: if you adopt Jesus teaching, and for you the Two become One, united you immediately enter the Kingdom of Heaven:- *He said to them, "What you are looking forward to has come, but you don't know it."* Gospel of Thomas 51. And again: *When asked by his disciples "When will the Kingdom come?" Jesus said "It will not come by waiting for it. It will not be a matter of saying 'here it is' or 'there it is'. Rather, the kingdom of the father is already spread out upon the Earth, and men do not see it."* Gospel of Thomas 113.

15.36   Unfortunately, for the vast majority of humans, we fail to love our neighbours as ourselves, thus we will experience the second death and separation of soul from spirit. Once dead, we lose the ability to unite – separated from our Spirit, containing our free will and intellect, our Soul has no power to reach out but can only rely upon habit and memories. *Jesus said, "Look for the living one while you are alive, lest you die and seek to look for him then and find you do not have the power to look."* Gospel of Thomas 59.

15.37   Jesus also gave interesting insight into how we will perceive the Father, who as noted elsewhere (15.86 to 15.97), may or may not be the Creator God. It seems that after the second death, which occurs for most of us, our Spirit remains aware of its Soul (containing the memories of all its past lives) but sees it as an inert and lifeless 'image'. Jesus contrasts our bodily existence when we see the 'image' of others, their personalities but not their spirits which remain hidden, with the afterlife where we do see Father's spirit, but the brilliance of his light obscures his image (soul). Apparently, the Father also exists as a duality – comprising a 'light' and an 'image'. Our Spirits are drawn to the light of the Father which is so bright as to hide his image. *Jesus said, "Images are visible to people, but the light within them is hidden. The image of the Father's light will be disclosed, but His image will be hidden by the light."* Gospel of Thomas 83. It seems God is a Duality, a spirit (light) and a soul (image), not a Trinity.

15.38   All is not lost however, Jesus also taught that his mission was to save the souls which suffered the second death. At some point, when is unclear, these souls will be resurrected and brought to open Judgment. At Judgment, the Souls (one from each mortal life) of each Spirit are all resurrected (from the dark locked depths of our Soul) and invade our awareness simultaneously. This is likely to be a horrifying experience, as all our unleashed past life Souls chastise and punish our Spirit for the sins it has committed. Each mortal life our Spirit experiences in which it fails to embrace its Soul, compounds the tribulations at Judgment – when your Spirit is eventually reunited with the Souls from each of your sinful lives. For our Spirit this must be quite a sobering thought.

15.39   The first thing Jesus taught us was that if you can unite your Spirit and your Soul you become a Son of Man, whole and perfect, like him. Gospel of Thomas 106 records: *Jesus said "when you make the two become one, you will become the Sons of Man"*. Jesus is explaining that he personally had previously lived in a mortal body but had united his Spirit with his Soul and, when dying, had escaped the second death – the definition of his frequently self-proclaimed description as "a Son of Man".

15.40   The alternative, which happens to the overwhelming majority of us, is that we suffer the second death and when our Spirit is reborn, it is united with a new blank image within our Soul, devoid of any memories, a state Jesus described as being 'born of woman' – code for being a <u>divided duality</u>. The description 'born of woman' Jesus even applied to John the Baptist. John was described as the greatest amongst those born of women – Luke 7:28 and Matthew 11:11. In the Gospel of Thomas 46 the quote extends to add: *"But I have said that whoever among you becomes a child* (innocent and united) *will recognize the Father's kingdom* (within themselves) *and will become greater than John."* Given the evidence that the Gospel of Thomas was circulating long before either Luke or Matthew had been written, the source is clear and the later truncation of the quote might reflect a lack of understanding outside the apostolic circle.

15.41 Jesus taught that he would help those who believed by 'whispering' to their soul, to help our soul tame and pacify our spirit. In the canonized gospels, Jesus is recorded as saying that his Father had 'given' him those who follow him. In gospels banned by Rome, Jesus quoted more specifically, as in the Gospel of Thomas saying 100: *They showed Jesus a gold coin and said to him "Caesar's men demand taxes from us". Jesus said to them "Give Caesar what belongs to Caesar, give God what belongs to God and give me what is mine".* This verse is explosive for Roman doctrine – firstly Jesus is clearly stating he is not God and secondly that whilst our Spirits belong to God, our Souls belong to Jesus.

15.42 At face value, Jesus message about how to save our soul and how he would help us to do so required teaching the good news and supporting life coaching which focused the early church on assisting the poor and sick in society and generally loving others – rather than raising funds for impressive places of worship and lavish accommodation for the priesthood.

15.43 The importance of our soul is set out in detail in the Gospel of Thomas and referred to in many other texts – including The Holy Book of the Great Invisible Spirit, The Apocryphon of James, The Exegesis on the Soul, Gospel of Philip, Gospel of Mary, Gospel of Truth, The Book of Thomas the Contender and The Tripartite Tractate. Of course, all these texts were later ruled heretical by Rome and almost all copies destroyed. The Gospel of Thomas is referred to in numerous early church writings, so we know that originally it circulated widely and indeed is even quoted by Paul. Yet until the middle of the 20th Century, no copies were known to have survived the Roman church's purge. It was known to be a collection of Jesus sayings. Initially, a Greek copy of 20 sayings was found, and at Nag Hammadi a complete text of 114 sayings, written in Coptic was recovered.

15.44 The message of Jesus teaching in the Gospel of Thomas and other important early texts that were almost completely destroyed, differs markedly from the Pauline tradition in the most important aspect. The teaching recorded in Thomas focuses on people being able to save themselves by making the Two become One (i.e. enable your Spirit to embrace and unite with your Soul); with Jesus telling us how to live so that we could avoid the second death, avoid losing our memories and thereby ensure that our personal memories and selves become immortal. If we fail to achieve this, then at the end times we face a horrific mental battle as all our past souls are reunited with our spirit simultaneously – and they (not God) judge us harshly. *'And Jesus said, "When you see your image (unite with your Soul), you rejoice. But when you see your images (your previous souls) which come into being before you (i.e. from your previous lives), and you neither die nor become manifest, how much (pain) will you have to bear!"* Gospel of Thomas 84.

15.45   The absolute conviction that took many believers to martyrdom may be understood to reflect their belief that having adopted Jesus teaching and given all their worldly goods to the church – their spirit and their soul would be unifying – so when martyred they escaped the second death and achieved immediate immortality.

15.46   As we have seen, Greek culture had a muddled view of the role of soul and spirit whilst there is no clear evidence that Roman culture had absorbed the ancient concept of a soul and a spirit. Therefore, it is possible that Jesus references to his being a Son of Man and not born of woman might also have contributed to the growth of the idea of a virgin birth.

15.47   Surprisingly, evidence remains in the canonical texts of the centrality of the 'binary soul doctrine'. James states in 1.15 *"When lust has conceived, it gives birth to sin and when sin is accomplished it brings forth death."* Sin is spiritual not material. Sin does not cause bodily death but death of the soul (at least its separation from our Spirit). In verse 1:21 James continues: *"Therefore, putting aside all filthiness and all that remains of wickedness, in humility receive the **Logos** implanted, which is able to save your souls."* Clearly, Jesus is saving souls not bodies, and his teaching helps the soul unite with the spirit. And, the last verse, James 5:20, states *"he who turns a sinner from the error of his way will save his **soul** from death and will cover a multitude of sins."* James is stating that Jesus saves our soul, our personality, from the second death and from the torment by that soul for those sins we had committed. In contrast, when James writes about people's relationship with God, he states: *"He (God) jealously desires the Spirit which He (God) has made to dwell in us"* – for context read James 4:4-8. James is unequivocally saying our freewill, our Spirit, belongs to a jealous God who desires to have it returned.

15.48 After discussing the need for works, faith without works is nothing, in 2:26 James states *"For just as the body without the Spirit is dead, so also faith without works is dead."* James is clearly describing the body, soul and spirit as separate and distinctive. We know many people have described 'out-of-body' experiences – e.g. some describe rising above and looking down at their own body during a medical operation whilst under anaesthetic – the Soul can temporarily wander from the body but not the Spirit – when the Spirit departs our body, we are dead.

15.49 Peter also makes a clear reference to Jesus role in relation to our souls. In 1 Peter 2:25 he notes: *"For you were like sheep going astray, but now you have returned to the Shepherd and Overseer of your souls"*. Jesus guides our souls and they belong to him.

15.50 The contrast is clear when referring to our Spirit. In Paul's 2nd epistle to the Corinthians, he wrote: *"God put his Spirit in our Hearts"* (1:22) and *"God has given us the Spirit as a deposit"* (5:5). Some OT texts also follow the older belief *"and the dust returns to the ground it came from, and the spirit returns to God who gave it"* as in Ecclesiastes 12:7. Psalm 146 describes death as the body returning to dust, the Spirit departing (returns to God) and that very day ones' thoughts perish as the soul (Hebrew *nephesh*) descends to Sheol, cut off from God for all eternity. Paul knew the three-part human entity, in 1 Thessalonians 5:23 he wrote: *"May God himself, the God of peace, sanctify you through and through. May your whole spirit, soul and body be kept blameless at the coming of our Lord Jesus"*.

15.51 In 1 Corinthians 2:9, Paul seems to directly quote Gospel of Thomas 17, with Jesus saying he will give us what has never occurred to the human mind. The whole of Paul's chapter is clearly written from the perspective of God being the source of our Spirit and Jesus focusing on the mind (i.e. our Soul). In 2:12, Paul writes that *"What we have received is the Spirit who is from God, so that we may understand what God has freely given us."* In 2:16 Paul refers to us having the 'mind' of Jesus, which may be taken as Jesus soul being linked to ours in ways we cannot understand. Conventionally, Paul's quote has been linked to Isaiah 64:4 but the reference is partial and out of context, Paul is clearly writing from the perspective of humankind hosting dual spiritual forces. Paul's quote in 2:9 is almost identical to Gospel of Thomas saying 17 – which points towards:

(i)   Paul regarding the Gospel of Thomas as highly authoritative;

(ii) The Gospel of Thomas being authored and in circulation so that it was widely accepted before Paul wrote the First Epistle to the Corinthians – generally dated to 53 or 54;

(iii) Therefore, the Gospel of Thomas is likely to be the earliest NT text that we have – and accordingly (a) plausibly written by Judas Thomas, and, (b) something dated so early is more likely to be authentic.

15.52   John also wrote of our two spiritual elements dividing after death if they have not united during our lifetime. In Revelations 2:11, John wrote in a style reminiscent of the Gospel of Thomas: *"Whoever has ears, let them hear what the Spirit says to the churches. The one who is victorious will not be hurt at all by the second death."* And again in Revelations 21:8 John wrote *"But the cowardly, the unbelieving, the vile, the murderers, the sexually immoral, those who practice magic arts, the idolaters and all liars—they will be consigned to the fiery lake of burning sulphur. This is the second death."*

15.53   The then contemporary understanding of both the existence of soul and spirit and the close unity that is ideally formed between them are also reflected in Hebrews 4:12: *"For the word of God is living and active, sharper than any two-edged sword, piercing to the division of soul and of spirit, of joints and of marrow, and discerning the thoughts and intentions of the heart."*

15.54   Despite the clarity of both the Jewish scriptural heritage and statements surviving in canonised New Testament texts, the church has been remarkably successful in suppressing the idea that humans have two spiritual components. The Catholic Catechism specifically denies the existence of two spiritual elements. Statement 367 admits *Sometimes the soul is distinguished from the spirit: St. Paul for instance prays that God may sanctify his people "wholly", with "spirit and soul and body" kept sound and blameless at the Lord's coming.* Before going on to state: *The Church teaches that this distinction does not introduce a duality into the soul.* The Catechism makes frequent references to both soul and spirit in doctrine but seems to deliberately use the terms interchangeably as well as referring to man's 'spiritual soul' to deliberately muddy the waters.

15.55   The official denial of the separate existence of the Spirit and Soul within humans only occurred in 861 in the rulings of the Third Council of Constantinople. Chaired by emperor Constantine IV, the Church decreed that the existence of the Spirit as a constitutive part of the human being was ruled heretical and all texts stating such should be erased. From that moment, only the human Soul had spiritual quality as humans comprised only body and soul. Philosophically, erasing the immortal spirit from the concept of man also removed the possibility of evolution, thus man could be condemned to a single life and total dependence on the Roman church. One might speculate whether the Roman church suppressed the binary spiritual nature of man deliberately or from ignorance of the predominant Middle Eastern culture. But, as the distinction is clear from Greek culture this would seem unlikely, therefore one must conclude that the move was part of efforts to bury Jesus teaching of self-salvation – to ensure the church secured monopoly control over human lives.

15.56 However, the original meaning of souls being consigned at the 2nd death to Sheol lies uncorrupted in the Catholic Catechism's Statement of Doctrine 968 when describing Jesus mother, Mary: *Her role in relation to the Church and to all humanity goes still further. "In a wholly singular way she cooperated by her obedience, faith, hope, and burning charity in the **Saviour's work of restoring supernatural life to souls"**.*

15.57 The inconsistency of the editing of Doctrine is something to marvel – Statement 1014 refers to the second death, as in *Blessed are they who will be found in your most holy will, for the second death will not harm them* (St. Francis of Assisi 1181 to 1226, from his 'Canticle of the Creatures'.)

Saving our Soul – the route to immortality

15.58 Those that have studied the binary soul concept believe the key step is to unify the Soul and Spirit, so our two spiritual components become one – achieving wholeness, perfection, fulfilment and completion leading to redemption, salvation, divinity and immortality.

15.59 It may be helpful to set out the steps in this process:

1   We need to consciously confront all our repressed feelings and emotions – a painful psychological process – only those whose present-life Soul is free of division and defect can then proceed to:

2   Salvation through Repentance, the cleansing of the Soul, in order

to unite our Spirit with our Soul.

3   The 'Sacrament of the Imaged Bridal Chamber' initiates the return of all one's past life Souls (images) to unite with our current life united Soul and Spirit – achieving the final seal of salvation, the Chrism.

4   Jesus then helps us manage the orderly absorption of the memories of our previous lives – as our earlier life souls, previously locked away and buried in our Soul, are released. *"If then you abide in him, and are built up in him, you shall possess your Soul indestructible"* – Acts of John, 104

5   Becoming perfect and whole does not mean being sinless or without guilt but being fully open and honest to oneself.

6   In we don't unite with our Soul, it separates from us in a second death.

7   Without a body in which to unite, our Spirit must reincarnate again if it is to have a chance to unify with our Soul. When reborn, unknown to us, all our previous life souls are present but locked away and we have to learn everything afresh without knowledge of our past selves – a state Jesus described as 'born of woman'.

15.60   As humans, we seem to know instinctively what is good and what is evil, maybe it is written on our 'hearts', maybe these qualities are imprinted on our Souls. When our Freewill Spirit listens to the guidance of our Soul, we act to promote good, when our Spirit acts sinfully we are rejecting the pleading of our Soul and hardening ourselves against our Conscience. We acknowledge that repeated evil actions dull the senses – so called 'hardened' criminals are those who lack compassion; elite military units that are trained to become killing machines.

15.61   The Catholic Catechism contains Statements which help describe this process:

- 1832 *The Holy Spirit endows us with spiritual fruits, the Church identifies twelve: charity, joy, peace, patience, kindness, goodness, generosity, gentleness, faithfulness, modesty, self-control, chastity.* (I suggest our Soul brings these fruits to teach our Spirit)

- 1855 *Mortal sin destroys charity in the heart of man by turning man away from God, venial sin allows charity to subsist, even though it offends and wounds it.* (I suggest evil perpetrated by our Spirit destroys charity, and lesser evils damage our capacity to act charitably)

15.62 A large body of heretical texts described in detail how the damage caused by the second death could be rectified, including the Gospel of Thomas, the Gospel of Philip, the Gospel of Truth, the Secret Book of James, the Book of Thomas, the Teachings of Silvanus and The Tripartite Tractate.

15.63 The common themes in these texts include:

- Making ourselves whole, unifying our Spirit and our Soul can only occur whilst both are hosted within a mortal body, if we die divided – we have to wait for our next reincarnation and try again to unify within a mortal body. 2000 years ago, some worried that they either might not get reincarnated again or might reincarnate in an animal body. Today, one might speculate whether reincarnation might be into some alien species on a distant world – after all God's strategy to create relatable personalities is more likely to be on an inter-galactical scale than being parochial to our little planet Earth;

- To make the Two become One, we have to recall and confront all our repressed memories of actions and words we regret, resolving and repairing where we can;

- It is usually the actions initiated by our freewill Spirit, ignoring guidance from our Soul (our conscience), that damage our Soul, driving it apart from our Spirit and condemning our Soul to lonely imprisonment in darkness after our death;

- Each time we reincarnate, we inherit all our dead Souls from former lives, we unknowingly host their dreams, desires and fears which may leak into our present unconscious – maybe it is leakage from the Souls of our past lives that cause some of our dreams and nightmares;

- Once we are dead, our Soul has no power to rationalise and act to try to save itself – it can only fall back on its memories and fears;

- On a number of occasions during his ministry, Jesus claimed our souls had been given to him by his Father;

- Both orthodox and heretical texts claim that the crucifixion somehow resulted in Jesus own soul forging a connection with the souls of every person who has ever lived; giving us hope that he can resurrect all our souls. Therefore, as we are very likely to fail to make our Two become One, our salvation and immortality is utterly dependent upon Jesus;

- The final resurrection of souls that Jesus promised results in judgment – the process by which our Spirit, reunited with all its past life Souls, endures as a traumatic experience akin to excruciating torture. But this torture is not by God but entirely internal to ourselves – our Souls torture each other and our Spirit;

- Hence, we understand Jesus' mission was to teach how we might achieve unity within our mortal bodies in our current incarnation and then be helped to methodically assimilate each past life Soul until we reach wholeness and enter the Kingdom of Heaven in this life – whence upon our bodily death we avoid the second death and immediately enter immortal life;

- We need to 'put on' all our old Souls to become whole, to restore ourselves to perfection – meaning absorption of every single one of our past life Souls – only then will our *Image* become transparent and the *Light* of our Spirit become visible – meaning we qualify as achieving wholeness and eligibility to enter the Kingdom of Heaven.

15.64   A fascinating belief comes down to us from ancient Sumeria, from at least 4000 years ago. Inanna, (in Akkadian, Ishtar) warns that, at the end times, the dead arise to consume the living. The dead souls are resurrected and devour the living spirits in judgment of their sins. This is a very good description of the fallback salvation Jesus warned of, if we fail during our mortal life to make our Two become One, then before judgment all our past life souls are resurrected and come alive in our spiritual mind simultaneously – consuming it. Indeed there are many references to 'eating the dead' and 'let the dead bury their dead' in the Gospel of Thomas, the Gospel of the Truth, the Teaching of Silvanus and the Gospel of Philip. Inanna was the daughter of Sin and the sister of Shamash – both of whom are credible candidates for the Yahweh of the Old Testament (see the family tree of the main gods on the website for this series, and for more detail of these three 'gods', please refer to Part One of this series).

What was the purpose of Jesus crucifixion?

15.65 Pauline theology dropped the revolutionary part of Jesus message and focused on his death as a redemptive sacrifice. However, it is not clear from Jesus' teaching, or from the gospels, that Jesus' crucifixion was to provide an abiding sacrifice to absolve the sins of humanity. This is a Pauline theological development. Jesus taught that the route to salvation lies within us, giving us the simple rule of loving others as we love ourselves, thereby enabling our Spirit to unify with our Soul, saving us from the second death and gaining immortality for our Soul. Jesus said he would enter the souls of those who believe and help our souls guide our freewill spirits. However, Paul twisted this teaching and has led Christians to believe that Jesus will save people's mortal bodies, reviving bodies by their resurrection at some climatic End Time.

15.66 If we look at canonical texts, the purpose of Jesus death is less clear. Mark wrote that Jesus died to atone for our sins but although textual analysis argues for Mark to be a key source for Luke, it seems Luke wrote this key issue out of his gospel. Throughout Luke and Acts, the author ignored Mark's references to Jesus' death as an atonement. The only remnant of that teaching is in some manuscripts of the Lord's Supper, where Jesus says that the bread is his body to be broken "for you" and the cup is his blood poured out "for you". But in the earliest and best manuscripts, these words are missing – much of Luke 22:19 and all of 22:20 seem to be 4th Century additions. It appears that scribal copyists added these words to make Luke's view of Jesus' death conform to Mark's and Matthew's. In other words, it appears that Luke did not share with Mark and Matthew one of the most important theological claims. The implications are profound. Luke writes that Jesus death was important because it will remind you that the wages of sin are death and therefore you will repent.

15.67 Both the canonical gospels, as well as those declared heretical by the Roman church, make references to Jesus having an inner circle with whom he confided the most special knowledge. It is possible that Jesus did not explain to Paul how people could save themselves? After all, it seems Jesus only appeared to Paul for a short time and the main message Jesus gave Paul that has been handed down to us is "lay off my followers".

15.68   The gospels record Jesus telling his apostles that he had to die – but for what purpose? Because Jesus had already unified his Spirit and his Soul in a previous incarnation, upon mortal death he would remain united and retain his memories.

15.69   Conventional Christianity explains that Jesus death as necessary to redeem sinful humanity. God had originally created a perfect world and humans to live on it. Then the Devil, supposedly a 'fallen angel', had tempted man to sin and sin had therefore 'entered' the world. Mankind, being sinful was thereby 'cut-off' from God and only a perfect sacrifice could atone for the sins of humanity. One can readily detect the Israelite origin of this religious myth – but today it makes no sense at all. We know God had no direct role in the creation of either Earth or humanity – and that 'sin' is not something that exists 'in the world' but some act with negative consequences arising from the freewill actions of individuals. *The Saviour replied "there is no sin in the world, but it is you that make sin when you do things".*

15.70   The idea that a supreme intelligence that formulated the myriad forces and equations governing the evolution of our universe, leading to the formation of life supporting planetary ecosystems and species with potential intelligence somehow plots how to balance the ledgers of sin – is simply not credible. That such a supreme creator would devise a strategy to incarnate part of himself to live a perfect life on this planet in order to deliver a perfect sacrifice in a horrible death makes no sense at all.

15.71   The canonical gospels certainly record Jesus foreknowledge of his impending death at the hands of the authorities but the reason is not given. Various gospel verses describe Jesus telling his disciples that he will be betrayed, mocked and insulted and then sacrificed for the forgiveness of sins but he will then rise again. The synoptic gospels contain similar verses: Matthew 16:21-23, 17:22-23, 20:17-19 and 26:26-28; Mark 8:31-33, 9:30-32, 10:32-34 and 10:45; Luke 9:21-22, 9:43-45 and 18:31-34. John includes John the Baptist making a prophetic statement in 1:29.

15.72   The similarities of the synoptic gospels reflect the understanding that three authors used common source material. A number of biblical scholars have tried to piece together what the key source document, labelled 'Q', may have contained. The first attempt was by Adolf von Harnack in 1907, others followed and the latest, titled the *Critical Edition of Q* by John Kloppenburg was published in 2000, and has been translated from Greek into English, German and Spanish and contains a full database of all the arguments invoked by scholars regarding the reconstruction of Q since 1838. The most startling result of the work to reconstruct Q is the conclusion that it contained no references to Jesus death and resurrection. For readers of this chapter, this conclusion does not come as a surprise.

15.73   The earliest gospels we have such as the *Gospel of Thomas*, the *Gospel of Philip* and the *Gospel of the Saviour* focus on followers needing to gain the correct interpretation of Jesus sayings with no mention of Jesus death, atonement, salvation or resurrection. In stark contrast, Paul never mentions Jesus sayings or deeds but focuses only on the redemptive value of his death and resurrection.

15.74   We also have the earliest authoritative manuscripts of Luke – which do not include the references to Jesus death being for redemptive purposes.

15.75   Having concluded that Jesus death was a sacrificial atonement for the sins of mankind, conventional Christianity is undecided as to how this actually works. In his *Christian Theology: An Introduction*, Alister McGrath groups the theories into four themes:

- **the cross as a sacrifice**: The idea of sacrifice comes from Israelite tradition, a perfect sacrifice atones for sin in order to repair a broken relationship with God – Paul writes extensively on this and Augustine developed the idea.

- **as a victory**: The idea of a victory comes from the term 'ransom' used in Mark 10:45 – Origen suggested it was a ransom paid to the Devil, whilst Gregory the Great developed this into being a payment in exchange for the Devil giving up control over humanity. Really? This sounds like God capitulating to blackmail?

- **as forgiveness**: This was developed in the 11th Century by Anselm of Canterbury in his work *Cur Deus Homo* (Why God became Man) in which he argued that Jesus death represents the satisfaction or

penalty for sin. For Trinitarians this creates the bizarre logic that God
created creatures that sinned, so God arranged for his creatures to kill
himself as a sacrifice for the sins of his creations.

- and, *as a moral example*. The idea that Jesus meekly accepted a
  difficult and undeserved death demonstrates for us that love moves us
  to repent thereby re-uniting us with God. This theme was developed
  by Peter Abelard (1079-1142) *"Our redemption through the suffering of
  Jesus is deeper love within us which not only frees us from slavery to sin, but also
  secures for us the true liberty of the children of God, in order that we might do all
  things out of love rather than out of fear – love for him who has shown us such
  grace that no greater can be found"*.

15.76   For me personally, only the last of these makes any sense, and indeed
        chimes well with the original teaching of Jesus. The puzzle though
        is why Jesus, assuming he had powers, allowed his mission to be cut
        short the way it was. If Jesus had foreknowledge of the future spread
        of Christianity, he would also have known how his teaching would be
        distorted and the horrific acts perpetuated against his future followers by
        those claiming to act in his name. Please see chapters 10 & 11 above and
        Part Three chapter 23 for more on this point.

15.77   Conventional Christianity teaches that Jesus died, was buried, descended
        into hell and then rose again, resurrected by himself, being God. But look
        more closely at the Catholic Catechism and it is less clear. Ancient culture
        and modern beliefs share the understanding that the Soul may wander
        from the body when asleep or under anesthetic (out of body experiences)
        but departure of the Spirit equals death. In physical terms, the small
        electrical charge present in a live body – is absent from a dead body.
        Catechism 630 states that *During Christ's period in the tomb, his divine person
        continued to assume both his soul and his body, although they were separated from each
        other by death. For this reason the dead Christ's body "saw no corruption"*. Whilst
        internally contradictory:- *his divine person continued to assume* (remained
        present?) c/w *were separated from each other by death*, the main point is that his
        body *saw no corruption*.

15.78   Given the numerous biblical references to 'Jesus' descending to Sheol
        during the three day period between crucifixion and resurrection,
        the most logical explanation is that it was Jesus Soul having an out of
        body experience, visiting the other souls in 'Sheol', whilst his Spirit

remained in his body preventing its 'corruption'. This suggests Jesus did not die from the crucifixion but maybe was in a coma (allowing his Soul to wander) and, upon waking up, he bore the wounds of his ordeal (although as we saw in previous chapter, the traditional account sounds embellished) and could happily consume barbequed fish. The conventional account of the crucifixion is undermined by contemporary historical accounts of Roman justice (see 14.34 to 14.47 above) suggesting death from crucifixion normally took a few days – whilst all the gospel accounts say that Jesus was cut down after just 3 hours and therefore mostly likely remained alive.

15.79 The Catholic Catechism is a fascinating document. Many statements supporting doctrinal positions seem to adopt convoluted language which sometimes suggests writers were maybe trying to preserve an original meaning ruled heretical whilst outwardly supporting dogma. The use of phrases like *"the church teaches that"* adopting a third person perspective seems to imply *we teach this but we ourselves do not believe it!* The significant use of 'tradition' to justify a doctrinal position hardly represents rigorous scholarship – being tantamount to claiming that the *repetition of a falsehood many times converts it into truth.*

Good Works or Faith Alone

15.80 Another sharp difference between the teaching of the Nazarene church, led by James after Jesus crucifixion, is that salvation depends on good works, the Soul is united and saved because it is successful in doing good works in line with the principle of loving others. James writes that belief in Jesus alone is, in itself, barren. Paul however adopts the opposite approach – faith alone results in salvation, as in Ephesians 2:8-9 *"For it is by grace you have been saved, through faith—and this is not from yourselves, it is the gift of God – not by works, so that no one can boast."* Paul argues that it is important to show thanks for God's unwarranted grace but to perform good works on the basis that it helps earn salvation is actually insulting Jesus as it means that you think Jesus did not do enough to save you.

15.81 In contrast, James wrote that faith without works achieves nothing. James 2:14 states *"What good is it, my brothers and sisters, if someone claims to have faith but has no deeds? Can such faith save them?"* and in 2:17 *"In the same way, faith by itself, if it is not accompanied by action, is dead"*. James goes on to underline his point in 2:20 *"You foolish person, do you want evidence that faith without deeds is useless"* and answers his own question in 2:24 *"You see that a person is considered righteous by what they do and not by faith alone."* And if that is not clear enough he ended that chapter with: *"As the body without the spirit is dead, so faith without deeds is dead."* 2:26

15.82   Despite the clarity with which both authors wrote, articulate theologians attempt to paper over this glaring difference by simply saying that those who have faith will naturally do good works whilst those who do good works must by definition have faith – umm?

15.83   Paul's teaching that Jesus has done all the hard work for us and we only have to believe is an attractive marketing line. But many then concluded, ok, we can believe and then we are free to continue sinning as much as we like because it won't affect our salvation. Paul's epistles contain many sections seeking to combat this obvious reaction.

15.84   The bottom line is do you believe James, Jesus brother, who travelled with Jesus for three years during his ministry and whom Jesus appointed as his successor (Gospel of Thomas 12) with James recognized as head of the church in Jerusalem for almost 30 years, or Paul, who only met Jesus in a brief apparition on his way to Damascus? It's not a difficult decision.

15.85   Unless we devote ourselves to doing good works, we are unlikely to be really loving our neighbours and therefore we will fail to make our Two become One; on the other hand, as a backstop, faith alone might save us at the End Times resurrection of souls.

Did Jesus refer to God as his Father?

15.86   There are numerous references to Jesus stating that God is Spirit. At the same time, throughout the gospels, Jesus prays to his Father, states he is carrying out his Father's work, at the command of his Father and has been granted authority by his Father – Jesus seems to make a clear distinction. The church may have confused people by its policy of naming 'God, the Father' and 'God the Holy Spirit'. What if God is the Holy Spirit and the Father is another power that adopted Jesus as his son and commanded Jesus during his mission.

15.87   Luke 12:10 provides some interesting guidance on this – where Jesus says that anyone who blasphemes the Son of Man (Himself) will be forgiven – but anyone who blasphemes against the Spirit will not be forgiven. That shows a stark difference for Trinitarians! But the text of the Gospel of Thomas is explosive, GoT Saying 44 states: *Jesus said, "Whosoever blasphemes against the Father will be forgiven, and whosoever blasphemes against the son will be forgiven, but whosoever blasphemes against the Holy Spirit will not be forgiven either on earth or in heaven."* Given that the Gospel of Thomas is believed to have been written significantly earlier than any of the canonical gospels and is known to have been widely distributed given the many references to it in surviving texts – the verse in Luke may have been sourced from Thomas. ***Clearly Jesus is telling us that his Father is junior to God.***

15.88   Amazingly, the Catholic Catechism even quotes the above saying of Jesus but bashfully ignores the huge implication. Statement 1031 says *The Church gives the name Purgatory to this final purification of the elect, which is entirely different from the punishment of the damned. The Church formulated her doctrine of faith on Purgatory especially at the Councils of Florence and Trent. The tradition of the Church, by reference to certain texts of Scripture, speaks of a cleansing fire. As for certain lesser faults, we must believe that, before the Final Judgment, there is a purifying fire. He who is truth says that whoever utters blasphemy against the Holy Spirit will be pardoned neither in this age nor in the age to come. From this sentence we understand that certain offenses can be forgiven in this age, but certain others in the age to come.* I know, I had to read this a few times to understand the meaning: that tradition and church councils have determined thus:- apart from saints and the damned, all others have to pass through the cleansing fires of Purgatory because some sins may be forgiven (by ordained priests) during mortal life, others may be forgiven during the spiritual phase but some (such as blaspheming against the Spirit, i.e. God) are never forgiven.

15.89   Jewish scripture always describes God, YWHW, in human terms – he has a face; he speaks; he has a back; he eats – he is very fond of the aroma of roast lamb but allergic to yeast, so his bread must be unleavened; he loves wine – needing at least a *hin* each day. Jacob witnessed him descend a ladder from his spaceship and the Israelites wanted him to park his *shem* in Jerusalem. But Jesus described God as Spirit without human features – distinctly different from the Father figure whom he was obedient to. Therefore, it seems highly likely that synoptic gospel writers (who never met Jesus and who are generally believed to have written between the years 70 and 90) would simplify Jesus original statement, if found as in

15.87 above, and distinguish only between God and Jesus. Alternatively, scribal copyists in the early centuries, seeing a challenge to the trinitarian doctrine, cut out the offending phrase.

15.90 Another consideration flowing from the Binary Soul Doctrine, is that Jesus references to his Father may be to a dominant prior life soul that was now unified with his Spirit and thereby effectively made the rules for Jesus to live by. Imagine you live not only with all the issues arising in your current life but are also in discussion with memories and feelings of your prior lives – maybe one dominant prior life Soul has mastered your Spirit and subordinated your other souls, including your current life. Jesus may have had at least two persons in his head all the time. This would explain Jesus references to him being *in* his Father and his Father being *in* him. It would explain why he would naturally claim his Father and his current self were both present and both witnesses when the Pharisees brought the case against the woman caught in adultery – see John 8:14 and 8:18.

15.91 *Jesus said, "When you see one who was not born of woman, prostrate yourselves on your faces and worship him. That one is your father."* This intriguing statement is in the Gospel of Thomas, Saying 15. Using the term *'not born of woman'* indicates Jesus is referring to a Son of Man, someone reincarnated with full knowledge of their prior lives. That such a person would be your father and deserve worship may be linked to such a person having (i) huge knowledge and experience from all their past lives, and (ii) having lived so righteously as to unify their soul and spirit in a prior life. Any such person should certainly be honoured and seen as a source of great learning. The use of the term 'father' may indicate generational seniority or in the sense of pastoral care – the ancient model of emotional, social and spiritual support. Maybe the term 'worship' might mean something like "praise, pay attention to, support and learn from" rather than worship.

15.92 Alberto Zencanaro, a dear friend in Hong Kong, alerted me to two curious facts concerning Jesus and references by Jesus to his Father. Firstly, in the gospel texts that we have Jesus invariably refer to "my" father not "our" father, he is tasked, carrying out the wishes of and obedient to "his" father not "our" father, of all Christians. Taken together with references by Jesus to him being *in* his father and his father being *in* him could again point to Jesus referring to a prominent past life ancestral figure being alive and conscious in his mind alongside his current life soul.

15.93   In the Saying quoted in 15.91 above (Gospel of Thomas 15), Jesus appears to use the term 'your father' to signify the title of anyone we discover is a 'son of man', such person we should also 'worship'. Pointedly, again Jesus does not say "our' father – it seems more likely he is using 'father' in an ancestral sense – pointing to a past life soul. Certainly, anyone whom we discover is a 'son of man' has managed to unify their soul and spirt during a previous life and therefore has existed as an earlier generation – hence might be referred to as a father.

15.94   The only biblical use of "our" father by Jesus appears as the opening of the Lord's Prayer. But, of course, all is not what it seems. This, the most popular Christian prayer, is popularly referred to by Catholics as the "Our Father". The Catholic rite, which had a monopoly from c380 to c1520, always prefaced the reading of the Lord's Prayer with a short qualifying statement. The English version of this statement states *"Obedient to the word of the Saviour and formed in his divine teaching, we dare to say: Our Father"*. However, the official Latin (*Praeceptis salutaribus moniti, et divina institutione formati, audemus dicere: Pater noster*) makes no reference to either Jesus nor to his teaching. A better translation of the Latin might be: *"Warned by healthy command and ruled by divine design, we dare to say: Our Father"* – which, although silent on who is commanding and what divine design, sounds like a discharge of responsibility.

15.95   Let's dig deeper!! Back to the Greek – Matthew 6:9 and Luke 11:2 state "Πάτερ ἡμῶν ὁ ἐν τοῖς οὐρανοῖς,". The first word is "Father" but although most biblical translation software of the second word as "our" this looks like a fix. The ancient Greek word ἡμῶν (hemon) is the imperfect form of a verb which usually means to "gather" or "collect". So, the translation into "Our Father" appears to be a fiction – a real curate's egg! Even the NIV has recently dropped the word "our" from 11:2 – adding the footnote "some manuscripts read *'our'* Father".

15.96   Now one can appreciate why those who drafted the sacraments prefaced the recital of the Lord's Prayer with a qualification. The current Catechism statement 2777 summarizes the preface as "we dare in all confidence to say...Our Father". Of course, this caution was dispensed of by Protestants who adopted translations as being faithful to the original.

15.97 Jesus statements about the Spirit of God and in the Gospel of Thomas strongly indicate that God is the Spirit that Jesus refers to whilst the Father is Jesus boss, way above our pay grade but not the ultimate Creator God. Given the number of galaxies, 10 billion plus, **each** with hundreds of billions of stars, each with say ten orbiting planets – the potential number of intelligent species is beyond comprehension. The idea of there being a single sentient Creator God is credible but not that he has a single helper!

15.98 In conclusion, I will summarise that, for me, the teaching of Jesus is simple and clear – although not easy to implement. The entire purpose of life is to secure immortality for our Soul. Jesus came to teach us how to achieve this ourselves – by loving everyone else as we love ourselves. By doing so, our Soul may then tame our freewill Spirit and manage to unify with it. If we fail, as I'm sure most of us always will, then we may get another chance when we next reincarnate – but we have no knowledge about whether we have any choice in that process nor even if we reincarnate as a human. And, it seems at the end time we may get saved in a process which unites our Spirit with all our abandoned souls at once – which is the torment foretold as judgment.

15.99 The Gospel of Thomas is probably by far the most important religious text we have describing Jesus teaching. Without an understanding of the Binary Soul Doctrine, a reader of the Gospel of Thomas will be left greatly puzzled by the Sayings. But, once the BSD is grasped, the meanings of most Sayings immediately become apparent. So does Jesus key command – love thy neighbour as thyself.

15.100 When reading Gospel of Thomas 25 *Jesus said "Love your brother like your own Soul, protect him like the pupil of your eye"* the meaning suddenly jumps out:- your closest brothers are your previous Souls, locked down within your Soul, if you love your Soul, you may awaken and assimilate the Souls from your previous lives. The next Saying, 26, is reinforcing the same point: *Jesus said "You see the mote in your brother's eye, but you don't see the board in your own eye. When you take the board out of your own eye, then you will see well enough to remove the mote from your brother's eye"*. When we accept our own Soul, we open the door to our the Soul's of our previous lives.

15.101 There is an interesting link between righteousness, barrenness and chastity. The Jewish Patriarchs, supposedly righteous, were often recorded as suffering from barren marriages (Abraham and Sarah, Isaac and Rebekah, Jacob and Rachel) – something culturally frowned upon and signifying the withholding of God's blessings. One of Jesus sayings in the Gospel of Thomas (79) sounds typically inverted: *A woman in the crowd said to him, "Blessed are the womb that bore you and the breasts that fed you." He said to her "Blessed are those who have heard the word of the Father and have truly kept it. For there will be days when you will say, Blessed are the womb that has not conceived and the breasts that have not given milk."* This and other statements led early Christians to embrace chastity even within marriage as necessary to get closer to God.

15.102 However, from the perspective of the binary soul doctrine, the interpretation is very different. Those who manage to unify during their mortal lives thereby avoid the second death and never reincarnate as independent, alienated, subsequent generations of themselves but arrive knowing their former lives. Such Sons of Man arrive knowing their spiritual father. The result is that one Soul actively lives multiple generations. But those who reincarnate in a divided state produce alienated spiritual offspring – these new generation of children are produced from the sin of their spiritual forefather – not their birth parents. The sin comes from their spiritual forefather dying divided and suffering the second death. The church campaign to suppress the binary soul doctrine led to confusion and misinterpretation, even linking all sex with sin.

15.103 Jesus taught that we should seek him, seek the truth, within ourselves – for there we shall find him. *Peter asked Jesus 'Tell us what is the sin in the world', to which Jesus replied 'there is no sin in the world but it is you that make sin when you commit sinful acts'.* After greeting others, Jesus then warns against people being led astray by those urging them to go here or to go there for guidance – *"For the Son of Man is within you. Follow after him. Those who seek him will find him."* – Gospel of Mary. The teaching that Jesus is within us also comes from the Gospel of Thomas: *He said to them. "You examine the face of heaven and earth, but you have not come to know the one who is in your presence, and you do not know how to examine the present moment."* Saying 91. In gnostic texts, Jesus is often referred to as the Pearl, a treasure of great value and beauty stored within us.

15.104 Moreover, once you find the truth, Jesus tells us clearly our future is binary: *Jesus said, "Come to me, for my yoke is comfortable and my lordship is gentle, and you will find rest for yourselves."* Gospel of Thomas 90. The reference to accepting his 'yoke' is highly significant – a yoke binds two animals together to work in harmony, Jesus guides the Two to become One.

15.105 If Jesus mission was to be able to somehow create an interface with all our souls then this opens the possibility that all humanity is spiritually connected in some way. If all our Spirits are from God and return to God, and all our Souls belong to Jesus, he is *"in us"* and we are *"in him"* – then does Jesus being *"in"* all of us mean that all humans are in some way connected? If all humans are in some way connected then the command to love our neighbours as ourselves is even more profound.

15.106 Whilst we may only fantasize about the afterlife, the Gospel of Thomas points to a very different spiritual existence – maybe humans form a vast interlinked neural network of experiences working in unison to accomplish ends we cannot currently fathom. Forget choirs of resurrected humans singing hymns of praise – our task will be far more awesome.

15.107 Even in the Middle Ages many people knew the truth – as immortalised in the cry SOS originally meaning "Save our Souls".

15.108 Also solved is the theological debate that thought some early Christians were confused in believing in both resurrection and reincarnation – surely you could only have one, not both. Now it appears the Spirit may reincarnate multiple times but if your two never become one, each time your Spirit has no memories of its prior lives. The Soul memories of each prior life being locked away until you unify or your Souls are eventually resurrected at judgment.

16

The Creator's strategic plan
reveals key characteristics

16.1   The conventional Christian view is that God made mankind in order for mankind to learn and mature into a species that desired a relationship with its maker. But humanity went astray because God also invented the Devil which then successfully tempted humanity to sin prolifically. To correct this, God then sent his 'only' Son to teach us how to get back on track and as an atoning sacrifice for our sins because God can neither abide sin nor leave it unpunished.

16.2   The conventional view is both incredibly arrogant and amazingly self-serving. However, a significant percentage of humanity does believe this view of our purpose.

16.3   Let us sweep aside the dogma and start from first principles. What has human endeavour established as a credible base line?

16.4   Firstly, there are very strong indications that the universe we live in was designed by an intelligent Creator, aka God. The breathtaking mathematical complexity built into the attributes of atomic structures and molecular combinations is proof of the hidden hand of a Creator. (Please see Part One chapter 2 for more detail)

16.5   What can we deduce of the style of the Creator? For me, three aspects stand out as hallmarks of creation:- evolution, unlimited bounty and great beauty.

16.6   Ironically for folk in the Southern states of the US, evolution really does appear to be the principal tool of God. The basic nuclear forces are designed so that primordial matter, plasma, cooled into atoms (overwhelmingly of) hydrogen, forming clusters which after accumulating to a critical mass, ignite as giant nuclear power plants generating energy from fusion whilst producing heavier elements as waste products. Eventually, these power plants run out of fuel and explode in supernovae which, by exploding, disperse vast quantities of a range of heavier elements into the surrounding space. From the debris, new stars gradually form, accompanied by collections of planets. Planets capture other left-over material as moons – which are essential to the evolution of life. So, the master plan creates collections of orbiting planets accompanied by climate inducing orbiting moons, which together orbit their own local power source. Gravity and the weak nuclear force combine to sort these planets into a stable elliptical plane to minimize collisions once the system has stabilized.

16.7   There is a clear design in grouping stars into galaxies, giving each power source (each star), a collection of planets formed from the heavier material left out from the coalescence of the star, which form into planets and these planets then capture smaller clumps of material to form moons. The existence of an orbiting moon (or moons) results in that moon's gravitational power generating tidal forces on the planet it orbits. These tidal forces exert currents within the core of the planet which is more likely to remain molten if stirred. A moving molten core maintains the planet's magnetosphere which in turn helps retain an atmosphere of gases whilst the same forces slosh surface liquids in tidal patterns. The combination of heat, light, movement and electrical discharges from weather events in the atmosphere – provide a crucible for the spontaneous creation of the building blocks of life.

16.8   Already we can see that matter itself is designed to lead inevitably to conditions conducive to the creation of lifeforms. The basic structure of stars, planets and moons is perfection – without all three, intelligent life could not form. It seems that no life of any kind could evolve inside a nuclear reactor, even if some form of bacteria could thrive in that combination of extreme heat, pressure and radiation – it could hardly evolve into anything intelligent enough to create something and only exist in a sea of broiling plasma. Planets cannot sustain life without both a source of energy (a star) and the provision of adjacent tidal energy (one or more moons) to maintain a liquid core, magnetosphere and the resulting weather to engineer a ecosystem. Random variation in the distribution of the primordial mass of hydrogen and later in the distribution of debris from supernovae result in a wide range of sizes and lifespans for stars. As we saw in Part One, the laws of physics are specially crafted to ensure stars only ignite when achieving a threshold mass (so they can burn for aeons of time) and the burn rate for hydrogen is set to ensure stars burn for many billions of years. Is it just a coincidence that planetary terraforming also requires a few billion years? The timescale for terraforming, the emergence of suitable climates and an ecosystem teeming with life required to support the emergence of intelligent life, would seem to be matched to the life-cycle of stars. Taking Earth as an example it took 4543 million years for intelligent life to emerge, at present homo sapiens sapiens looks unlikely to survive even 1 million years – but Earth will be around for maybe another 4500 million years. Even time is provided at a scale of unlimited bounty!!

16.9   Evolution means constant change – a planet may not evolve conditions suitable to support an ecosystem, it may orbit outside the Goldilocks zone, it may lack moons. We have a great example, next door to us – Mars, which in only 500 million years did evolve a suitable climate to support life – with an atmosphere, climate and plentiful water. But early on in the life of our star, Mars lost out – its two feeble moons were unable to keep Mars small central core molten. When Mars core begun to solidify, around 4 billion years ago, it was doomed. A solidifying iron core led to the failure of its magnetosphere and then the progressive loss of its atmosphere. (See the Prequel, chapter 3 for more detail)

Unlimited bounty

16.10   The second key aspect is the unlimited bounty in creation. As far as we can determine from our current instruments and technology, there appear to be some 10 billion galaxies across our universe. Each galaxy contains hundreds of billions of stars – our own Milky Way is estimated to hold between 200 and 400 billion stars – the wide range stems from our relative ability to estimate the total mass (how is complicated) but not agree on the average mass of individual stars. Another galaxy, Andromeda, which is on a collision course to hit our Milky Way, is estimated to contain one trillion stars. Don't worry too much, the collision is forecast to occur 4.3 billion years in the future. Thus, the total number of stars in the universe is way beyond our mental ability to conjure – bounty beyond our imagination.

16.11 Each star is a local power station of free energy available to its orbiting planets. We now understand that star formation is inevitably accompanied by the formation of orbiting planets. Wherever we point our instruments to detect exo-planets we find abundance. True, we cannot yet detect exo-moons but we are still discovering additional moons orbiting the planets in our own solar system – we have now identified over 200. That's around 20 per planet – so the overall design generates lots of moons. For many reasons, Earth is very fortunate to have one big moon – many other planets have far lower relative orbiting moon mass than we do.

16.12 It is worth considering that our moon is probably near the maximum relative size to the planet it orbits. If significantly bigger, the moon and the earth would start to pull each other apart. Originally, the moon orbited much closer to earth – creating high levels of volcanic activity and of tectonic plate movement. Earth would become much more stable if the moon orbited at twice its current distance. On the other hand, its previous proximity created tidal ranges far greater than today and twice as frequently, as well as far more turbulent climatic conditions – perfect conditions for the spontaneous formation of amino acids that could naturally link up to form RNA.

16.13 The evidence all around us indicates that matter is pre-programmed to evolve into potentially life supporting planets. We can identify likely precursors that are preconditions for life to emerge – a planet more rocky than gaseous, in the Goldilocks zone (not too close and not too far from its star) and with a moon or moons of sufficient mass to exert sufficient gravitational waves to maintain a molten core, and thus both a magnetosphere and thereby an atmosphere. The preconditions will not of course always lead to life – at least in any recognizable form. When Mars was looking very inviting for life we would instantly recognize, Earth presented a highly toxic stew of noxious gases and global volcanic activity. No one visiting our solar system 4 billion years ago would have looked for signs of life on earth – and none existed here at that time.

16.14 Wherever we look in nature, meaning earthbound life forms, we see examples of unlimited bounty. It seems that life's organizing principle is to reproduce in vast numbers to overwhelm natural barriers and predators – so that sufficient always survive. As geology is constantly being weathered, the ecosystem has to constantly evolve to keep adapting – for most of the time such changes occur infinitely slowly, gradually moving the ideal mix of abilities required for each new generation to survive. Of course, life is generally blissfully unaware that evolution of the physical environment is a constant on-going process. When we learn that our ecosystem is actually changing before our eyes, as with global warming – we become very concerned. Humans now understand that when change is speeded up, it will easily outrun our (and most other earthly species) ability to adapt.

16.15 We have found plenty of evidence that events can cause cataclysmic changes in our climate and mass extinctions of species on our planet. In chapters 4 to 6 of the Prequel, we looked at numerous extinction level events on Earth over the most recent few hundred million years. Indeed, the most recent was not long ago – only around 10765BC and seared into our memories as hundreds of tribal myths all around the world.

Beauty

16.16 The third factor I detect in creation, which may again reflect the style of the Creator, is beauty. The most universal form of language is maths, our brains seem wired to recognize symmetry as beauty. When we look at natural life, what we discern as beautiful is usually something presenting as symmetry and symmetry flattered by curves reflecting the Golden Ratio or the Fibonacci sequence make us swoon. We have similarly resolved music into numbers, which enable us to replicate and construct electronically patterns of sound which stimulate our brains.

16.17 Thus, for me, it seems we may discern three aspects of the character of the Creator summarized above – evolution, unlimited bounty and great beauty. The Creator appears to be a polymath intellect beyond our comprehension which designed a delicately balanced series of physical laws which set in motion a constantly evolving physical environment of vast dimensions (our universe), these laws produce unlimited variety and quantities of variations and lifeforms (many millions of species have already been identified on earth alone). And, having set this 'mechanism' in motion, one might expect the result (after 13 billion years) to be chaos and confusion – but most humans see great beauty presented by nature wherever they look – whether at galactic scale or at planetary scale – landscapes, forests, butterflies or flowers.

16.18   I wonder at the causal link between the natural creation of symmetry governed by the rules of molecular engagement verses the rules of pattern recognition stimulating pleasure in our brains. Most of our species take pride and pleasure in creating order out of chaos, we instinctively want to tidy our possessions, clean our living spaces and make any land we occupy neat and tidy. We can all think of younger people who seem to relish living in chaos, leaving things untidy, like some teenagers, but we know this is normally a rite of passage not the long-term default mode. When we view the product of human endeavor, say walking down a road passing the gardens of different folk – we automatically identify and mentally approve those gardens that present neat, tidy and interesting vegetation. Why do we have this innate bias towards order? Is it in some way linked to that aspect of the Creator which demonstrates a bias towards beauty?

16.19   That idea reminds me of Genesis 1:27, "*the gods created man in their own image*". Leaving aside the fact the Hebrew speaks of multiple gods creating man in their (plural) image, which we looked at in Part One, the central issue is whether man in some way reflects some characteristic of the Creator? Whilst undoubtedly there are fundamentalists that do subscribe to the notion that this phrase means God is some form of Superman, serious theologians interpret the notion as meaning humans moral, spiritual and intellectual nature is to some extent a reflection of God.

16.20   Interestingly, many leading early church fathers opined that the biblical idea of man being made "*in the image of God*" related to the soul not the body. In some books deemed heretical, Jesus used the term 'image' when referring to the soul and these texts probably influenced various early church fathers to do likewise, including Origen of Alexandria (185 to 254), Gregory of Nazianzus (c325 to 389) and Didymus the Blind (313 to 398).

16.21   Whilst we now understand that many species seem to exhibit features which we used to think of as purely a human capability – such as emotions, speech and memory – we have yet to find examples of other species gazing at the stars, staring at the waves breaking or studying a flower, nor creating landscapes for no purpose other than to look attractive. Does our combination of expressed characteristics imply a spiritual component to our individual being?

16.22　Mankind has gained enormous insight into the physical world, knowledge which would have astounded our grandparents is almost daily news. Some understanding is truly profound: that the physical laws applying where we have already explored appear to apply uniformly across the entire universe – e.g. H^2O will always transition from metal to gas in an Earth mix of gases at one atmospheric pressure at 100^0C. All life on Earth uses DNA as its operating system – on balance, we believe DNA must have evolved elsewhere (otherwise there should be some variety in the operating systems different Earthly lifeforms use) and was carried to Earth via panspermia, or, was deliberately seeded here aeons ago.

16.23　In the same way that humanity has gradually understood and gained mastery over inorganic matter – learning how to create compounds from a mixture of elements to fashion a cornucopia of products – we recently started to gain mastery over organic matter. We have learned DNA is constructed much like operating software code and now we can edit DNA to create repair, add or delete functions within an organism. A recent example has been designing mRNA based Covid vaccines which provide a genetic upgrade to the immunology section of the human genome. We have already made new DNA based lifeforms using novel amino acids for the commercial production of bacteria and enzymes. We are now contemplating the creation of lyfe, forms of life which use an operating system other than DNA.

16.24　The physical world of matter is rapidly becoming our playground – our advancing knowledge giving us enormous potential. But matter only accounts for 4% of the mass energy of our universe. Does this imply the other 96% includes the spiritual universe?

16.25　All religions claim there is a spiritual realm which humans have a stake in. Given what we can see is evidence of a clear master plan for matter to evolve into the creation of intelligent species – it points to there being a purpose. Effort and ingenuity far beyond our understanding went into devising the physical laws of our universe and the performance characteristics of each element – this strongly suggests a purpose.

16.26   At this point, I have to speculate. It seems to me that the creation of
        the universe does have a purpose, perhaps that purpose is to evolve (not
        directly create) species that can exploit a material existence to learn to
        grow into divine entities. By divine, I mean existing outside of matter.
        Hence one can speculate on the truth of the ancient belief system of
        the spiritual duality – that humans have been granted freewill, a dose
        of divine spirit to allow our intellectual development far beyond basic
        physical needs for our existence, and a portable soul to record our
        activities and experiences for posterity.

16.27   One mystery is how this strangely sophisticated belief managed to be
        adopted in all parts of the world in ancient times – how was it developed
        by so many far-flung cultures? Does it point to an earlier global
        civilization that was overcome by climatic change or a meteor impact?

17

If I am a conventional Christian, what am I to make of all this?

17.1   If like me, you are a Christian, you believe your theology is based upon what Jesus taught. It is therefore disturbing to discover that unfortunately most doctrinal beliefs that the churches teach do not originate from Jesus but have been developed by man. Worse, it seems key elements of Jesus original teaching have been suppressed by the churches who claim to be teaching his massage.

17.2   In writing this series, particularly this final book, I have come to realize that actually whatever Protestants believe – they are actually far more Catholic than they might think. Starting with the Reformation, some Catholic priests challenged the biblical basis for many Catholic doctrines – alarmed that there was no biblical basis for many beliefs and practices.

17.3   However, the Reformation, initiated by revulsion at the luxurious lifestyle of senior clerics and serial abuses for monetary gain and political ends, only peeled away the first layer of falsehood. The Reformation revealed many Catholic practices were simply invented by the Roman church – such as indulgences, relics, papal authority, the daily Eucharist and excommunication.

17.4   This focus on comparing Roman doctrine with the bible completely overlooked what should have been obvious – Rome had also enjoyed monopoly control over biblical texts for more than a millennium. With the advent of the printing press and widespread dissemination of bibles in the vernacular, many academics begun to question the idea that the bible constituted the true words of God – as many begun to see errors of fact and numerous contradictions.

17.5   Textual analysis begun to reveal many questions about the veracity of much of the Old Testament – particularly in the light of evidence from archaeological excavations. Thus, in the 19th and 20th centuries many begun to realize the texts of the bible were not at all historically reliable and that Jewish redaction (editing) of Old Testament texts had been a regular practice.

17.6   The education system in 'Christian' countries teaches a composite story about Jesus birth and death which, later when reading individual books of the New Testament, we find we know the broad details in advance so we tend to overlook contradictions and omissions. We grow up believing the three synoptic gospels were written by Jesus disciples – it is never pointed out that these were written at least 40 years after the crucifixion and that none of these authors had ever met Jesus.

17.7   Whilst we accept all versions of the bible are based upon translations, we are led to believe that these translations of the bible all try to faithfully replicate the meaning of the original texts. In fact, we do not have a single original autograph – and the earliest versions that we do have contain vast numbers of textual variations. For example, the early manuscript copies of Greek texts contain more than 70 versions of the Lord's Prayer – we have no way of knowing definitely if any of these is the authentic original. It appears many versions of collections of Paul's epistles were in circulation. Current bibles reflect a choice made soon after Nicaea on which collection to adopt.

17.8   But, are these textual variations of any significance? Most certainly, as we can see numerous edits being made by scribal copyists to support doctrines adopted by Roman church councils and to suppress evidence that points against such doctrines and supports doctrines held to be heretical. A big example of this is the idea of the virgin birth.

17.9   Issues of huge significance are now accepted as late developments even in official Catholic publications – e.g. that Jesus came to be regarded as divine only around the end of the first century. The Catholic church covers this by explaining that "tradition" is an essential part of how the Holy Spirit guides the beliefs of the church through a process of progressive revelation.

17.10   Paul (e.g. in his epistle to the Galatians) and his friend Luke (who wrote the Book of Acts) both record disagreements on doctrine between Paul and Jesus church in Jerusalem headed by James. Paul specifically boasting he avoided meeting with Jesus' apostles for the first three years of his ministry and was right to do so as he could learn nothing from them. It is generally held that the main issues causing the dissent were over whether the Gentile converts should adhere to the Mosaic Law's regarding food. Paul understandably rejected these food laws because refusing to partake of food with those he was preaching to would have been seriously counterproductive. But two points stand-out:

- Paul's theological journey may be measured by his progressive change in attitude towards circumcision. Initially, he was so keen that he personally circumcised his assistant, Timothy, prior to an early mission dated in Acts to probably the year 49 (Acts 16:3). Yet by the time he wrote Galatians only one or two years later, Paul writes that those getting themselves circumcised risk cutting themselves off from God (Galatians 5:2-4). Near the end of his ministry c62, Paul is writing in Philippians 3:2 that anyone who gets themselves circumcised is a dog (Jewish term for a male prostitute) and in doing so cuts themselves off from God and Jesus redemptive salvation. That is quite a pivot.

- Paul's rejection of the Mosaic Law in its entirety was a relatively late development, central to his long epistle to the Romans which was not written until 56 – when he concluded that the Mosaic Law was only for Jews and that Gentiles were not only exempt but only needed to have faith and would then be saved by grace alone. Given his early missionary trips relate his frequent visits to synagogues, early dismissal of the Mosaic Law would have closed down his preaching very quickly.

17.11   It is therefore clear that Paul's theology was not a completed thing when he started his missionary journeys but evolved radically during his missionary work. It is also clear that Jesus had little regard for the Mosaic Law, teaching his disciples that laws against healing and gathering food on the Sabbath were not God's laws, that circumcision was not from God and that the food and purity laws were not sources of sin but that sin is something that comes only from men's hearts. So, Paul's total rejection of the Mosaic Law actually came later in Paul's missions and, moreover, would not have been much of a surprise to the church in Jerusalem. So, what were the issues that Paul refers to as causes of the rift occurring with James at the beginning of Paul's work?

17.12   It is noteworthy that Paul is silent about a virgin birth, which may confirm it was not a belief during Paul's period of writing, i.e. before 70. However, three other key doctrines may be traced to Paul and even his very early epistles:

- To me it seems that Paul was probably the inventor of Jesus promise of **bodily** resurrection, a belief of the Pharisees, rather than resurrection of our souls;

- Paul may also be responsible for the dogma that Jesus crucifixion was **required** for our salvation – clearly stemming from a tradition of a vengeful god demanding settlement of outstanding liabilities;

- Paul developed the idea that our salvation only required *faith* in Jesus being the Son of God – an extraordinary claim that Jesus himself never made. Jesus plainly taught that salvation comes from treating others as one treats oneself, salvation comes from works **not** faith – a point reinforced by James "*faith without works is dead*" (James 2:26)

17.13   As described in chapter 1, the incredible aspects of Jesus conception and birth described in Matthew and Luke – the miraculous conception, Mary's perpetual virginity, the star in geostationary Earth orbit and the three kings all appear to be copied from very popular culture of the time – e.g. the cult of Isis. Actually, Christians should view this positively, it is helpful to strip away the obvious bogus material which defies medical and scientific knowledge – but removing this 1st century marketing 'guff' is only one step in peeling away the various man-made myths encrusting Jesus real message.

17.14   Those describing themselves as Christians have invariably been indoctrinated, almost from birth by references to the Bible as the 'Word of God'. I suggest that those claiming the bible in inerrant, devoid of errors of any kind, do a great disservice to the faith. We looked at the main types of argument put forward by Inerrantists in chapter 18 of Part Two, concluding that the impact of these authors is the opposite of their intent – they seriously undermine the credibility of the bible.

17.15   A very critical question is whether we can consider the Gospel of
        Thomas to be authentic? Whilst references to this gospel are plentiful
        amongst early Church Fathers, many are negative as such denunciations
        were aligned with Roman objectives. Certainly Church efforts to suppress
        the text were extensive and almost completely succeeded. Even the name
        has been left untranslated so that the Hebrew meaning of 'twin' was
        lost on listeners. How many questions would have been raised about the
        apostle called Twin and the Gospel of the Twin – whose twin? Once
        the complete text became available again from the discovery at Nag
        Hammadi, the radical nature of the purported Sayings of Jesus attracted
        dismissal by Christian apologists – many asserting late authorship (maybe
        3rd or 4th century) and that the writings were gnostic. The term Gnostic
        tends to be used as a term of abuse, that such 'sects' believed Jesus was
        not really human but an apparition assuming human form. In reality
        gnostic simply means 'secret' – and probably resulted from growing
        persecution by the Roman church!

17.16   As some have argued, the three 'heretical' gospels of Thomas, Philip
        and Truth, known as the Coptic Gospels, are demonstrably not gnostic
        because each author is explicit in describing the reality and sanctity of
        human incarnate life – the very opposite of gnostic as defined by the
        Church.

17.17   Stepping aside from the inevitably biased views both for and against,
        there are grounds for considering the Gospel of Thomas as being *more*
        authentic than any of the four canonized gospels. Whilst each of the four
        gospels included the New Testament suffers from many instances of late
        editing to reflect arguments over dogma (e.g. the frequent inclusion of
        the phrases such as 'Jesus Christ, Son of God'); the birth narrative copied
        in many respects from the then popular story of Isis and Horus; the
        clearly fake genealogies; etc – there are no such obvious edits, copying of
        popular myths and clearly fake narratives in the Gospel of Thomas.

17.18   To conclude, there are strong grounds to take the Gospel of Thomas
        seriously. Once you understand the teachings embodied in the Sayings,
        then many statements contained in the canonized gospels take on new
        meanings. One is then left with an overall teaching more elegant and
        coherent than the conventional dogma, much of which when examined
        in the cold light of day lacks credibility or logic.

17.19   So what parts of the bible may still be regarded as reliable? From the work undertaken for this series, I reach the following conclusions:

- The key to Jesus teaching is the Gospel of Thomas

- From the canonized bible, I believe James and Peter to be instructive and Acts to be an accurate record.

- The gospel coverage of Jesus missionary work to be largely accurate but not coverage of Jesus birth, genealogy, crucifixion and resurrection.

- Paul's letters reveal the historical evolution of his theology but also reflect his limited contact with, and knowledge of, Jesus theology. Collections of these letters circulating in the early centuries show numerous variations inserted when they were copied – further reducing their reliability.

- The Old Testament is basically a national foundation myth of the Jews containing some good moral teaching amongst much rather dubious material. The cold hard truth is that the numerous gods referred to in the OT do not include the power worthy of the title 'God'.

17.20   Out of this wreckage one may identify clarity, Jesus did teach:

- The imperative to love ones' neighbours as one loves oneself;

- By doing so we can save ourselves;

- If we fail, he will resurrect our souls at some future time;

- Judgment is unavoidable but the punishment is done by ourselves – not by God

17.21   For Catholics in particular, some comfort may be derived from the remarkable statements of recent popes. Pope Benedict XVI, in his book *Jesus of Nazareth*, makes a very profound statement comparing the central thrust of Jesus teaching with the central focus of Christian teaching. In Jesus teaching, the central focus concerns the Kingdom of God becoming present inside each person. Benedict sees Christian teaching as making church and community are central, concluding that Jesus focused on God but missionaries have focused on Jesus and Christology. Without touching on the issues of duality and reincarnation addressed in this book, Benedict has zeroed in on the core issue – the need for each one of us to establish the 'Kingdom of God', i.e. a unified spirit, within ourselves in this life.

17.22   The corollary of what Pope Benedict says is also profoundly correct – conventional Christianity, particularly Catholicism has focused far too much on making the role of the church central to belief – forging a role acting as an intermediary between man and God.

18

Conclusions – who was Jesus and what did he teach

18.1 The window opened into Jesus original teaching by the study of some
of the early texts deemed 'heretical' provides a more coherent view of
his mission on Earth. From my research, it appears that Jesus original
message was that man could save himself by adopting the key rule of
loving ones neighbour. Salvation and immortality may be attained by
actions taken during our bodily life, avoiding the second death and
thereby keeping our spirit and soul united after bodily death. If one
failed, and it seems inevitable that most of us will do so, then Jesus taught
that a second chance of salvation comes later – through the resurrection
of our souls (reawakening the soul memory of each past life). This
resurrection of our past life souls, after our bodily death, results in our
spirit suffering painful torture as all our souls berate our spirit for all its
past misdeeds – this is the Judgment.

18.2 Therefore, it appears that Jesus taught that there were two routes to
eternal 'life', let us say 'eternal awareness'. Firstly, the immediate route
for those able to fully apply the teaching in this life, which avoids the
second death and in a managed process endows us with the cumulative
awareness and memories of all our past lives. Secondly, the later
route involves the eventual resurrection of all our souls at once for a
tumultuous and painful end times Judgment. Paul only hinted at the
first route and his focus on the second 'end time' awakening of our souls
meant the Roman church concluded the first route would undermine its
authority, and naturally the church soon decided it was heretical.

18.3   Orthodox Christianity was developed for political control purposes.
        The idea that one could save oneself, independently of the church
        was an anathema, so the involvement of the church was held to be
        mandatory. In the 4th century, when the Roman church and the Roman
        state effectively merged, any idea that there was a route to personal
        salvation outside the church, circumventing the state apparatus, had to
        be suppressed. Orthodoxy taught that salvation could only come from
        resurrection after death as a result of the mediation of the church.
        Avoiding the church meant excommunication and eternal damnation.

**Conventional Christianity teaches God is in control and all creation
is for a purpose**

18.4   You must have questioned why so many humans are born into very poor
        life chances – suffering hunger, ill health, disabilities, war and abuse?

18.5   Most East and South Asians believe in reincarnation – with blessings
        in this life being a reflection of good deeds in previous lives, whilst
        sins committed in past lives result in afflictions in this life. Denying
        reincarnation, Christian doctrine also dismisses chance, describing
        random distribution of well-being as a naturalistic and atheistic
        worldview, not a Christian worldview. Conventional Christianity holds
        that God is sovereign and in control of His creation seeing purpose
        in God's creation. However, divine purpose and control is difficult to
        reconcile with what we actually witness, what purpose does a significant
        minority of humans living in abject poverty fulfil? Some believe that God
        will intervene as a response to prayer. But, if God is in control, why does
        he fail to act in the face of so much human misery?

18.6   The fact is, there is no evidence that God intervenes in life – such
        intervention would have to be inexplicable to be by God's action –
        otherwise it is the inevitable cause and effect of atomic motion. So
        interventions by God would constitute magic – and even the Pope agrees
        God does not do magic. The only control God clearly has over Creation
        is the original design and in pushing the start button.

18.7   That is not to say that God does not hold any reserve power – but
        looking at the history of this planet, God's design of the interactions of
        matter and energy has led to numerous mass extinctions – some quite
        recently when proto humans roamed the plains. Numerous very large
        scale disasters have happened during the short span of human existence

– there is no evidence God has ever intervened. God allowed nearby supernovae to bathe the planet with deadly radiation causing extinction of numerous species and meteorites to almost wipe out humanity on a continental scale. Most of these people died in prolonged agony – from slow starvation in darkness or from their bodies becoming increasingly deformed. Death by atomic bomb is painless by comparison. Thus one has to conclude that God is not in control, or if he has such power, he must either be disinterested or not care – hence God needs to be reappraised, conventional Christianity has misled itself.

Is humanity able to improve itself, in terms of ethics, morality and values?

18.8   Power and absolute power seem an inevitable outgrowth from civilisation. Civilisation requires specialisation in order to optimise output as no one can excel at everything. This inevitably leads to unequal distribution and unequal control of resources amongst people. Some people have thought wisely about these forces – e.g. Hammurabi, Solon, Aneurin Bevan, Jean Monnet, etc, to promote a sharing and supportive community. Others have used their leadership solely to accumulate and retain power, oblivious to the welfare of people they control. Is humanity improving? The record is patchy: look to where strong institutions can hold leaders to account, supported by freedom of speech and quality journalism free to speak truth to power. Looking at history, humanity has certainly waxed and waned: the voluntary surrender and pooling of national sovereignty by the majority of European countries is a shining example of what can be achieved. The populations of some countries increasingly rise up spontaneously to try to overthrow selfish leaders – e.g. Egypt, Sudan, Belarus, the colour revolutions, etc. Sadly, large parts of the global population have generally been controlled by corrupt dictatorships.

Why do I appear to give credence to heretical texts at the expense of orthodox canon in the NT?

18.9   This book has explored some of the most intriguing 'heretical' texts revealing ideas that were originally mainstream but later ruled 'illegal' not always even by leading theologians but often first by political leaders with the church catching up later. Let's look at just a few of the key beliefs of early Christians which became outlawed. Summarising what we have already explored, I am sure you were surprised to find politicians ruling out reincarnation centuries before the church did. Similarly, it took over 800 years before the teaching that humans housed a spirit and a soul was declared 'heretical':

Jesus and God being one	Minority view at Council of Nicaea, 325, championed by Emperor Constantine, who then recanted on his deathbed.
God being a Trinity	Invented in 381 by an Imperial Edict of Emperor Theodosius I describing the Holy Spirit as a power emanating from God. However, when translated into Latin by the Vatican, it was edited to say that the Holy Spirit emanated from both God and Jesus. This is the foundation of the schism between Catholic and Orthodox churches existing to the present day.
Reincarnation	Belief first banned in 543 by Emperor Justinian, who took 8 years to overcome papal resistance before the heretical status of reincarnation was established in Canon Law in 553. The rejection of reincarnation was confirmed in 1274 by the Council of Lyons and condemned in 1439 at the Council of Florence as being pagan.
Binary spiritual nature	Denial of the separate existence of the Spirit begun in 869 at the 4th Council of Constantinople.

18.10   The above should alert readers to how Christianity changed fundamentally. We have already identified numerous edits that were made to texts of the New Testament, particularly to support evolving Christology – developing the virgin birth and Mary's perpetual virginity, elevating Jesus to a (indeed 'the') son of God, supporting the concept of a Trinity, etc. We have traced the rise of Mary as Theotokos to the point where the Trinity may, with perhaps a little more 'revelation', become a Quaternity. We have noted that early manuscripts contained a vast range of alternate wordings – for example no less than 70 variants exist of the

Lord's Prayer.

18.11   By contrast, the text of the key books held to be heretical lack the tell-tale edits of later centuries, without references to Son of God or to a virgin birth. This makes them feel more authentic and original, we also have references to some key texts in the writings of early church fathers – showing these texts were highly regarded and the earliest references predate any references to canonical texts. It is true that the sparse numbers of extant copies of the heretical books may conceal the variety of wordings that originally circulated. But, what we do find, is a number of key sayings of Jesus which are corroborated by canonical texts. This is helpful both in supporting the heretical text and in confirming the relative authenticity of parts of canonized texts. Sometimes we find more extensive quotes in heretical texts which have been truncated in the canonized versions because they conflicted with elements of dogma which developed later.

18.12   To conclude, whilst some heretical texts like the Gospel of Thomas appear to date from the earliest times, even being quoted by Paul, and are devoid of any later edits to conform to emerging dogma – canonized texts are a proverbial curate's egg. The reliability of gospels included in the New Testament is undermined by blatant plagiarism from pagan stories, fake genealogies and easily recognized 4th and 5th century edits – with large chunks of some chapters and even whole chapters generally accepted as late additions. Such late additions are not a few years after the original but are known to have been added in the 5th century as the oldest bibles do not include them.

Fundamental conclusions from my research for this series

18.13   Eight fundamental conclusions may be drawn from my research for this series:

   A   that the nature of Jesus has been misrepresented by the church ever since the merger in AD325 that gained Christianity recognition across the Roman Empire

   B   that the complex doctrines developed by the Roman church are almost entirely man-made and have either no or very tenuous theological basis – even in the canonised scriptures that have been edited to try to provide such support

C Jesus Second Coming was in 4BC, maybe earlier

D Paradise, aka the Kingdom of Heaven, exists in the present, if we make our Two become One we enter right now.

E Jesus teaching gained rapid traction because it was aligned with then contemporary cultural understanding and it was simple to understand – although difficult to apply

F Is salvation and immortality a human right?

G The explanation of Biblical lifespans

H The salvation taught by Jesus is not only far more amazing than that now taught by the church but is available now to those who seek it

A The nature of Jesus

18.14 For me, the research for writing this series has been an interesting journey. As a child, I had swallowed the conventional Protestant teaching (my primary school was a Church of England school) that Jesus was miraculously conceived as Mary's firstborn and grew up with siblings. I recall questioning the contradiction between both (i) Jesus father being the Holy Spirit at the same time that Jesus was also God and also the Holy Spirit and (ii) having two gospels which included (almost entirely different) bloodlines – and I remember being fobbed off with the explanation that the two bloodlines represent in one case Mary's and, in the other, Joseph's ancestors – which adds nothing to their authenticity!

18.15 I could never get comfortable with the idea of a Trinity, of one being in three forms. I was being informed that the Old Testament Yahweh was God (which made God seem like a really nasty human – angry, jealous, inflicting terrible things on both his so called chosen people as well as their enemies, obsessed with humans making sacrifices and complying with endless petty rules; whilst making frequent promises which he always broke within a few centuries). But Jesus, another manifestation, happened to be gracious, merciful and intelligent. I saw two major problems with the Trinity – the characters of Yahweh and Jesus seemed to be polar opposites, whilst Jesus kept telling us 'God is Spirit' – so how do we differentiate between God and the Holy Spirit – Houston we have a nomenclature problem!

18.16 My next challenge was puzzling over how Jesus could be wholly human, his mission being to experience what mankind experiences, if he only had one set of chromosomes – from his Mum. It also struck me that if Jesus incarnation was, at least in part, for him to experience what man faces, i.e. the temptations of sin, then his experience would be seriously deficient if he had not married and fathered children. After all, the whole point of a life form is to procreate.

18.17 When, only a few years ago, I started studying Catholic doctrines I was frankly astonished: to discover that, according to Catholic belief, Mary herself had been born by a virgin, and was one of only three humans born without Original Sin – can you name the other two? According to Catholic doctrine, Mary was brought up in seclusion by priests in the Temple complex and had conceived only once, courtesy of a magical intervention by the Holy Spirit. Despite biblical references to marriage and to having other children, Mary remained a virgin for her entire period on this planet. Not only that, Mary never died but ascended bodily to heaven, without dying, to be made divine as the Theotokus (God bearer). I wonder if anyone is making a market in the odds of the Trinity becoming a Quaternity, or maybe, from the Greek – a Tetrad?

18.18 My research into early Christian beliefs and the extent to which original biblical texts were edited during the early centuries to conform to Roman doctrine, reveals a far more credible picture. Even official Catholic publications admit that originally Christians believed Jesus was born a normal human from two human parents whilst the notion Jesus is divine was a belief that grew towards the end of the 1st century. Early Christians believed that the baptism by John marked the point that Jesus was vested with a special dose of Spirit and immediately commenced his ministry. The earliest surviving copies of the canonised gospels and those deemed heretical all state that the voice from heaven at Jesus baptism stated *"today,* I have adopted you as my son" – which surely rules out a divine conception.

18.19 The original *Gospel of Matthew*, in Aramaic, held in the ecclesiastical library at Caesarea according to Eusebius – started with chapter 3 of the canonised gospel. Similarly, texts and fragments recovered in the past century of the gospels *'of the Ebionites'*, *'to the Hebrews'* and *'According to the Egyptians'* are all similar to the text of Matthew although with many variations – but all start with Jesus baptism by John as marking Jesus adoption by a divine power.

18.20 For me, this strongly indicates that the first two chapters of the canonised Matthew (covering the genealogy of Jesus and the virgin birth) were later additions – maybe in the 2nd or 3rd centuries. The majority of Christian Jews living in Judea and Samaria were killed during the deliberately genocidal campaigns by Roman forces between AD66 to 70 and again between AD132 to 136. The destruction of the Temple in 70 eliminated the genealogical records which may have supported Jesus eligibility to be a messiah – as a descendant of Aaron and/or of David. Jesus triumphant procession into Jerusalem strongly suggests the people recognised Jesus to be a king messiah, eligible through descent from David to be anointed messiah and crowned as king.

18.21 The Gospel of Matthew believed to have been written in Antioch (3rd largest city in the Roman empire at that time, now in modern Syria) and the Gospel of Luke believed to have written in Ephesus or Smyrna (both in modern Turkey) were written by authors who had never met Jesus. Writing after the Jerusalem Temple records were destroyed, both contain crude attempts to manufacture genealogies. Both relied upon contemporaneously available texts to assemble their gospels – most likely the sources included the three 'heretical' gospels referred to in 17.10 above, the earlier 'Gospel of Matthew' in Aramaic and the supposed 'Q' document. They both faced two key problems – how to prove Jesus was a messiah in the absence of the Temple records and how to make Jesus competitive with other contemporary gods who were all believed to be of divine descent.

18.22 It seems that fake genealogies of Jesus were circulating even before the Temple was destroyed – as Paul (whom all agree died before the 66-70 military campaign across Judea) warned his followers to ignore such fake genealogies. In Jesus time, everyone worshipped the local territorial god in whose area they lived, plus gods of cities they were visiting or travelling through as well as maybe a favourite god whom they liked. The common principal being that all gods were the progeny of other gods, although some might be from a union of a god and a human female. Frankly, it would not be credible to claim that Jesus was a god if he was born of two ordinary humans. Hence, for Gentiles, impregnation by God rather than Joseph was much more convincing.

18.23   Thus I believe the scene was set for doctrinal arguments. The original Christians within Judah were largely massacred, the Nazarene church spread largely outside the Roman empire and maintained Jesus had a normal birth from two human parents. Whilst Matthew's gospel, generally believed to address a Jewish audience, may have influenced survivors of the 66-70 war in Judea. Across the rest of the Roman empire, the Lucan story became adopted and the Johannine alternative of Jesus as the *intermediary* sent by the Creator God to convey God's instructions to humanity, known in the Greek culture as *the Logos*, simply mistranslated to conform to the emergent new orthodox doctrine.

18.24   Transmission errors, mistranslation and probably sheer marketing necessity all contributed to Jesus message being twisted. The idea that Jesus forgives wholesale all the sins of those who repent and believe in him could be viewed as too good to be true. Well guess what, that's most likely correct. As we have discovered, what Jesus actually taught was how we can forgive ourselves the sins we try to ignore and cover up inside. Only once we have recognised all our sins and reconciled our Soul to our Spirit are we ready to go forward to Judgment.

18.25   As the Catholic Catechism points out (Statements 430 and 431 – see paragraph 5.101), only God can forgive our sins. Gospels claiming that Jesus could forgive sins contributed to the need to deify Jesus. John's description of Jesus being the already well understood intermediary created by God to communicate God's message to humanity, the Logos, was simply mistranslated to read that Jesus was *the* God (instead of *a* god, as written by John). Centuries of fierce debate ensued, leading to the excising of references to Jesus being made an adopted son by God at his baptism by John or at his resurrection, which clashed with the idea he was conceived by a union between God and Mary.

18.26   One unintended consequence of 'victors write the rules' is that the only remaining evidence of many early texts completely eradicated by the Roman authorities is often quotes of heretical statements which are berated in writings by theologians regarded as orthodox. These quotes open a narrow window into the original and probably more accurate teaching of Jesus before it was corrupted by the Roman church.

18.27   The obvious lesson is one we all learn very early on – once you start to lie, the sin grows as you are forced to spin ever more complex lies to maintain the first lie. However, before one jumps to apportion blame solely to the Roman church – how does one justify the alumni of Protestant seminaries who also preach beliefs they have learned are not the truth.

18.28 AND, if all this has still not made you choke on your morning croissant or your 油揸鬼 (oily ghost), consider the evidence that suggests Jesus was not referring to the Creator God when he referred to his 'Father'. Suppressed early Christian texts indicate Jesus differentiating between the Spirit (or Holy Spirit) which he regarded as the Creator God and his 'Father', the party who had instructed him and whose mission he was carrying out. This suggests that maybe my idea of there being multiple levels of divinity in the universe, tasked with husbanding emergent intelligent species whenever they emerge, might have some truth in it. My alternative explanations include the possibility that when Jesus referred to his 'Father' he was referring to a past life ancestor whose soul memories were alive within him or perhaps simply alluding to his own moral compass – love.

18.29 The weight of evidence points overwhelmingly to the conventional concept of Jesus as one of a Trinity comprising three 'expressions' of God as being a man-made confection. This is explored in detail in chapters 16 and 17 of Part One and also chapters 19 and 20 of Part Three. Now, we can add two very clear Sayings from the Gospel of Thomas – a source which is regarded as written earlier than any text contained in the New Testament. The same sayings are included in canonised gospels but appear to have been edited by deleting short phrases to conform with later doctrine. Both older statements by Jesus make clear that Jesus does not regard himself as equivalent to, or as part of, God:

- Saying 44 *"Jesus said: "Whoever blasphemes against the Father will be forgiven and whoever blasphemes against the son will be forgiven, but whoever blasphemes against the holy spirit will not be forgiven, neither on earth nor in heaven."*

- Saying 100 *They showed Jesus a gold coin and said to him "Caesar's men demand taxes from us". Jesus said to them "Give Caesar what belongs to Caesar, give God what belongs to God and give me what is mine".*

18.30 In addition, both original statements reflect the tripartite nature of man – our Spirit belongs to God and our Soul belongs to Jesus.

18.31   Generally we tend to think the word 'divine' applies only to God. But if you think about it, any being clearly superior to humans could be justifiably described as divine – certainly 2000 years ago, any being descending from the sky would be described as a divine godly being. Today, the number of humans on Earth is approaching 8 billion – but that is a tiny number when compared with the c300 billion solar systems in our galaxy alone. On this planet, humans play god – dominating the other billion odd species of life also sharing this ecosystem. Why do we believe there is only one single entity in the spiritual world? We speculate about angels, God's army, but surely across the universe it is more realistic to think there may be many levels of spiritual beings from novice ex-humans to other spiritual beings that will be millions of years old and, almost definitely, some that are billions of years old.

18.32   The most likely reality is that Jesus was purely human but very special. He was a reincarnation of a person who, in a previous life, had managed to live by loving others as himself and unified his Soul with his Spirit – exactly as he kept telling us, he was a Son of Man, rather than Born of Woman. This meant Jesus was fully aware of all his previous lives, his memories of all his lives and experiences were open to him. Jesus may have lived on Earth many times – in the Gospel of Thomas, Jesus warns those who fail to make the Two become One in their current life, will find that at the end times hundreds or thousands of resurrected past life memories will be awakened in our soul. The lifetime memories previously locked away at each of our many second deaths, will all be awakened and terrorise our Spirit for the sins committed in all those past lives.

18.33   What we have no idea of is whether Jesus past lives, or indeed our own, were in human bodies or maybe in other creatures – or even whether we were here on planet Earth or somewhere else in the cosmos!

B   Esoteric man-made doctrines of the Roman church

18.34   The complex theological constructs developed to try to support Catholic doctrine reflect the elevated status enjoyed by the church from the time Christianity was adopted as the official religion of the Roman Empire – from the Edict of Thessalonica, issued by Emperor Theodosius I in 380 (not long before the collapse of the Western Empire) right through until challenged by scientific discoveries during the Enlightenment in the

18th Century. For almost the whole of this period, the Catholic church was a beacon for those with intellectual ability. It was the largest and richest organisation the world had ever seen, those with ability (not just intellectual) could ascend the ranks through contacts and relationships, collecting 'livings' as they went, to achieve a life of unparalleled luxury. The residence of a bishop is called a Bishop's Palace for good reason. Lambeth Palace, close by the British Houses of Parliament, was originally bought for the Archbishop of Canterbury c1200 so he could be close to the centre of power when he was visiting London.

18.35 When Emperor Constantine merged his Sol Invictus religion with Christianity he maintained his position as Pontifex Maximus (High Priest) to whom the Bishop of Rome became subordinate. Politicians continued to shape and change church dogma. It was Emperor Justinian who decreed by edict that reincarnation was illegal (belief became a crime against the state) in 543. Justinian then commanded the pope to sign a confirmation and when Pope Vigilius refused he was imprisoned for eight years!! Finally, the 2nd Council of Constantinople adopted a church canon outlawing reincarnation in 553. It took a decade for even a powerful emperor such as Justinian to change church doctrine! To confirm his overlordship, Justinian also made the church Council pass a motion that the church would "make no changes to doctrine contrary to the will or opinion of the emperor". Today, this sounds unbelievable – but it demonstrates that fundamental church dogma was not necessarily laid down even by theologians – let alone by Jesus or by apostolic teaching.

18.36 You might question why a Roman emperor would want such power and certainly why an emperor would declare a belief such as reincarnation to be illegal. It points to exactly why the State took direct command of religion – the state religion was viewed as the most effective tool to control the citizens. Historical and biblical evidence shows belief in reincarnation was widespread in the ancient Middle East, amongst Jesus disciples and early Christians. So, this was the original context in which Catholic dogma became codified. However, reincarnation was seen to represent an existential threat to the church. The emerging dogma sought to control the population by placing the church between God and one's salvation (immortality). If you were not baptised, did not attend Mass frequently, failed to confess your sins and were not buried in sacred ground – you could not be saved. To reinforce this, those seriously in breach of canon laws were excommunicated and burnt – so that their ashes could not be resurrected nor, being excommunicated, could they even be saved by God.

18.37 What Justinian realised was that the idea of reincarnation blew away all the above controls – one could simply ignore the church in this life and then, when returning in the next life, consider it another time. If this view became widespread, the control of the church would dissolve and for the Emperor this would be a grave political blow. Therefore, reincarnation was condemned as heretical. I think most readers will be astonished to read this decision was made by a Roman emperor, Justinian in 543, and also that banning reincarnation was fiercely resisted by the papacy. Pope Vigilius was held captive for 8 years before consenting to sign the Edict and convene a Church Council (2nd Constantinople) to enforce it.

18.38 The concentration of intellectual power led to increasingly esoteric justifications for doctrine. The overarching importance of otherwise obscure aspects of doctrine is well illustrated by the issue which caused the failure of the most ardent attempt to reconcile the Orthodox and Roman churches. The Great Schism was triggered on 16 July 1054, when a papal envoy pressed an Article of Excommunication into the hands of the Patriarch of Constantinople – whilst he was in the midst of celebrating Mass. The ill-fated Council of Ferrara-Florence, 1438-1445, negotiated reconciliation between Rome and Constantinople. Attended by the Eastern Emperor and the Orthodox archbishop, key concessions were hammered out :- such as married clergy being accepted in eastern provinces but the effort ultimately failed due to an irreconcilable difference over whether the Holy Spirit could be deployed only by God or by both God and Jesus. For more details see section 5.88 above.

18.39 Proof of the human origin of the overwhelming majority of Catholic doctrine lies in official Catholic publications. The Catholic Catechism sets out in great detail the doctrinal beliefs of the Catholic Church and has been subject to periodic updating. Every element of doctrine is set out, as well as the source of such doctrinal belief. One might assume the most authoritative source of doctrinal beliefs would be Jesus himself, then perhaps his closest apostles, his inner circle of James, John and Peter. But no, statements by Jesus and his inner circle account for maybe 5% of citations. Paul, who as far as we know only met Jesus for a brief moment on the road to Damascus, takes a much bigger share – quoted as the authority for maybe four times the number of instances as Jesus. And what is the authority for the overwhelming majority of doctrinal statements – the Catholic church itself – popes, church councils, church fathers and 'tradition'. So, if you want the source of Catholic teaching, it is quite clearly set out by the Vatican – it is mostly from the popes and their council meetings. The Catholic justification for this reliance on church tradition and officials for developing doctrine is that the church is herself guided by the Holy Spirit and it 'learns' deeper understanding over time from study and reflection – critics note this definition is highly convenient.

C   Jesus Second Coming

18.40   Conventional Christianity teaches that Jesus will reappear in a Second Coming to herald the End Times and the establishment of the Kingdom of Heaven (maybe on Earth). Jesus own statements shed a different light on this. *When asked by his disciples "When will the Kingdom come?" Jesus said "It will not come by waiting for it. It will not be a matter of saying 'here it is' or 'there it is'. Rather, the kingdom of the father is spread out upon the Earth, and men do not see it."* Gospel of Thomas 113.

18.41   One staggering conclusion from the Binary Soul Doctrine is realization that Jesus must have lived previous lives on Earth – maybe also teaching on those occasions. In the texts recovered, Jesus teaches that a person may only unify their Spirit and their Soul during cohabitation within a physical body. Therefore for Jesus to come to Earth as a Son of Man he must have previously lived here, at least once. Of course, there are also other possibilities:- maybe there are other creatures on Earth that house a spirit and a soul, or maybe humans on other planets that may house a spirit and a soul.

18.42   The internal layout of the Giza pyramid represents the distinctive features of the Binary Soul Doctrine ('BSD' better described as Binary Spiritual Doctrine as humans have two spiritual components not two souls) whilst lacking any other purpose. There is absolutely no evidence it was ever intended as a tomb. Was it built as a lasting monument to future generations to remind them lest they forgot? What we examined, in the Prequel to this series, suggests this knowledge of BSD must have originated from the survivors of the relatively advanced pre-Flood culture – brought to Egypt by those who may have designed and directed the construction of the Giza pyramids around 9500BC. The obvious question is from where did those survivors gain this obscure knowledge?

18.43　The Giza complex was built by 'gods' around 9500BC (see the Prequel for details) – but these gods were mortal beings, the Egyptian records describe the special cemetery constructed for them which the priests guaranteed to maintain and preserve for eternity. These gods were definitely mortal! The interior of the Giza has been interpreted, by Peter Novak and a few others, as a representation of the BSD. The pyramids appear to have had no other purpose than to be a diagrammatic illustration of the BSD – deliberately constructed as a massive edifice to survive for millennia – presumably to warn/teach future generations.

18.44　This suggests some staggering implications – when Jesus arrived in 4BC, as a perfect, unified, Son of Man, he would have arrived with memories of his previous lives intact within his conscious Soul. Jesus memory of his past lives maybe the real source of his wisdom? Did Jesus have previous incarnations on Earth – or elsewhere or maybe both? Jesus sayings recorded in the Gospel of Thomas quote him referring to the possibility that a human may have hundreds or even thousands of past lives. Given Jesus impact in Judea around AD30-33, we might look for the impact he had during other incarnations. Was Jesus in fact a serial instigator of, not religions per se, but of ways of life by which people search for higher meaning and seek to live righteously?

18.45　Was Jesus here around 9500BC when Giza was built? If Jesus was not here then – where did the ancients get the idea of the BSD from? Certainly knowledge of BSD was prevalent not only across the ancient Middle East but evidence indicates it was known globally in ancient times. This points to the possibility that Jesus, or perhaps another Son of Man, had developed the belief system before the last major climate events of 10765BC and 9600BC (bookending the Younger Dryas interval).

18.46　In the Prequel to this series, we looked at evidence of advanced stone age cultures which have bequeathed us megalithic constructions, mostly 'temples' clearly used as celestial calendars. The celestial alignments of these megaliths enable us to use the Earth's nutation cycle to determine construction dates. Recently, geological examination of the area of western Mauritania has revealed severe water erosion which points to a climatic upheaval. Smack in the midst of the area affected lies the Richat Structure – a huge curiosity, visible from space, which appears to be the remains of a series of concentric circles separated by water which left deep salt deposits. Many physical aspects of the structure closely resemble the description of Atlantis given by the leading Athenian, Solon, which he learned from records at the Egyptian temple at Sais. None of Solon's works survive but are quoted by Plato – who named the fabled lost capital city as Atlantis. Intriguingly, the date Solon was told Atlantis was destroyed is our 9600BC – a very close estimate for the abrupt end of the Younger Dryas period. The next edition of the Prequel will include far more detail of this intriguing structure – meanwhile articles are appearing on the web and even Google maps now identify Richat as the 'Eye of Africa' and as 'Atlantis'.

18.47   Now, a moment of personal speculation. The Edfu Building texts (also covered in the Prequel) tell of Egypt's civilisation being wiped out by catastrophic storms and flooding leaving the Nile valley devastated. The texts tell of recovery and reconstruction being led by a few skilled refugees from another devasted place. If the Richat Structure is the remains of Atlantis and was destroyed c9600BC then the huge tidal waves of water that are indicated to have flowed south east over the area might be linked to similar flows southwards up the Nile valley – pointing to an epicentre in the Mediterranean where possibly a meteor impact created huge tidal waves. At that time, it is understood that the climate of North Africa was far wetter than today and any desert would have covered a far smaller area. Perhaps some of the sand was carried from the Mediterranean – maybe, as in the Badlands of Washington, the entire area was stripped to bedrock, scouring away all the soil and vegetation. This would account for the deep ripple impressions left in the sand surrounding the Richat structure. Just imagine the headlines if, one day we conclude that, the people of Atlantis practised the original version of what we call Christianity.

18.48   The level of devastation apparent from what remains of the Richat structure means it will never yield any evidence of an early civilisation – but lidar mapping of parts of the Sahara might reveal other ancient settlements that might yield something helpful.

18.49   It is possible that science may vindicate the binary spiritual nature of mankind – developments in psychology have led to our current understanding of a binary nature existing in our brains. The specialisation between the two halves of our brain exhibits close similarity between the allocation of functions attributed to the spirit and the soul. Can this be a coincidence or did an ancient civilisation on Earth gain this understanding? Did primitive man gain this understanding on his own? And, how did it become an almost global understanding?

D   **Where and when do we experience Paradise?**

18.50   Paradise, also described as the Kingdom of Heaven, is here and now. Despite Jesus numerous statements that he was here for at least a second time and that the Kingdom of Heaven was already spread out over the Earth 2000 years ago, the conventional church continues to teach that these are future events. Jesus taught that the Kingdom of Heaven is a state existing within our minds waiting for us to enter. A moment's thought may lead you yourself to concur that Paradise may be the here and now rather than somewhere we might aspire to inhabit in the afterlife.

18.51   Paradise might be what we experience during our incarnate phase. Whilst we have mortal bodies, we interact with the physical material world. We can enjoy delicious food, slake our thirst, enjoy the sensual arousal of love making, the inspiration of music, the joy of entering sleep, the sensations of cool breezes and warm sunshine, the gorgeous vistas of trees, flowers, birds, coastlines and seas.

18.52   In the afterlife, we may have awareness but lack physical sensations derived from interacting with the material world – we may have unlimited vision and information but no tactile senses – no touch, no taste, no smell, no hearing – as these require life in the physical world.

18.53   Be very careful what you wish for.

E   **Jesus teaching struck a contemporary chord**

18.54   So, where has this contemplation got us? In chapter 15 we looked at the binary soul doctrine and how it appears to tie in so well with Jesus original but suppressed teaching. We have identified the most famous architecture in the world appears to be a diagrammatical representation of the same doctrine and the most widespread and long-lived epic tale also seems to be based upon the binary soul doctrine. The Epic of Gilgamesh, which dates back at least as far as 2600BC, tells of one person who was 2/3rd god and 1/3rd human (i.e. spirit, soul and body) accompanied on his quest for immortality by his alter ego. Gilgamesh is clearly the Spirit, the extrovert dominant decision maker, sparring with his partner, Enkidu, but usually ignoring his advice. Enkidu is always trying to help Gilgamesh but always submits to being overruled. Enkidu represents the Soul of Gilgamesh, Enkidu dies and Gilgamesh fails in his quest – clearly illustrating that separation at the second death denies us immortality.

18.55　One important take away is the idea that the bonding of Spirit and Soul needs to occur within a mortal body. Those of us whose Spirit and Soul suffer the second death, find our Spirit reincarnated into another body without access to any of the past life memoires locked away in our Soul. Devoid of memories – we start each earthly life anew with a fresh opportunity to gain enlightenment. Here we may speculate – do we really gain nothing from each life we fail to unify? I have a theory, as you might expect! Perhaps, our freewill Spirit does gradually learn to be more righteous, an instinct or muscle memory rather than detailed learning from its past experiences which remain locked away in its Soul. Any evidence? Perhaps the record of Elijah and John the Baptist points to such a possibility. As discussed above in 14.13, 14.14 and 14.70, there are strong grounds for believing that John the Baptist was a reincarnation of Elijah but when Elijah had died he not yet unified. What this suggests is that Elijah, although quite righteous, had not perfected and therefore suffered the second death – resulting in his Spirit reincarnating in John the Baptist but with the memories of life as Elijah locked away in his Soul – hence Jesus references to John being the best of those 'born of woman'. That John the Baptist lived a very righteous life points to some learning from his life as Elijah – so the Spirit must retain some good learning, even if its mortal memories are locked away. This is quite encouraging.

18.56　Presumably, once unified, the Spirit (unified with all its prior life Soul memories) would not need to reincarnate any more but might enjoy the spiritual realm. It seems Jesus was one of the very few who did come back, as a unified Spirit & Soul, as Jesus labelled himself, a Son of Man. Maybe the Father sent Jesus back to Earth because the yield of unified spiritual beings from amongst Earthlings was so very poor.

18.57   One might ponder whether it is our Soul, with our personality and memories, that needs to be saved or our Spirit which has the freewill ability to sin or do good? The *Apocalypse of Paul* indicates that it is the Soul that sins but given the mass of other evidence it would seem that it is the Spirit that sins and in doing so pushes the Soul away. Jesus implied he entered our Soul and acts 'behind the scenes' to counsel our Soul how to manage our Spirit. Jesus described the impact of resurrected past life souls awakening to flooding the spirit, with each past soul believing it owns the spirit – resulting in our mental tumult (Gospel of Thomas 16).

18.58   My conclusion is that our freewill Spirit, wielding the power to do good and evil, is responsible for the sins we commit but our Soul, merely guiding and recording what we do, is the party that suffers for those sins.

F   Is salvation and immortality a human right?

18.59   The conventional view is that all believers will be saved, and most clergy will extend that promise to all of other faiths, or of no faith, that live according to Christian principles. However, there are statements in the canonised gospels which shed doubt on the totality of the salvation:

   •   Mark 16:16 *"He who believes and is baptized will be saved; but he who does not believe will be condemned"*

   •   Statement 1021 of the Catholic Catechism identifies a number of New Testament texts which speak of the final destiny of the soul depending upon people's actions during their lives:

      Luke 16:22-23 *"The time came when the beggar died and the angels carried him to Abraham's side. The rich man also died and was buried in Hades, where he was in torment"*;

      Matthew 16:26-27 *What good will it be for someone to gain the whole world, yet forfeit their soul? Or what can anyone give in exchange for their soul? For the Son of Man is going to come in his Father's glory with his angels, and then he will reward each person according to what they have done*;

      2 Corinthians 5:8-10 *We are confident, I say, and would prefer to be away from the body and at home with the Lord. So, we make it our goal to please him, whether we are at home in the body or away from it. For we must all appear before the judgment seat of Christ, so that each of us may receive what is due us for the*

things done while in the body, whether good or bad.

18.60   As set out in paragraph 15.28 above, there are references in Mark, Matthew and Luke which suggest Jesus told the apostles that his message was not for everybody.

18.61   There are also Sayings from the Gospel of Thomas which, in plain English, imply that many will be cast aside:

• *Jesus said, "the kingdom of the father is like a man who had good seed. His enemy came by night and sowed weeds among the good seed. The man did not allow them to pull up the weeds; he said to them, 'I am afraid that you will intend to pull up the weeds but pull up wheat along with them'. For on the day of the harvest the weeds will be plainly visible, and they will be pulled up and burned".* Gospel of Thomas 57

• *Jesus said, "A grapevine has been planted apart from the Father. Since it is not strong, it will be pulled up by its root and will perish."* Gospel of Thomas 40

• In the Shepherd of Hermas, Ch 13 & 14, – *many stones, rough and broken left from the new building as unrepentant sinners; the round stones are those who are wealthy – these cannot be used until something is cut off.*

18.62   However, read in the context of our having binary spiritual components, an alternative interpretation may be deduced. In other Sayings, Jesus noted that an individual may have lived thousands of lives during which they never achieved unity – meaning that their Soul now contains thousands of hidden soul memories of past lives. For most of us, all of these past life souls will be resurrected at once at the time of our Judgment. We can mentally understand our mind managing the memories, relationships, issues and problems arising in our current life. Try to imagine two or three 'persons' sharing our mind simultaneously – that would be a novel experience. But if hundreds or thousands of past lives arrive together, and start to judge our past – we would go crazy. So, perhaps in Gospel of Thomas Saying 23 (*Jesus said, "I shall choose you, one out of a thousand, and two out of ten thousand, and they shall stand as a single one"*), Jesus is telling us that he will choose which of our past souls he will resurrect or perhaps that he will choose which he will allow to become dominant in our future spiritual life. Presumably by selecting the one or two souls from the more exemplary lives that we have lived? Saying 40 uses a grapevine to illustrate our past lives, perhaps indicating that there are entire lines of our past lives which will be found of no value and cast away at Judgment.

18.63 The paragraph above leads to consideration of a stunning possibility – that, when Jesus referred to his Father, he was referring to a dominant past life soul which as a senior ancestor he deferred to. This explains for example Jesus claiming he presented as two witnesses (himself and his father feeling very much alive and present) during the trial in John 8:14 & 18.

18.64 Man bears the responsibility to utilise his freewill wisely to secure his eternal destiny. Jesus is recorded in Matthew 7:13-14 as stating: *"Enter by the narrow gate; for the gate is wide and the way is easy, that leads to destruction, and those who enter by it are many. For the gate is narrow and the way is hard, that leads to life, and those who find it are few."*

G   An explanation for the incredible lifespans in early Egypt and Sumer

18.65 I left this question dangling in an earlier Part of this series. Now I am able to posit two explanations for the incredibly long lives recorded in the various King Lists of Egypt and of Sumer as well as the more modest but still extremely long life spans claimed for some of the early Jewish patriarchs in the bible.

18.66 The common feature of the King Lists is the assertion that the original rulers were the gods – for Egypt including Ptah (Enki) and his son Ra, ruling for tens of thousands of years, giving way to demi gods (hybrid god/human people) and finally to mere mortals with normal life spans from the establishment of the First Dynasty c3200BC. Similarly in Sumer, originally ruled by gods with reigns of 30,000 years or more, then by demi gods (such as Gilgamesh) and finally by mere humans from 3760BC when kingship was 'lowered from heaven' to King Etana. The Jewish patriarchs also lived superhuman lives – with 969 years claimed for Methuselah but falling to a more reasonable (imagine your diet comprised dates, figs, honey and grapes!) 175 years for Abraham.

18.67 I have two theories for you to ruminate upon:

18.68 That the smart survivors of the climate change event triggering the Younger Dryas Period (see the Prequel of this series) saw the opportunity to perpetuate their rule by institutionalising their status as the elite (aka gods). This they achieved through the adoption of elaborate tunics and headdress which allowed the leader to age unseen and for a scion of the family to take over the leadership role whenever needed. Given the superior technology, health knowledge and living conditions – these rulers would tend to live natural lives far longer than the local natives they had brought civilisation to. Those who credibly claimed to live for a few thousand years would have natural authority over lesser mortals.

18.69 The other possibility stems from the apparent global knowledge of the binary soul doctrine – see chapter 15. If these ancients were somehow smart enough to work out the BSD theory, then could they have also worked out how to (i) achieve unity in during their earthly life, and, (ii) then somehow influence where and when they reincarnated, and were reborn incorporating detailed memories of their past lives? They would need a placeholder and a regent for a few years but their detailed intimate knowledge of their forebears would be highly convincing of their claim either of longevity or of reincarnation.

18.70 Indeed, this is exactly the Tibetan belief – the five senior enlightened Lama's always reincarnate, and being enlightened, have avoided the second death and returned with the knowledge of their past lives. Accordingly, they know the answers to the special questions put to them when found as very young children.

H   Jesus message is more exciting than the conventional church teaches

18.71 Firstly, the 'kingdom of heaven' is here now, just waiting for us to wake up and smell the coffee! True, applying the rule of loving ones neighbours as oneself feels like it directly contradicts of all the economic rules we are taught for self-preservation and advancement in the material world.

18.72 Secondly, if we fail, as probably most of us will, then we do get a second chance (at some later stage) although our task will be equally forbidding – to reconcile our Spirit with all our past life Souls that we have ignored and abused. Jesus described the process as terrifying – purgatory and hell wrapped up together – but at least mental anguish rather than the physical pain of burning in purgatory. It seems that when all our past life Soul memories are reawakened/resurrected, it is not God that judges us but we ourselves who carry out the judgment – and we shall be brutal. Our Soul will have already suffered in the darkness, tortured for aeons by nightmares – maybe our past life memories attack our guilty Spirit and rip it apart.

18.73 Only once we are reconciled, 'fully clothed' with all our past life Souls, is the Light of our Spirit revealed. Then we go before the Father and enter into the eternal light. We can only speculate as to our activities – chatting with others will be fascinating – with each of us being a collective of thousands of past lives we will have known a vast number of others with whom to reminisce shared memories whilst we gently vibrate in the slipstream of a local supernova.

18.74 Maybe, having become a Son of Man, we might get selected for a 'special mission' like Jesus – and sent to help teach a promising species on some distant planet.

Summing up – the final conclusions

18.75 So, where has all this contemplation got us? In chapter 15 we looked at the binary soul doctrine and how that appeared to tie in well with Jesus original but suppressed teaching. We have identified the most famous architecture in the world appears to be a diagrammatical representation of the same doctrine and the most widespread and long-lived epic tale also seems to be based upon the binary soul doctrine. The Epic of Gilgamesh, dating back over 4500 years, tells of someone two thirds god and one third human – i.e. spirit, soul and body. Gilgamesh is clearly the Spirit, the extrovert dominant decision maker, sparring with his soul partner Enkidu but usually ignoring his advice. Enkidu dies and Gilgamesh fails in his quest – illustrating the separation of past life memories from our Spirit at death denies us awareness of immortality.

18.76 In chapter 16, we considered whether there is a purpose for humanity and identified human discoveries which point to the physical laws of the universe being purposely designed to create stars, planets and moons capable of nurturing lifeforms with adequate timelines to allow the development of sophisticated species. All of this strongly suggests a purposeful design. My speculative conclusion is that the purpose of humanity is to enable the growth of spiritual entities suitable for graduation from the very small material realm of physical matter into the wider universe of dark energy.

18.77 How might this work? Binary concepts seem fundamental to the laws of our universe, as a polymath artist maybe God loves symmetry? Therefore, when lyfe (as defined by NASA) results in a species capable of organizing itself into a civilization, perhaps God seeds each specimen with a fragment of Spirit (our freewill). To teach righteousness to our Spirit, we each also get a Soul in which to store our personal lifetime experiences.

18.78 Jesus appears to have taught that the bonding of our Spirit and our Soul needs to occur within a mortal body. Those of us whose Spirit and Soul 'part' at the second death, find our Spirit reincarnated into another body and the memories of our previous lives locked away and inaccessible – so that we start each earthly life with a fresh opportunity to gain enlightenment. Once enlightenment is achieved, the unified Spirit & Soul would not need to reincarnate any more but enjoy the spiritual realm. It seems Jesus was one of the very few who did come back, as a unified Spirit & Soul, as Jesus described himself, as a Son of Man. Maybe the Father sent Jesus back to Earth because, although the yield of spiritual beings from amongst Earthlings was very poor, He was intrigued by our creativity.

18.79 That's it my friends, I hope at least I have given you plenty of food for thought as you have struggled through these rather dense booklets. I hope you have enjoyed the material and that you are now left with much to ponder and some feeling of enlightenment. May the Force be with You!!

Key – colours indicate name of each 'god' in principal languages:
Sumerian; *Akkadian*; *Egyptian*; Hebrew

* Until Moses met the Burning Bush, the god of Genesis was named El Elyon, the Canaanite
name for Enlil. From Moses up to Saul, the Hebrew deity appears to have Nannar but by the
Psalms of David the title had passed to Shamash. In all translations of Jewish scripture into Greek,
Latin, English, etc., all names of 'god' are assumed to refer to a single entity.

Appendix

Selected family members of ruling elite – survivors of 'the Flood' or perhaps ET's?

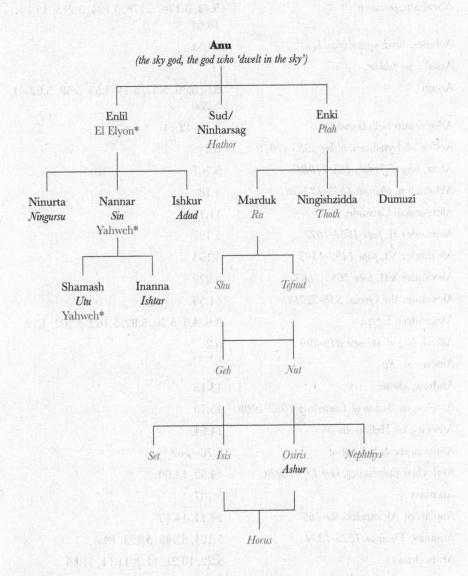

Anu
(the sky god, the god who 'dwelt in the sky')

Enlil
El Elyon*

Sud/
Ninharsag
Hathor

Enki
Ptah

Ninurta
Ningursu

Nannar
Sin
Yahweh*

Ishkur
Adad

Marduk
Ra

Ningishzidda
Thoth

Dumuzi

Shamash
Utu
Yahweh*

Inanna
Ishtar

Shu

Tefnut

Geb

Nut

Set

Isis

Osiris
Ashur

Nephthys

Horus

Index

317

Biblical References

Catholic Catechism references

Statement 58	5.260
Statement 65	5.253
Statement 66	5.253
Statement 73	5.253
Statement 100	5.254
Statement 105	5.254
Statement 106	5.254
Statement 181	5.259
Statement 246	5.255
Statements 250-252	5.256
Statement 262	5.257
Statement 299	5.263
Statement 324	5.263
Statement 328	5.263
Statement 343	5.263
Statement 358	5.263
Statement 366	5.206, 10.18
Statement 367	10.19, 15.54
Statement 389	5.65, 5.259
Statement 402	5.38
Statement 430	5.101, 18.25
Statement 431	5.101, 18.25
Statement 446	5.263
Statement 454	5.259
Statements 464-469	5.263
Statement 491	5.231, 5.261
Statement 500	5.261
Statement 575	5.207
Statement 630	13.9, 14.39, 15.77

Bibliography

Durant, Will. *The Story of Civilisation, Vol4, The Age of Faith 1950*. Simon Schuster, 1980

Ehrman, Bart D. *Lost Scriptures: Books That Did Not Make It Into the New Testament*. Oxford University Press, 2005

Ehrman, Bart D. *Misquoting Jesus: The Story Behind Who Changed the Bible and Why*. New York, HarperOne, 2005

Ehrman, Bart D. *The Orthodox Corruption of Scripture*. Oxford University Press, 2011

Elledge, C.D. *Resurrection of the Dead in Early Judaism, 200BC to AD200*. Oxford University Press, 2019

Epp, Eldon. *The Theological Tendency of Codex Bezae Cantabrigiensis in Acts*. Cambridge University Press, 1966

Frend, W.H.C. *The Rise of Christianity*. Fortress Press, Philadelphia, 1984

Guitton, Jean. *Great Heresies and Church Councils*. Harper & Row, 1965

Harari, Yuval Noah. *Sapiens, A Brief History of Humankind*. Harper Perennial, 2014

Justice, Ginny. *The Role of Indulgences in the rebuilding of St Peter's Basilica*. Rollins College, 2011

Latourette, Kenneth. *Christianity Through the Ages*. HarperCollins, 1965

Montefameglio, Gianni. *Paolo e la Sua Teologia*. Centro Universitario di Studi Biblici, 2018

Murdock D. M. (Acharya S.). *Christ in Egypt: The Horus-Jesus Connection*. Stellar House Publishing, 2008

Novak, Peter. *Original Christianity*. Hampton Roads Publishing Company, Inc., 2005

Ratzinger, Joseph (Pope Benedict XVI). *Jesus of Nazareth*. Ignatius Press, San Francisco, 2007

Reeves, Michael. *The Unquenchable Flame*. Inter-varsity Press, 2009

Stevenson, Ian. *Reincarnation and Biology: A Contribution to the Etiology of Birthmarks and Birth Defects (2 volumes)*. Praeger Publishers, 1997

The Truth Will Set You Free – Series

Prequel: The Flood and the Origin of 'Pagan' Gods

We now have compelling evidence of the devastating event which spawned hundreds of tribal memories of a terrible and rapid change in the Earth's climate. In the aftermath of the Flood, 'men of renown' appeared and the leading family literally became immortalized, forming the pantheon of 'pagan gods' worshipped across the ancient Middle East. First Edition published August 2020.

The Torah and the Trinity

Proof of a divine Creator is not to be found in the Bible. However, the real identity of Yahweh may be discerned from biblical texts. The most memorable figures from the Old Testament include Noah, Abraham, Moses and kings David & Solomon – one might expect these find international recognition, with references to their exceptional feats in the historical record of surrounding affected cultures. But only one of these hero's has been verified, one appears to be adopted from another culture, one surprises by his total invisibility and the kings are acknowledged only by an isolated and obscure fragment. Second Edition published January 2021.

Part Two: The Levant in the Second Millennium BC

The Old Testament books covering the time of Abraham to David (c2000BC to c1000BC) tell of the Israelites led from slavery to conquer the Promised Land. However, clear evidence reveals these books were largely written during the Babylonian captivity, after 596BC, by priests with only hazy notions of geography and history. The biblical story overlooks the fact that the entire area of the Promised Land formed part of the Egyptian Empire for the greater part of the entire millennia. Second Edition published September 2021.

Part Three: Jesus, the Nazarene

Arguably, Jesus has had the most formative impact on humankind. Today, the New Testament stands as the only authoritative source of his life and teaching – but almost all of the books written about him in the first century have been destroyed. How authentic and reliable are those texts selected for the New Testament? The Old Testament is reputed to contain hundreds of prophesies concerning Jesus – are they credible? We name him Christ, meaning Messiah, a term the church has allowed to be widely misunderstood. Is Jesus part of a Trinity? Second Edition published in July 2022.

Part Four: Truth Revealed, Jesus original teaching

This final work identifies many significant changes made to the Gospels to mould Christian beliefs in line with Church dogma. The majority of early Christian texts were ruthlessly destroyed by the Roman Church – why? What did they say? Aided by the earliest uncorrupted manuscripts and the few surviving examples of texts declared heretical, we can piece together Jesus original teaching. What is revealed dovetails well with ancient belief systems, explaining why Nazarene teaching spread like wildfire in the first century. Many of the difficult to grasp elements of conventional Christianity are exposed as being man-made. Many clues have survived, even in the New Testament, which support these findings. First Edition published August 2022.

Thomasine Creed: A radical update of the Nicaean Creed

Available for download on the Series website:
www.truthpublications.co.uk

CPSIA information can be obtained
at www.ICGtesting.com
Printed in the USA
BVHW082142280722
643318BV00013B/129

9 789887 448983